SOCIOLOGY FOR EDUCATIO

Sociology for Education Studies provides a fresh look at the sociology of education, focusing on themes such as *habitus, hegemony* and *intersectionality*. It supports students in applying sociological theory to their own educational experiences and developing an understanding of why social orders appear to be predetermined, why the state continues to create education policy in certain forms and, crucially, how to make it better.

The book explores the multi-faceted perspectives that influence the sociology of education and presents examples of the applications of sociology to a wide variety of different educational contexts, including education in schools and in the community. Chapters cover topics such as:

- Morality, education and social order
- Spaces of invisibility and marginalisation in schools
- The global political economy of education
- Rethinking the 'international perspective' in Education Studies

This accessible book is an essential read for students of Education Studies as well as those involved in teacher education and training.

Catherine A. Simon is Programme Leader for Education and Childhood Studies at Bath Spa University, UK.

Graham Downes is Programme Leader for Education Studies at Liverpool John Moores University, UK.

The Routledge Education Studies Series

Series Editor: Stephen Ward, Bath Spa University, UK

The **Routledge Education Studies Series** aims to support advanced level study on Education Studies and related degrees by offering in-depth introductions from which students can begin to extend their research and writing in years 2 and 3 of their course. Titles in the series cover a range of classic and up-and-coming topics, developing understanding of key issues through detailed discussion and consideration of conflicting ideas and supporting evidence. With an emphasis on developing critical thinking, allowing students to think for themselves and beyond their own experiences, the titles in the series offer historical, global and comparative perspectives on core issues in education.

https://www.routledge.com/The-Routledge-Education-Studies-Series/book-series/RESS

Inclusive Education
Edited by Zeta Brown

Gender, Education and Work
Christine Eden

International and Comparative Education
Brendan Bartram

Contemporary Issues in Childhood
Zeta Brown and Stephan Ward

Psychology and the Study of Education
Edited by Cathal O'Siochru

Philosophy and the Study of Education
Edited by Tom Feldges

Sociology for Education Studies
Edited by Catherine A. Simon and Graham Downes

SOCIOLOGY FOR EDUCATION STUDIES

Connecting Theory, Settings and Everyday Experiences

Edited by
Catherine A. Simon and Graham Downes

Routledge
Taylor & Francis Group

LONDON AND NEW YORK

First published 2020
by Routledge
2 Park Square, Milton Park, Abingdon, Oxon OX14 4RN

and by Routledge
52 Vanderbilt Avenue, New York, NY 10017

Routledge is an imprint of the Taylor & Francis Group, an informa business

British Library Cataloguing-in-Publication Data
A catalogue record for this book is available from the British Library

Library of Congress Cataloging-in-Publication Data
Names: Simon, Catherine A., editor. | Downes, Graham, editor.
Title: Sociology for education studies : connecting theory, settings and
    everyday experiences / edited by Catherine A. Simon and Graham Downes.
Description: Abingdon, Oxon ; New York, NY : Routledge, 2020. | Series: The
    routledge education studies series | Includes bibliographical references
    and index.
Identifiers: LCCN 2019044842 (print) | LCCN 2019044843 (ebook) | ISBN
    9780367028381 (hardback) | ISBN 9780367028404 (paperback) | ISBN
    9780429397585 (ebook)
Subjects: LCSH: Education–Sociological aspects.
Classification: LCC LC191 .S66147 2020 (print) | LCC LC191 (ebook) | DDC
    306.43–dc23
LC record available at https://lccn.loc.gov/2019044842
LC ebook record available at https://lccn.loc.gov/2019044843

ISBN: 978-0-367-02838-1 (hbk)
ISBN: 978-0-367-02840-4 (pbk)
ISBN: 978-0-429-39758-5 (ebk)

Typeset in News Gothic
by Cenveo® Publisher Services

Contents

Contributors

Dr Dan Bishop is a Lecturer at the University of Leicester. Having previously worked as a teacher in further education, his academic interests focus on adult and workplace learning in particular, and on sociological and policy issues within education and learning more broadly. His research is concentrated in this area, and includes recent projects on degree apprenticeships, and the interaction of context and agency in workplace learning.

Dr David Blundell led the Education Studies programme at London Metropolitan University until his retirement in early 2019. With origins in the New Social Studies of Childhood, David's work is concerned to encourage curiosity surrounding children's lives in education and schooling.

Dr Jessie A. Bustillos Morales is currently employed as a Senior Lecturer in Education Studies at London Metropolitan University where she is also Course Leader for the BA in Education and Social Policy. Jessie has extensive experience of teaching at undergraduate and postgraduate levels. She has written a series of book chapters and journal articles on aspects of economics and education, including the effects of neoliberalism on education and learning.

Dr Graham Downes is the Programme Leader for Education Studies at Liverpool John Moores University. He has taught the sociology of education for a number of years and he has a particular interest in inequality and education.

Dr Joe Gazdula is Senior Lecturer in Education at Edge Hill University. He was a founder member of the British Education Studies Association and is Managing Editor of their Academic Journals. His research interests include the sociology of education, enterprise, entrepreneurship, accounting, management, employability, e-learning and education and innovation. Joe is be the REED Global External Consultant for staff training programmes.

Prof Martin Levinson is Professor of Cultural Identities at Bath Spa University. Much of his ethnographic research has been with Gypsy traveller communities, but he has also focused on other traditionally nomadic groups, including Indigenous Australian and Sami communities. A consistent area of exploration has been in the impact of alternative cultural values on orientations towards education and the outcomes of engagement with mainstream education upon cultural identities.

He is also interested in the processes of marginalisation, and this has led to inter-disciplinary studies with migrant groups and with children who have been excluded from schools.

Dr Victoria Showunmi is an Assistant Professor in Education at UCL Institute of Education, UK. She focuses on Gender and Educational leadership and Black young women and their wellbeing through an intersectional lens. She is currently leading an educational leadership partnership with colleagues on projects that are based in Pakistan, Germany and the USA.

Dr Ben Simmons is a Senior Lecturer in the School of Education at Bath Spa University and co-directs the Centre for Research in Equity, Inclusion and Community (CREIC). Ben's research examines the social and educational inclusion of children with profound and multiple learning disabilities (PMLD).

Dr Catherine A. Simon is Programme Leader for the Education Studies Undergraduate Awards at the School of Education, Bath Spa University, where she is also a Teaching Fellow. Her research interests are concerned with education policy, school systems and leadership and management and contribute to her undergraduate and post-graduate teaching and supervision.

Prof Stephen Ward is Emeritus Professor of Education, Bath Spa University, formerly Dean of the School of Education and subject leader for Education Studies. A founder member of the British Education Studies Association, he has published on the primary curriculum, primary music teaching and Education Studies. His research interests are education policy and university knowledge.

Dr Tingting Yuan is a Senior Lecturer in International Education at Bath Spa University. Her research interests include globalisation, international aid of education, China-Africa cooperation, higher education policy and other educational issues in relation to the contemporary global political economy.

Series Editor's preface

Education Studies has become a popular and exciting undergraduate subject in some 50 universities in the UK. It began in the early 2000s, mainly in the post-1992 universities which had been centres of teacher training, but, gaining academic credibility, the subject is being taken up by post-1992 and Russell Group institutions. In 2004 Routledge published one of the first texts for undergraduates, *Education Studies: A student's guide* (Ward, 2004), now in its fourth edition (Simon and Ward, 2020). It comprises a series of chapters introducing key topics in Education Studies and has contributed to the development of the subject. Targeted at the levels 5, 6 and 7, the Routledge Education Studies Series offers a sequence of volumes which explore such topics in depth.

Education Studies is concerned with understanding how people develop and learn throughout their lives, the nature of knowledge and critical engagement with ways of knowing. It demands an intellectually rigorous analysis of educational processes and their cultural, social, political and historical contexts. In a time of rapid change across the planet, education is about how we both make and manage such change. Education Studies, therefore, includes perspectives on international education, economic relationships, globalisation, ecological issues and human rights. It deals with beliefs, values and principles in education and the way that they change over time.

It is important to understand that Education Studies is not teacher training or teacher education, although graduates in the subject may well go on to become teachers after a PGCE or school-based training. Education Studies should be regarded as a subject with a variety of career outcomes, or indeed, none: it can be taken as the academic and critical study of education in itself. At the same time, while the theoretical elements of teacher training are continually reduced in PGCE courses and school-based training, undergraduate Education Studies provides a critical analysis for future teachers who, in a rapidly changing world, need so much more than simply the training to deliver a government-defined school curriculum.

Since its inception in the late 1990s there has been continuing discussion about the roles of the so-called 'contributory disciplines' in Education Studies. Some have argued that Psychology, Sociology, Philosophy, History even Economics should form its theoretical basis. Others urge that Education Studies should be seen as a 'discipline' in itself that the other disciplines should be less prominent and make the study of education too difficult and complex. This book is based on the former assumption that, for a rigorous analysis of education, a grounding in the disciplines is essential: students should have an understanding of the nature of each of the disciplines, be aware of the theoretical issues in the subject and familiar with its methodologies and publications in education.

Intended for second- and third-year undergraduates and masters students, the book is the seventh in the Routledge Education Studies series, which builds on the introductory guide and looks in depth at sociology in education.

Stephen Ward, Series Editor
Bath Spa University

Books available to date in the series:

Zeta Brown (Ed.) (2016) *Inclusive Education: Perspectives on pedagogy, policy and practice*. Abingdon: Routledge.

Christine Eden (2017) *Gender: Education and Work: Inequalities and Intersectionality*. Abingdon: Routledge.

Brendan Bartram (Ed.) (2017) *International and Comparative Education: Contemporary issues and debates*. Abingdon: Routledge.

Zeta Brown and Stephen Ward (Eds.) (2018) *Contemporary Issues in Childhood: A bio-ecological approach*. Abingdon: Routledge.

Cathal Ó Siochrú (Ed.) (2018) *Psychology and the Study of Education: Critical perspectives on developing theories*. Abingdon: Routledge.

Tom Feldges (Ed.) (2019) *Philosophy and the Study of Education: New perspectives on a complex relationship*. Abingdon: Routledge.

Jessie Bustillos Morales and Sandra Abegglen (Eds.) (2020) *The Study of Education and Economics: Debates and Critical Theoretical Perspectives*. Abingdon: Routledge.

Titles forthcoming:

Brendan Bartram (Ed.) *Contemporary Issues in Higher Education: Contradictions, Complexities and Challenges*. Abingdon: Routledge.

Nicholas Joseph (Ed.) *History of Education*. Abingdon: Routledge.

British Education Studies Association (BESA)

Many of the editors and contributors to Education Studies book series are members of the British Education Studies Association. Formed in 2005, BESA is an academic association providing a network for tutors and students in Education Studies. It holds an annual conference with research papers from staff and students; there are bursaries for students on Education Studies programmes.

The website offers information and news about Education Studies and two journals: *Educationalfutures* and *Transformations*, a journal for student publications. Both are available without charge on the website: https://educationstudies.org.uk/

Acknowledgements

To all students of education

The editors wish to thank Stephen Ward for his invaluable help and guidance in the creation of this book.

List of abbreviations

CBD   Central Business District
CRT   Critical Race Theory
CTC   City Technology Colleges
CCPEE   Critical Cultural Political Economy of Education
CCTA   City Colleges for the Technology of the Arts
CWEC   Common world educational culture
DCSF   Department of Children, Schools and Families
DES   Department of Education and Science
DFID   Department for International Development
DfEE   Department for Education and Employment
DfE   Department for Education
EFA   Education for All
EKE   Education for Knowledge Economy
GPE   global political economic
GSEA   Globally structured educational agenda
IMF   International Monetary Fund
IPE   International political economy
MDG   Millennium Development Goals
OECD   Organisation for Economic Co-operation and Development
PE   physical education
PISA   Programme for International Student Assessment
PMLD   profound and multiple learning difficulties
PRSP   Poverty Reduction Strategy Papers
PRU   pupil referral unit
SDG   Sustainable Development Goals
UNESCO United Nations Educational, Scientific and Cultural Organization
UN   United Nations
UNDESA United Nations Department of Economic and Social Affairs
UPE   Universal primary education

Introduction

This book on the sociology of education is one of five in the Routledge Education Studies series designed to address the need for students to know and understand the form and methods of the disciplines, with examples from the wide range of topics for analysis.

Education Studies began as the theory for teacher training in the Bachelor of Education (B.Ed.) degrees in the 1960s. The validating universities insisted on a strong formal theoretical basis for the degree courses, and it was agreed that the disciplines of Psychology, Sociology, Philosophy and Economics should be the theoretical basis. Economics was subsequently dropped in favour of the History of Education (Crook, 2002). There was at the time a very limited research base for the disciplines in education in the universities and little academic competence in the subjects in the training colleges. Pedagogy was excluded and Crook details the historical problems which Education Studies encountered alongside demands for practical teacher training:

> ..the absence of pedagogy as a core component of Educational Studies in the undergraduate degrees established during 1965-68 was indicative of the general difficulties of educationists making a decisive theoretical contribution to practical problems in education.
>
> (2002: 23)

The initial result was complaints of teacher training being 'over-theorised' and giving insufficient practical guidance for teachers. When non-teacher-training Education Studies programmes emerged in the early 2000s there was some reluctance among course leaders to explicitly include the disciplines as the theoretical grounding for their courses. There were suggestions that Education Studies as a free-standing university subject should have its own discrete theoretical basis (Ward, 2006). In recent years, however, Education Studies degrees have turned to the disciplines to ensure a depth of critical analysis and understanding.

The sociology of education considers education as social institution. In most western societies education is considered the route to personal freedom, economic success and social mobility. Thus the sociology of education explores the contribution education can make to society. However, it also takes a critical view of the impact made by social structures on the educational outcomes, policies and practices of formal and informal schooling. Emile Durkheim (1982: 52), considered the father of sociology, emphasised 'social facts' in other words 'a category of facts which present very special characteristics: they consist of manners of acting, thinking, and feeling external to the individual, which are invested with a coercive power by virtue of which they exercise control over him. A number of social and cultural factors including moral values, religious beliefs, and social and cultural norms, therefore, influence education and educational outcomes.

Other sociological perspectives on education have persisted over time. From a Marxist viewpoint, the very institution of education reproduces social hierarchies and inequality diminishing the prospects of those from marginalised groups. In this way, the sociology of education is a multifaceted and complex domain and, for some, should be considered a discipline in its own right. This complexity is reflected in the chapters that follow.

Summary of the chapters

We believe we have taken a fresh look at the sociology of education moving away from traditional accounts of gender, race and social class to consider themes such as *habitus*, *hegemony* and *intersectionality*.

In the opening chapter Graham Downes presents the case for a sociology of education in its own right and, as such, demonstrates the multi-faceted perspectives that influence the sociology of education, considering in particular the *how* (methodology) and *what* (knowledge-base) of such a field of enquiry. The theme is continued by Jessie Bustillos Morales in Chapter 7 which takes an historical perspective on the various discourses that have shaped the education debate over time with particular reference to the notion of a 'deserving poor'.

Indeed the backdrop too much of our recent understanding of education and its role within society has been the rise of neoliberalism in the West and its enactment through education and social policy since the 1970s. Joe Gazdula charts the growth of a global political economy in education from its earliest inception in the eighteenth century. In Chapter 8 he takes an historical perspective exploring the influence of authors such as Adam Smith, J.S. Mill and John Maynard Keynes. The chapter considers some of the Marxist and neo-Marxist critiques of neoliberalism. It is this corpus of literature that provides the socio-political theoretical lens through which to analyse the ascendency of neoliberalism charted through Chapter 9. For Gazdula the key questions are whether the needs of industry and commerce, the need for social justice, or the needs of individuals have primacy in education.

How and why people make judgements and act in particular ways is the focus of Chapter 5 on the Sociology of Morality. There is a close association here with the philosophy of education and debates about notions of right and wrong, justice and injustice. What is right for the individual may not be right for the wider community or society as a whole. The positioning of schools and education within this debate is far from straightforward. Should schools be the guardians of social morality as codified in the British values taught in all English state schools, or should they be part of the social structures that challenge and change moral behaviour?

Thus far it should be self-evident that education policy and the social structures of formalised schooling do not exist within a vacuum and, within a world closely connected through cyber-space, opportunities to borrow from other nations or to be influenced by global organisations such as the World Bank or the Organisation of Economic Co-operation and Development (OECD) are many. Competition between nations for recognition of the education systems and contributions to the national economy are enhanced through league tables such as the Programme for International Student Assessment (PISA). Tingting Yuan in Chapter 10 considers whether a universal model of education is possible, if indeed desirable.

However, as David Blundell highlights in Chapter 11, nine out of ten children now live in non-western majority-world settings. As such the universal currency of western constructions of childhood and 'the child' found in the work of critical sociologists, children's geographers and post-colonial theorists would no longer appear to be fit for purpose. He therefore posits post-colonial challenges to the dominance afforded western 'global cities' and assumptions surrounding economic developmentalism, along with their concern to reveal the diverse social realities found in *ordinary cities* for the *ordinary child.*

In Chapter 4, Martin Levinson uses evidence from his own ethnographic research to demonstrate how students marginalised by the institutional organisation of formal schooling can acquiesce, resist and/or challenge the structures that position them as 'outsiders'. What is it that makes school an unkind place for some students? How can we make mainstream schooling kinder and more relevant to all pupils? Levinson argues that the creation of more flexible spaces in schools can reap positive rewards in terms of pedagogical and social outcomes.

In Chapter 12 on disability, Ben Simmons highlights the tension between international policy, which promotes inclusive education as a human right, and the challenge of including learners with profound intellectual impairments in the current neoliberal education system. The chapter introduces social complexity to the debates about whether children with profound or moderate learning difficulties (PMLD) are 'includable' and again challenges normative educational responses that separate children according to type and judge them according to competitive subject knowledge acquisition.

Debates about inequality are inextricably linked with notions of power. Indeed it is the power of the post-world war two human rights agenda, coupled with the individualism of neoliberal economics, that argues against social inequality and for the equality of all citizens. However, how such equality is conceptualised and measured is open to debate. In Chapter 2, Dan Bishop explores the notion of 'habitus' with particular emphasis on the work of Pierre Bourdieu. Defining the concept of habitus and exploring related notions of 'capital' and 'field' in relation to social class inequality, the chapter critiques the usefulness of habitus as a concept for explaining educational inequality. In Chapter 3, Graham Downes foregrounds the work of Poulanzas in exploring the power relations perceived to exist in the English state system of education. Through this particular lens, individual wants and rights are set in tension with economic desires at the individual and national levels. It is the role of the state rather than the individual in community with others to resolve this particular dichotomy.

These chapters offer a fresh and at times challenging account of the role the sociology of education in understanding complex human systems and institutions in the field of education.

Catherine A. Simon, August 2019

References

Crook, D. (2002) Education studies and teacher education. *British Journal of Education Studies,* **50**(1), pp. 55–75.

Durkheim, É. (1982) [1st pub. 1895] *The Rules of Sociological Method and Selected Texts on Sociology and its Method.* W. D. Halls (trans.). New edition edited by Lukes, S. (Ed.) (2013). New York: Free Press.

Ward, S. (2006) *Undergraduate Education Studies as an Emerging Subject in Higher Education: The construction and definition of university knowledge.* (Unpublished PhD Thesis). Bath: Bath Spa University.

1   Sociology and education

Graham Downes

Introduction

The academic study of education and society has always suffered from something of an identity crisis. Part of the problem is that education itself is a nebulous set of concepts that traverse social practices, political debates, moral issues and social theories. What Education Studies do have in common is a tendency to focus on context: they are always bounded so that one can say what education is at the moment it is being discussed. This complexity is something that should be celebrated rather than excessively problematised. The relationship between theory and context provides an interaction that can generate new contextual insights (through the application of theory) and new theorisations (through the application of context.). What emerges from this process is what Merton terms 'middle range theory' (Merton, 1967: 39). Such theories mediate between more abstract ideas and social systems and, as such, can be subjected to empirical scrutiny. By contrast, deductively constructed grand theories are often difficult to verify (Merton, 1967). As such, education can become a useful tool in bridging the gap between overly instrumental empirical approaches that purport to be value free and over-abstract grand theories that are, in Popper's terms, beyond falsification (Popper, 2002).

Sociology in Education Studies

With reference to the study of education, perhaps a more applied set of academic categories might be more productive in reflecting the importance of context in the field, for example: education policy (applied political science), pedagogy (applied psychology) and sociology of education (applied sociology). Such academic approaches, we argue, offer the potential for the development of radical and purposeful insights into how we educate and how we *should* educate. This, we propose, is the basis for the existence of Education Studies as an academic endeavour in its own right. This book focuses on one such applied discipline that potentially constitutes Education Studies. Whilst the sociology of education has traditionally been an essential part of sociology writ large, we suggest that it should be seen as more detached from the more general discipline of sociology and in doing so, it can find its own methods and knowledge that, whilst referencing grander theorisations and approaches, produces something distinctive. For example, it is worth noting that whilst relevant to a discussion of education, the concept of 'discourse', as defined by Foucault, is not specifically about education. However, subjecting the theory to scrutiny in education contexts generates new theoretical parameters, nomenclatures, values and tensions. This is useful both for wider theoretical discussions and for developing new insights into educational practice.

The obvious questions emerging from this bold set of assertions are: (a) What constitutes a sociology of education? (b) How might this be bounded in the study of education (Education Studies)? For us, the question can be broken down into 'How?' (methodology) and 'What?' (knowledge base).

The 'how' is relatively straightforward: educational methods inevitably have to follow those dictated by wider sociological theories and the accepted, discipline-specific methods of working. However, it should be noted that the relative value of these received methods should be open to challenge and reordering based on context-specific problems as they present themselves. For example, theories of morality may well need to be applied in different ways because morality in educational contexts tends to play out in distinctive ways compared to other contexts. This is because (a) education has its own, distinctive normative discourses and (b) these discourses tend to have their own distinctive patterns of linguistic modality in relation to such discourses. In this sense, retroductive approaches to knowledge have significant potential in the field of sociology of education (Danermark *et al.*, 2002). In acknowledging the complex and polyvalent nature of the empirical domain, researchers can develop new insights through consideration of the world as it can be, rather than the world we can observe. In order to do this, it is necessary to consider theoretical possibilities alongside observable phenomena. As such, empirical observations alone are not enough to generate meaningful insights about educational knowledge (Collier, 1999).

With reference to 'what', sociology of education is distinctive because it focuses on the external conditions that affect educational outcomes. By this we are referring to the social structures that exist beyond the educational institution but are internalised by and/or have a significant impact on what happens in education. We contrast this with the narrower focus of psychological theory and its application through pedagogy. This is important because we know that the main tenets of sociological analysis (class, ethnicity and gender) have a significant impact on educational outcomes (Dorling, 2015; Feinstein, 2003; Savage *et al.*, 1995). However, explaining the link between wider social structures and such educational outcomes is much harder to explain. Part of the issue here is that theorisations of social structures themselves are multi-dimensional, tending to be reducible to economic, political and/or cultural causes. A potentially fruitful way of creating a more coherent set of theorisations is the generation of intersectional social accounts that cross-reference these dimensions (Gillborn, 2010). As such, more modern approaches to both statistical analysis and critical theorisations tend to generate intersectional social models (Hancock, 2015).

Social structures and educational institutions

Whilst intersectionality helps to potentially complexify the evidence base from which social scientists work, it does little to resolve the seemingly intractable debate between structural approaches to social issues and agentive approaches. Although this debate plays out across the sociological discipline, it takes on a distinctive form within the educational field. With reference to Durkheim, specific organisations of rituals and enacted practices constitute educational institutions in unique ways (Durkheim and Fields, 1995). Specifically, education has a tendency to be highly ritualistic with a strong emphasis on routine and symbolism that is, for the most part, easily identifiable. For example, schools are predicated on timetables that are constructed from a set curriculum.

This curriculum and its organisation are easily transferable between schools and easily recognisable from outside the school environment, and thus exhibit a high level of linguistic modality (Fairclough, 2003). Such constructs are further reified through the extensive use of symbolism such as the use of bells, specific resources, as well as practices that necessitate the shifting of behaviour from one part of the school day to another. There are also strong boundaries between different actors and the division of labour (Bernstein, 2003). Teachers are easily identifiable from pupils and, likewise, head teachers are distinguishable from both. But these ritualised elements of education only represent some of the social structures that constitute education. Wider social structures are also internalised by educational institutions that, in turn, become internalised by wider social structures. Perhaps most prominent amongst these is social class. A plethora of data has demonstrated the strong historical link between educational outcomes and social status (Feinstein, 2003; Wilkinson and Pickett, 2011). Those such as Bourdieu have theorised about the various ways in which education has a tendency to discriminate against those from lower socio-economic status groups (Bourdieu and Passeron, 1990). Some of these issues can be attributable to ritualism but, for the most part, their roots are in wider, culturally constructed elements. In particular, normative values that are closely associated with status are played out through various discourses that include moral and aesthetic dimensions (Bourdieu, 1984). Education itself is synonymous with such a cultural milieu, and it is worth noting that it is not universally seen as a social good by all social groups (Willis, 1977).

Wider sociological debates centring on the 'cultural turn' (Hall and Morley, 2019: 9) take on a unique significance in the study of education. This debate has historically focused on a humanist/structuralist dichotomy that emerged in the field of cultural studies (Hall and Morley, 2019). Whilst the relationship between social structures and social agency cannot be reduced to a unified approach, more contemporary approaches have attempted to ameliorate the division between the two and at least recognise the existence of both within social formations. These approaches tend to focus on what might loosely be referred to as 'social reproduction': the reproduction and evolution of existing social structures through human actions (Bourdieu and Passeron, 1990). These models tend to emphasise that whilst we have the ability to choose between almost limitless possibilities of social agency, our actions have a strong tendency towards the reformation of existing patterns of interaction: we tend to reproduce what is familiar to us (Bourdieu and Passeron, 1990). Some approaches emphasise the material aspect to this phenomenon. The existing material boundaries that define the social world mean that we can only act in ways that they afford (Olssen, 2010). For example, whilst we have the choice to drive a vehicle in almost any direction we like, in reality this is very difficult and we tend to constrain our activity in ways that adhere to the materiality of the environment; that is, we tend to stick to the road. This is also true of education contexts. For example, schools also have material constraints, partly because they are inherited (building new educational structures is very costly), partly because they have to exist within wider pre-existing structures (they cannot be built anywhere), and partly because historical social relations have required children to be together in a manageable collected space so as to enable other forms of activities to occur, such as work.

It can be argued that such materiality is the historical material product of pre-existing economic relations, but this should not detract from the significant role that such materiality plays in reproducing existing social structures. Even if the political/economic systems changed radically, it is difficult to envisage how education systems could reflect such changes through a concomitant radical shift in the way they are organised. In this sense, schools are distinctive in their relatively fixed state. Other social practices – such as those associated with medicine – have been able to evolve in a way that makes them unrecognisable from their historical antecedents. Education has developed very little since elementary state education was introduced in 1870.

Compulsory state education

It should also be noted that material and cultural dimensions of education cannot constitute the entirety of the education system as we know it. The very fact we have a compulsory education system is a state-sponsored act that has endured over time. Many will point to the link between education and economic productivity as a reason for the need for universal education, and there are plenty of examples of political justifications that refer to economic issues as the reason for investing in compulsory education (Blair, 2002; Forster, 1870; Gove, 2012). Others have provided more complex accounts that refer to the need to address new social outcomes produced by the expansion of capitalism. Such justifications point out that the concomitant rise in urbanisation and social relationships whereby workers were not tied to landlords, as in previous feudal arrangements, had led to a greater need for social control (Green, 2013). Thus, education can be seen as an outcome of capitalist economic arrangements as much as it is as an intervention in such arrangements.

This model has been made more complex by those who point out that, whilst one can attribute political interventions (such as education) to capitalist economic arrangements, they cannot be predicted and are thus contingent (Jessop, 2010). Put more simply, whilst many causes of action can be attributed to capitalism, it is not possible to identify which of the outcomes that are possible within a capitalist society will come to pass. For example, whilst state education came into being in Britain in 1870 and can be attributed to the conditions created by capitalism, there were many capitalists who did not feel it was an action that was in their interests and who opposed the idea (Gillard, 2011).

Foucault on power

Such complexity has led to the foregrounding of approaches that attempt to recognise the importance of both structure and agency in society. Often referred to broadly as 'poststructuralism' (Young, 1981), these approaches tend to focus on the exercise of power and how this shapes and redefines existing social structures. Such theorists also attempt to develop new methods by extending the range of disciplinary approaches offered by classical sociology. In particular, they turn to fields such as psychoanalysis and linguistics to generate innovative ways of understanding society (Jessop, 2004). Perhaps most prominent amongst these theorists is Michel Foucault. Central to Foucauldian theory of social relations is the concept of power. Rather than understanding power as a simple causal relationship between those who hold power and those who submit to it, Foucault sees power as complex and multifaceted. More specifically, he portrays power as contingent on previous relationships and actions (Jessop, 2004). Foucault *et al.* (1995) referred to the various methods by which power is exerted as technologies of power. These are essentially discursive: that is, power is exercised through the various ways the world is constructed and communicated through language. With reference to education, schools themselves can be seen as essentially discursive because the very word connotes a number of associated concepts and practices. Furthermore, these discursive elements are highly value-driven – we usually talk about the practices associated with school in terms of good or bad, right or wrong. For example, the debate about whether parents should take their children to school in pyjamas is as much a moral issue (whether it is good or bad) as it is an instrumental one (whether it creates better measurable outcomes) (Halliday, 2016). Foucault's work is distinct from Marxist approaches in that he rejects the idea of a general theory of power predicated on a single causal effect. Power in Foucault's terms is always heterogenous and can only be mapped out from the ground up, that is, to examine the way power is exercised in specific institutional sites and then to consider how the discursive formations evident in a specific site are articulated elsewhere (if at all) to broader constructions of power (Foucault, 1972).

Importantly, Foucault's work rejects class as a totalising concept of power and the significance of economic relationships in general (Jessop, 2004). In terms of education, this is potentially problematic because educational outcomes are so obviously linked to socio-economic status (Blanden, 2008). However, it is worth noting that status does not necessarily have to be linked to relationships generated through a capitalist mode of production. It is possible to use Foucault's approach to make sense of the link between educational outcomes and status because new educational relationships are always predicated on what has come before. By such logic, one can consider ways in which educational institutions discriminate against certain groups *discursively*. That is, certain groups are not familiar with the discourses of education and are therefore put at a disadvantage. These groups will naturally consist of those born into a world where those around them were similarly disadvantaged. Sociologists such as Diane Reay have provided rich accounts of the ways in which certain groups are excluded from education in this way (Reay, 2006; Reay *et al.*, 2011).

Marx and hegemony

Whilst Foucault's emphasis on discourse is potentially fruitful in understanding the complex ways in which people can be excluded from educational institutions, it seems errant to omit economic considerations altogether, particularly as economic considerations are foregrounded within the political sphere with regards to compulsory education (Blanden, 2008). Whilst the economic determinism associated with traditional Marxism has become less fashionable, many theorists have looked to develop Marx's work in a way that acknowledge the more complex social elements identified by those such as Foucault. With reference to education, the concept of 'hegemony' seems particularly prescient because the state education system was imposed from the top down (through the imposition of law) and has existed as such ever since (see Chapter 3.) In Foucauldian terms this means that education as a discursive formation is extensive with a high level of articulation. However, such an explanation ignores the importance of economy to the discourse. By its own admission, the state sponsors education to benefit the capitalist state (Green, 2013). The case that education is part of a capitalist hegemony is therefore an easy one to make. Broadly, hegemony can be referred to as a dominant set of political arrangements at the level of the state. In this sense, education can be seen as a political act designed to meet the needs of capitalism (and capitalists). This could be seen in a deterministic way – the existence of education is inevitable under the conditions of capital – and the prevalence of state-sponsored education systems globally would certainly support this assertion. However, such a view ignores the contestable nature of education systems: not all who have interests in capital benefit from education policy. For example, many of those who represent the business sector have historically voiced opposition to compulsory education and an emphasis on academic subjects (Gillard, 2011). Here, the work of Poulantzas is important. For Poulantzas, capitalist democracies ensure universal interest through universal representation (Jessop, 1985). Not everyone can have their needs met; in particular, workers' needs will always be usurped by the needs of capital and capital's needs are secured through the colonisation of political spaces by the capitalist classes. Whilst capitalists do not speak with one voice, they are in turn unified by capitalist arrangements so that they essentially agree on fundamental issues (Poulantzas and Martin, 2008). Education in this sense has its place within the capitalist state and, whilst there will always be debate over the exact nature of education policy, it will essentially stay the same under the existing hegemonic arrangements.

Conclusion

Thus material, cultural, economic and political dimensions are all essential to understanding educational contexts. Each must be addressed in turn, but it is also essential that educational contexts help us to understand these dimensions and how they interrelate. In doing so, Education Studies has a significant role to play in the social sciences. This book hopefully makes a useful contribution to this progression.

Summary points

- The study of education involves the relationship between theory and practice and can bridge the gap between empirical approaches and over-abstract grand theories.
- To understand education it is necessary to consider theoretical possibilities: empirical observations alone are not enough to generate meaningful insights about educational knowledge.
- In contrast with psychology, the sociology of education focuses on the external conditions and social structures that exist beyond educational institution and have a significant impact on what happens in education.
- Social structures are internalised by educational institutions that, in turn, become internalised by wider social structures, creating, for example, the strong link between educational outcomes and social class.
- Compulsory state education can be seen as a means to sustain the status quo of capitalism.
- Michel Foucault's concept of power is multi-faceted and can be used to explain the more complex ways in which education operates to maintain social class.
- The concept of 'hegemony' is important in understanding the way in which education is part of the state power structure.

Questions for discussion

- How do psychology and sociology differ in their approaches to the study of education?
- Why does education tend to replicate inequalities? What can be done to reverse this?
- It is sometimes argued that compulsory state education exists to sustain capitalism. Do you agree?
- Can you think of examples of Foucault's concept of power in education?

Recommended reading

Dorling, D. (2015) *Injustice: Why Social Inequality Still Persists*. Bristol: Policy Press.

Green, A. (2013) *Education and State Formation: Europe, East Asia and the USA*. Basingstoke: Palgrave Macmillan.

Reay, D., Crozier, G. and James, D. (2011) *White Middle-Class Identities and Urban Schooling*. Basingstoke: Palgrave Macmillan.

References

Bernstein, B. (2003) *Class, Codes and Control - Volume I Theoretical Studies Towards a Sociology of Language*. London: Routledge & Kegan Paul.

Blair, T. (2002) Speech on education at Abraham Moss High School, Manchester. Online. Available at: https://webarchive.nationalarchives.gov.uk/20080909002007/http://www.number10.gov.uk/Page1706 (Accessed 6 August 2019).

Blanden, J. O. (2008) Social mobility: Concepts, measures and policies. *Political Quarterly*, **79**, pp. 57–69.

Bourdieu, P. (1984) *Distinction: A Social Critique of the Judgement of Taste*. Cambridge: Harvard University Press.

Bourdieu, P. and Passeron, J-C. (1990) *Reproduction in Education, Society and Culture*. (2nd ed.). London: Sage.

Collier, A. (1999). *Being and Worth*. London: Routledge.

Danermark, B., Ekström, M. and Karlsson, J. C. (2002). *Explaining Society: Critical Realism in the Social Sciences*. London: Routledge.

Dorling, D. (2015) *Injustice: Why Social Inequality Still Persists*. Bristol: Policy Press.

Durkheim, E. and Fields, K. E. (1995) *Elementary Forms of the Religious Life*. K. E. Fields (trans.). London: George Allen & Unwin.

Fairclough, N. (2003) *Analysing Discourse: Textual Analysis for Social Research*. London: Routledge.

Feinstein, L. (2003) Very early cognitive evidence. *CentrePiece*, Summer 2003, pp. 24–30.

Forster, W. E. (1870) Elementary education bill. First reading. *Hansard 1803–2005*, **199**, pp. 438–498.

Foucault, M. (1972). *The Archaeology of Knowledge, and the Discourse on Language*. New York: Pantheon Books.

Foucault, M., Sheridan, A. and Smith, A.M.S. (1995) *Discipline and Punish: The Birth of the Prison*. London: Penguin.

Gillard, D. (2011) *Education in England: A brief history*. Online. Available at: www.educationengland.org.uk/history (Accessed 3 August 2016).

Gillborn, D. (2010) The white working class, racism and respectability: Victims, degenerates and interest-convergence. *British Journal of Educational Studies*, **58**(1), pp. 3–25.

Gove, M. (2012) Michael Gove's autumn address to Politeia. Online. Available at: http://politeia.co.uk/other/michael-goves-autumn-address-politeia (Accessed 6 August 2019).

Green, A. (2013) *Education and State Formation: Europe, East Asia and the USA*. Basingstoke: Palgrave Macmillan.

Hall, S. and Morley, D. (2019) *Essential Essays, Volume 1: Foundations of Cultural Studies*. Durham and London: Duke University Press.

Halliday, J. (2016) Wave of support for school's ban on parents wearing pyjamas. *The Guardian*, 26 January 2016.

Hancock, A. M. (2015) *Intersectionality: An Intellectual History*. Oxford: Oxford University Press.

Jessop, B. (1985) *Nicos Poulantzas: Marxist Theory and Political Strategy*. London: Macmillan.

Jessop, B. (2004) Poulantzas and Foucault on power and strategy (Pouvoir et stratégies chez Poulantzas et Foucault). *Actuel Marx*, **36**, pp. 89–107.

Jessop, B. (2010). Cultural political economy and critical policy studies. *Critical Policy Studies*, **3**(3-4), pp. 336–356.

Merton, R. K. (1967). *On Theoretical Sociology: Five Essays, Old and New*. New York: The Free Press.

Olssen, M. (2010) Discourse, complexity, life: Elaborating the possibilities of Foucault's materialist concept of discourse. *Beyond Universal Pragmatics. Interdisciplinary Communication Studies*, **4**, pp. 25–58.

Popper, K. (2002) *The Poverty of Historicism*. London: Routledge.

Poulantzas, N. A. and Martin, J. (2008) *The Poulantzas Reader: Marxism, Law, and the State*. London and New York: Verso.

Reay, D. (2006) The Zombie stalking English schools: Social class and educational inequality. *British Journal of Educational Studies*, **54**(3), pp. 288–307.

Reay, D., Crozier, G. and James, D. (2011) *White Middle-Class Identities and Urban Schooling*. Basingstoke: Palgrave Macmillan.

Savage, M., Barlow, J. and Dickens, P. (1995). *Property, Bureaucracy and Culture: Middle-class Formation in Contemporary Britain*. London: Routledge.

Wilkinson, R., and Pickett, K. (2011) *The Spirit Level: Why Greater Equality Makes Societies Stronger*. New York: Bloomsbury.

Willis, P. E. (1977) *Learning to Labor: How Working Class Kids Get Working Class Jobs*. New York: Columbia University Press.

Young, R. (1981) *Untying the Text: A Post-structuralist Reader*. London: Routledge and Kegan Paul.

2 Education and habitus

Dan Bishop

Introduction

Of all the sociological concepts employed in the study of education, 'habitus' is one of the most commonly used. It is a concept that has a long history, with roots in ancient Greek philosophy, and was developed through the work of nineteenth and twentieth centuries sociologists such as Emile Durkheim and Norbert Elias. Through these and other authors, habitus gained in popularity as a means of explaining how large-scale social structures, such as social class, are reproduced (and modified) through the smaller-scale attitudes, values, actions and interactions of individuals.

Yet it is through the work of French sociologist Pierre Bourdieu that the concept has found its widest audience and, broadly speaking, it is his discussion of habitus that is most frequently applied to the study of education. Bourdieu spent much of his life investigating and challenging social inequality, and trying to explain how and why it persists over time. In particular, he was interested in how the advantages and disadvantages of social class background are passed on from one generation to the next – not just in the form of economic wealth, but also in terms of access to important social networks, and the 'right' attitudes and cultural environment. Through such means, he argued, the wealthy and powerful retain their privileged position, while the disadvantaged are denied the same opportunities to move up the ladder. In exploring this issue, his focus fell upon many areas of social life, including the education system and its role in reproducing these inequalities. By the late 1990s, Bourdieu's work had become so widely used in studies of education in the UK (and elsewhere) that it even received particular attention in a government report (Tooley and Darby, 1998). While this report was critical of Bourdieu's work, his concepts and theories remain as popular as ever in the study of education.

The aim of this chapter is to focus particularly on the concept of habitus – primarily as described by Bourdieu – and its role in understanding how social inequalities are reproduced through the medium of the education system. It begins by defining habitus and the related concepts of 'capital' and 'field', before moving on to explain how researchers have linked these concepts to social inequality in the education system. The focus falls firstly upon social class inequalities, and then turns to a discussion of how habitus is implicated in ethnic inequalities in education. Towards the end of the chapter, a critical eye is cast over habitus: to what extent is it really a useful concept in studying and explaining inequality in education?

What is 'habitus'?

Bourdieu, like many other sociologists, was interested in the interaction between 'structure' and 'agency'. That is, the relationship between large-scale social structures, on the one hand, and individual thoughts, attitudes, values and actions on the other. So, for example, how does a person's social class background shape their decisions about what school their child should attend? And how do these tastes and decisions, in turn, strengthen and reproduce social structures and inequalities? Some sociologists, including Bourdieu, have used the concept of habitus to help us understand this relationship.

While a consistent and universal definition of habitus can be hard to pin down, Bourdieu (1990: 53–54) describes it as a collection of 'durable, transposable dispositions... a present past that tends to perpetuate itself into the future'. So, our individual 'dispositions' (our attitudes and inclinations) are central to Bourdieu's notion of the habitus. These dispositions, which mainly operate below a conscious level, provide us with a powerful template of largely unspoken preferences and routines regarding how to think, act and respond within the situations that we encounter. We acquire these dispositions over time through processes of socialisation – particularly during our early upbringing – and gradually they come to inform everything from our ideas about what sports or music we like, or what kind of career we could and should aspire to, to who we are, where we 'fit into' society and our wider sense of identity.

Furthermore, Bourdieu argues that we share much of our habitus with other people who have similar backgrounds to us. So, while no two people will share *exactly* the same habitus – because no two people share exactly the same social experiences and upbringing – many aspects of social experience are shared. People of the same social class, ethnicity, gender, or nationality will, says Bourdieu, share certain background experiences and will therefore share certain aspects of their habitus. In his view, this helps to explain why people of (for example) similar class backgrounds often think, act and make decisions (e.g. about whether or not to go to university) in similar ways. So, we can begin to see how Bourdieu saw habitus as a means of explaining how large-scale social structures impact upon, and are reproduced through, individual thoughts and actions.

Habitus may therefore help us to understand why there are often observable patterns and regularities in the way that people and groups behave. This patterning suggests that there are some unwritten 'rules' that we understand, though not at a fully conscious level, about how it is appropriate for us to act and think if we are of a particular class background, nationality, gender, age, etc. This leads to identifiable commonalities in behaviour between people who share a social characteristic or attribute. As Maton (2014) explains, for example:

> social practices are characterized by regularities – working-class kids tend to get working-class jobs... middle-class readers tend to enjoy middle-brow literature, and so forth – yet there are no explicit rules dictating such practices.
>
> (2014: 50)

The habitus can therefore be seen as the social structure within us: our upbringing within a particular (for example) class, ethnic or national environment that guides our thoughts, feelings and actions, even though we may not be fully aware of it.

However, as Costa and Murphy (2015) point out, Bourdieu did not claim that our background and our habitus *entirely* determine our thoughts and actions; rather, they provide us with a set of flexible and implicit preferences, which also allow room for more conscious and reflective action. So, Bourdieu argued, we aren't just unthinking machines automatically acting out the programming of our upbringing. That background, through our habitus, does exert a powerful influence on what we do, but it does not dictate it completely. We can, in his view, exercise some freewill (or 'agency') outside of it.

Bourdieu is also keen to point out that we cannot understand the habitus in isolation from the environments within which it is formed, and within which it takes effect. In this sense, it is a 'relational' concept. This means that habitus can only truly be understood in relation to the various social environments of which we are a part. Bourdieu called these environments 'fields'. Fields could include things such as the school, the university system, or the teaching profession, and our habitus may be more aligned and 'in tune' with some of these fields than it is with others. Each field has its own 'rules', value systems and competitive struggles. They also have their own sources of advantage, which Bourdieu called 'capital'. The more aligned our habitus is with the fields we encounter, the more comfortable and successful we are likely to be within them. This relationship between habitus, field and capital is explored in the following section.

'Field' and 'capital' in relation to habitus

Bourdieu's contention was that the habitus develops as we interact with the different fields that we encounter in our lives (e.g. our neighbourhood or our school). Each field has its own 'rules' about how to act and be successful, and the more we experience a particular field, the more likely we are to understand its rules and achieve some level of status and success within it. We become part of the field and start to think and act as other members of the field do. However, when we encounter a new and unfamiliar field – for example, on our first day at university – our habitus may be 'out of sync'; we do not yet know the rules, the political games that are played or the criteria for success. Bourdieu described this as feeling like 'a fish out of water' (Bourdieu and Wacquant, 1992: 127). Over time, however, we might gain a firmer grasp of these things, and our habitus may gradually change in response to our new environment.

For some people, this process of change may be easier than it is for others. If the habitus that we develop through our early upbringing is in tune with the fields that we encounter later in life, then these transitions are likely to be more straightforward. For example, those whose parents and siblings have attended university, and who have attended a school where progression to university is encouraged, expected and supported, are themselves likely to possess a habitus that is inherently more in tune with the field of higher education. Crucially, for Bourdieu, fields are often dominated by certain social groups – e.g. a particular social class, gender or ethnic group – and they thus align more with the habitus of individuals who come from those groups. For example, professions such as law and medicine tend to be dominated by those from wealthier or middle-class backgrounds. In Bourdieu's terms, this creates a situation where access and transition to such high-status fields becomes considerably easier and more appealing for those who are already middle-class, and more difficult for those from lower-income backgrounds. This has the effect of strengthening and reproducing class inequalities.

Another central concept in Bourdieu's theory is 'capital'. In day-to-day life, we often understand 'capital' simply in economic terms; that is, as money that we can spend on goods and services or invest in things that may provide us with some advantage or benefit in the future – for example our education and qualifications. However, for Bourdieu, capital can also take on *social* and *cultural* forms. These are the resources that individuals can draw on in order to further their chances of achieving status and success within that field; Bourdieu (1985: 724) describes them as being 'like the aces in a game of cards'. Each field, he claims, has its own valued forms of cultural and social capital.

Broadly speaking, *social capital* refers to the social contacts and networks to which we have access, which can provide us with some kind of advantage in a particular field. For example, if a child's parents are well networked within the local community and school system, then this is likely to provide the child with some advantage in terms of accessing the best schools. 'Cultural capital', on the other hand, essentially refers to the cultural tastes, attitudes, behaviours, abilities and values that may signify and provide some kind of advantage for the individual. For example, the ability to talk in a well-spoken accent or demonstrate an interest in certain cultural interests (e.g. sport or classical music) might benefit us when applying for a high-status job.

Bourdieu claimed that these forms of capital tend to be dominated and controlled by powerful groups; they are not distributed equally throughout society. So, it tends to be more powerful groups (e.g. wealthier people, men and/or ethnic majorities) who have greater access to these advantageous resources, and who therefore are more likely to gain entry to more powerful and high-status positions. And crucially, for Bourdieu, capital is closely integrated with habitus. Being socialised into a particular habitus also gives us (or denies us) easier access to particular forms of capital. For example, as Papapolydorou (2016) argues, a characteristically middle-class habitus is more likely to be in tune with access to middle-class networks (social capital) and middle-class ways of acting, thinking and talking (cultural capital). This is a theme that will be developed in the following sections.

Habitus and the study of education

Much of Bourdieu's work – particularly during the 1960s and 1970s – focused on habitus within the specific context of education. He was particularly interested in how, despite having some progressive and transformative aims, education systems actually succeed in *perpetuating* social inequalities, by providing a context within which the economic, cultural and social resources (or *capital*) of privileged groups are converted into ongoing advantage. His work on education has received international interest; according to Murphy and Costa (2016: 4), this popularity 'derives from the universality of his concepts in helping to unearth engrained educational issues, such as inequalities regarding access to educational or educational trajectories of the social classes, and the ramifications of the different opportunities derived from such differentiations'.

Across the world, students from privileged backgrounds inherit not just money, but also cultural know-how, useful contacts and networks and an understanding of the cultural 'tastes' they are likely to need in order to be successful in the future.

Thus, in Bourdieu's view, the education system (or field) supports and reproduces social inequalities by valuing and rewarding the habitus and capital of powerful groups, 'while the capitals of the lower classes are systematically devalued' (Stahl, 2015: 22). In this way, educational institutions have the effect of ensuring that 'ability' and the 'right' kinds of attitude and aptitude are defined in terms of the cultural capital and habitus of more powerful and dominant groups. What we understand as 'ability', 'aptitude' or 'intelligence' is not simply a self-evident fact; these concepts are, says Bourdieu, defined in ways that reflect and support the values, habits and norms of dominant groups. The next two sections unpick and illustrate these issues by focusing on two sources of social inequality: social class and ethnicity.

Social class and habitus in education

It is in relation to *social class* inequalities that the concept of habitus has been most widely used in the study of education. Many researchers have used habitus to describe the way in which the values, attitudes and interests of the middle-and upper classes – the wealthier portions of society – are much more likely to be encouraged and rewarded within education than those of the working classes. Diane Reay (2001), for example, argues that the subjects taught in schools, and the forms of knowledge, attitudes, values, aspirations and 'cultural capital' that are valued within the education system are rooted firmly in middle-class culture. The working classes (broadly speaking, those from lower-income backgrounds) are, of course, educated and schooled, but only (claims Reay) in order to provide a functioning, literate and numerate workforce for employers to use – not to advance their own interests or possibilities.

Reay's argument rests on the idea that people of different class backgrounds are likely to have different values and beliefs, as well as different social and cultural capital. That is, people of different class backgrounds are likely to have a different *habitus*, and she argues that it is the habitus of the middle-or upper-class child that is more in tune with – and more valued by – the education system. Working-class children, she argues, are more likely to encounter an unfamiliar environment in the education system – particularly higher education – with unfamiliar pressures and expectations. Their habitus is consequently out of sync with the educational field they find themselves within; this makes their academic journey more difficult than it is for the middle-class student whose background has provided them with a habitus that feels more at ease in the school and the university.

Of course, working-class students can – and do – excel academically, but Reay (2001: 341) argues that this involves losing part or all of their habitus in order to 'fit in': 'the working-class struggle for academic success', she claims, 'is not about finding yourself but rather losing yourself in order to find a new, shiny, acceptable, middle-class persona'. Conversely, she claims, the middle-class habitus is based on the *expectation* of academic success; such success is seen as normal, and failure to attain it is associated with feelings of fear. This emphasis on *aspiration* (see Riddell, 2010; Stahl, 2015) motivates middle-class families to use their social, cultural and economic capital in order to protect and maintain their middle-class position – for example, by demanding that schools prepare their children for selective entrance exams at elite universities, by paying for personal tutors or by moving to a house in a different (and more expensive) school catchment area.

Reay's work on working-class students in higher education (e.g. Reay, 2001; Reay *et al.*, 2009) closely mirrors Bourdieu's own interests. During the 1970s, he examined patterns of access to higher education, and asked why people from working-class backgrounds were less likely to attend university – particularly elite universities – than those from middle-class backgrounds (see Bourdieu and Passeron, 1977). He found that it wasn't so much that working-class students were being deliberately excluded; rather, their own habitus led them to exclude *themselves*. As Maton (2014: 58) explains:

> Rather than the educational system blocking access to [working class students]... these social agents relegate themselves out of the system, seeing university as 'not for the likes of me'. Conversely, middle-class social agents are more likely to consider university education as a 'natural' step, as part of their inheritance. When at university they are also more likely to feel 'at home', for the underlying principles... within the university field – its unwritten 'rules of the game' – are [similar] to their own habituses.

As such, Bourdieu claims, the working-class student at a high-ranking university is much more likely than the middle-class student to feel like a 'fish out of water'. Consequently, claims Lehmann (2015), working-class students at elite universities often experience a transformation of their habitus, from its original form, into a new, more middle-class form that fully embraces academic success, new types of cultural and social capital and the professional career options associated with this. Lehmann argues that this shows how the habitus is not set in stone; it can modify and adapt as it encounters new and unfamiliar fields. Yet, this process of transformation is difficult, challenging and often involves a sense of loss; his interviews with working-class students at an elite university reveal:

> a complex and complicated mix of allegiances to and dismissal of their working-class roots, as many recognize this transformative process as having made relationships with parents or former friends and peers more difficult... as part of this transformation of habitus, the 'old' has become foreign and dislocating.

(Lehmann, 2015: 1–10)

Questions for discussion

- Think back to your first few weeks at university. To what extent did you feel 'at home'? Did you encounter and overcome any feelings of being a 'fish out of water'?
- How do you think your background and upbringing may have influenced such feelings?

Extending this line of investigation, Burke (2015) explores career choices and job-seeking activities among university graduates in Northern Ireland. He finds that both working-class and middle-class graduates were equally likely to be 'strategic' in their outlook toward career-building. However, the strategic working-class individuals experienced greater difficulty in navigating through the highly competitive graduate labour market. Their working-class habitus lacked the 'feel for the game' that the middle-class graduates had, in terms of mobilising their networks and cultural capital to get a high-status graduate job. The field of the graduate labour market, it seems, may still be one that tends to favour the middle-class habitus and its forms of capital.

Another aspect of education where habitus has been discussed in relation to social class is the question of how parents make choices about their child's schooling. For example, Reay and Lucey (2004) explore the ways in which parents of different social classes make choices about which school their children should attend. They studied children, parents and teachers at eight schools in London, and found that a 'classed subjectivity' (broadly speaking, a habitus) impacts upon this process. Middle-class parents, drawing on their habitus, are more likely to be intent on choosing the 'right' school, which contains the 'right' sorts of pupils and teachers that will enable their children to progress on to a good university. Working-class families, on the other hand, were found to share a habitus that often simply negates the concept of choice; they tended simply to assume (claim Reay and Lucey) that their children would go to the local school. Thus, habitus interacts with school choice to reproduce class inequalities (see also Ball and Nikita, 2014).

Levine-Rasky (2009) provides a further illustration of how class habitus can impact upon parental choices around schooling. In her study, based in Canada, she finds that the middle-class habitus, with its associated forms of cultural and social capital, is much more at ease with such choices than is the working-class habitus. Middle-class parents, she argues, are more 'strategic' and systematic in their approach to school choice, and have more cultural and social resources upon which to draw:

> In reflection over school choice, a [middle-class] parent will develop strategies based on preferences for kinds of schools, expectations about the children's future, and importantly on opportunities afforded by any particular school. Does the school emphasize arts or sports or core subjects? Are approaches to [children's classroom] placement and evaluation to their liking?… Does it have children that parents want their children to befriend?… Accomplished through their appreciation of the field, parents respond by formulating a strategy of choice.
>
> (Levine-Rasky, 2009: 332)

This helps us to understand the specific ways in which the middle-class habitus impacts upon parental choices. Armed with their class habitus, their cultural understanding of the school system and their influential networks, middle-class parents are more likely to desire and ensure that their children go to a particular school. The research cited above seems to suggest that this may be less of a concern or an option for working-class parents. Thus, within the increasingly marketised field of education, the middle-class habitus, with its reserve of different kinds of capital, is in a favoured position.

Questions for discussion

- Think back to when you first went to secondary school. How did you, and/or your parents, decide which school you would attend? Did you simply attend the nearest school, or was a more distant school chosen?
- What criteria or information was used in making that choice? Try to relate your answers to the issues discussed above, in terms of habitus, school choice and social class.

Ethnicity, language and habitus in education

Ethnic diversity and immigration, and their implications for education and schooling, have long been a subject of discussion in the UK and many other countries around the world. And, with levels of international immigration increasing in recent years (UN, 2017), such issues have received even greater attention. In a world of ever-expanding global mobility, where it is more common for people to move from one country to another, schools, colleges and universities are increasingly needing to under-stand and accommodate a wide variety of cultures, languages and ethnic identities. This presents both opportunities and challenges for educators and learners. The following sections will examine this growing area of research and will explore the potential for both tension and adaptation between the habitus of ethnic minority and migrant learners, and the educational fields they encounter.

Given the rising levels of immigration in recent years, researchers have increasingly focused on the ways in which learners from immigrant communities construct and manage their identities and habitus, and how this affects their experiences within their host country. For example, in a study based in Australia, Mu (2016) explores the ways in which a 'habitus of Chineseness' is maintained by Australian citizens of Chinese ancestry. This habitus, Mu observes, is based on historical aspects of Chinese culture which are often known as 'Confucianism', after the ancient Chinese philosopher Confucius. It includes elements such as:

> valuing mathematics, handwriting and academic performance; maintaining strong family ties and social hierarchies; hoping to have sons to continue the family line; and feeling embarrassed to refuse requests.
>
> (Mu, 2016: 20)

Mu argues that this 'habitus of Chineseness' promotes a particular set dispositions in learners who possess Chinese cultural heritage, and that these dispositions orient them in particular ways in rela-tion to education. In particular, all of Mu's participants expressed a desire to 'reproduce Chineseness in future through intergenerational Chinese learning' (Mu, 2016: 28). So, he observes, the participants in his study had chosen to follow educational programmes in 'Chinese Heritage Learning', in order to ensure that their ethnic identity, cultural values and the Chinese language were maintained over the generations. Thus, Mu argues, Confucian values, socialised into Chinese children from a young age, form the basis of the Chinese habitus, which is based on – and is reproduced through – the learning of Chinese cultural values and the Chinese language. This demonstrates how the habitus of immi-grant communities can find continuity and support through education and learning.

Other researchers have, however, focused more on the *tensions* that can emerge between the habitus of immigrant communities and the education system they encounter in their new country. Moskal (2014) observes that much of this research has focused on the uneasy relationship between the child's identity, their habitus, language and culture and the unfamiliar educational field they find themselves within. In her study of Polish children whose families had recently migrated to Scotland, Moskal found that there were actually some similarities between the habitus of the children and the field of the Scottish schooling system (e.g. in the way that they placed great value on hard work and academic achievement). However, she also found that the children's habitus was closely integrated with their own home language, and this sometimes brought their habitus into tension with the English-speaking field of the school. While the children had learned English quickly, they often lacked the cultural capital of being able to speak it fluently, and thus were relatively disadvantaged in comparison with their English-speaking peers.

Very similar findings are reported by Flynn (2013) in her study of teachers in England. Flynn focussed on teachers whose classes contained significant numbers of children from recently immigrated Polish families. She found that the teachers, under pressure from the demands of Ofsted, league tables and the national curriculum, felt that the Polish children in some ways had the 'right' kind of classroom habitus: they valued diligence, motivation and aspiration. At the same time, however, the children were still in the process of learning English; this led the teachers to define them as being 'in deficit' in relation to the requirements of the curriculum, and therefore not 'full' pupils in the same way that the native English speakers were. In Bourdieu's terms, as the children lacked fluency in English, their habitus therefore lacked access to the right kind of 'linguistic capital' (Flynn, 2013, 2016) that would enable them to fully integrate into the field of the school.

Chao (2013) provides a slightly different view of the immigrant habitus in host-country settings. In her study of Chinese families that had recently migrated to the USA, she finds – like Flynn (2013) – that a lack of fluency with the host language can indeed be a factor that brings the habitus of the immigrant learner into tension with a new and unfamiliar educational field. This, she says, prompts the learner to make a difficult process of adaptation to their new environment. Crucially, however, Chao argues that the *social class* of the learner is an important intervening factor in this process. She found that wealthier, middle-class Chinese parents had the inclination, aspirations and resources to assist their children in learning English and modifying their habitus so that it aligned more closely with their new social and educational environments. Therefore, we should not over-generalise about the experiences and habitus of 'immigrant communities', as social class differences mean that their experiences are actually likely to be diverse and varied. Middle-class families, of whatever nationality, are more likely than lower-income families to have access to resources and capital that ease the transition of their habitus. As Chao (2013: 69–70) explains:

> One of the key findings of this study is that the middle-class Chinese immigrant parents' class habitus and sociocultural resources may… enable them to respond with relative ease and flexibility to their newcomer adolescents' socialization in the United States… In other words, [middle]-class habitus provides the parents with more access, information, and resources for participation in their newcomer adolescents' integration into the mainstream schools.

The possibility of tensions between the habitus of immigrant and ethnic minority learners, and the field of the western education system is nothing new; research shows that even the more established immigrant communities tend to experience it. For example, Papapolydorou (2016) discusses the experiences of Black African and Caribbean students and their parents in inner-city schools in London. She finds a general dislocation between the lived experiences and culture of the black community and the white-dominated, euro-centric education system. This had the effect of discouraging black pupils, and their parents, from participating fully in school life and activities. As she explains:

> schools, as White British middle-class institutions… do not address the needs and interests of the Black African and Caribbean students… This gap between schools' culture and values on the one hand and Black African and Caribbean communities' needs on the other hand appears to hinder Black African and Caribbean empowerment and participation in the school community'.
> (Papapolydorou, 2016: 87)

Again, we can see how tension between the habitus of a relatively disadvantaged group, and the cultural 'rules' of a field defined by more powerful groups, can have the effect of reproducing inequalities.

Critiques of habitus

As the above discussions suggest, many researchers have found the concept of habitus – and related concepts such as social and cultural capital – useful in explaining how social structures and inequalities are reproduced over time. As encapsulated in Bourdieu's work, these ideas offer a means of understanding how large-scale social structures, such as class and ethnicity, impact upon small-scale dispositions, values and resources, and are thus perpetuated. Particularly within the study of education, many commentators have used habitus and capital as a lens through which to view the ways in which the values, social contacts and cultural tastes of, for example, the white or middle-class family find easier validation and success in the education system than do those of other social groups.

Yet, in spite (or perhaps because) of its popularity, Bourdieu's work has attracted significant criticism. For example, both Nash (1999) and Crossley (2013) highlight the often-repeated observation that the concept of habitus could be much more clearly and precisely defined. Indeed, Bourdieu offered different definitions at different times, and critics suggest that this inevitably confuses his theory somewhat. It is also sometimes unclear, argues Nash (1999), whether he sees the habitus as existing at the level of the individual (e.g. like a person's individual sense of identity), or at the level of a collective (e.g. an entire social class), or both.

Further critiques of habitus have focused more on how it has been taken on and used by other researchers. Reay (2004: 432), for example, argues that it is now over-used in educational research, in ways that Bourdieu never intended, to the point of it becoming almost meaningless: 'there is', she claims, 'an increasing tendency for habitus to be sprayed throughout academic texts… bestowing gravitas without doing any theoretical work'. Maton (2014) makes a similar point. He argues that one of the main problems with habitus is the way in which it has been applied – particularly in education research – where writers have often forgotten Bourdieu's assertion that habitus only really makes sense in relation to the 'field'. Many writers have forgotten, he says, that habitus can only explain the persistence of inequality in education if we show how the habitus of more disadvantaged groups is less likely to be in tune with the dominant form of educational field. Otherwise, argues Maton, habitus simply becomes another way of saying 'an individual's attitude', or 'their social background', and this makes it a much less useful concept.

Other critics have raised objections relating to the role of conscious freewill (or 'agency') in Bourdieu's conceptualisation of habitus. As noted above, Bourdieu wanted to avoid being deterministic; that is, he was keen to avoid the argument that individuals are like machines who unthinkingly follow the rules into which they have been socialised. He claimed that habitus was a way of getting around this problem as, in his view, it allowed room for the role of freewill. As Burke (2015) points out, however, some of his critics disagree, and argue that he actually fell into the same determinist trap that he was trying to avoid. Jenkins (2002), for example, claims that Bourdieu's theory underestimates the importance of rational thought and deliberative action, and fails to explain properly how individual agency can impact on social behaviour if the habitus is (as he argued) shaped by social structure. Bourdieu's response to these accusations of determinism is to emphasise that he sees habitus as being open to creative change in response to engagement with new and unfamiliar fields, but Jenkins points out that Bourdieu's work contains few genuine examples of change or resistance to dominant fields on the part of individuals. 'His social universe', claims Jenkins (2002: 91) 'remains one in which things happen to people, rather than a world in which they can intervene in their individual and collective destinies'. Thus, if we agree with Jenkins' criticism, then Bourdieu's notion of habitus represents an overly simplistic view of how individual learners experience and respond to education.

Conclusion

This chapter has provided an overview of one of the most important and influential sociological concepts in the study of education: the habitus. Bourdieu described the habitus as the enduring dispositions, values and attitudes that the individual acquires from their upbringing and social experience, and which they share with individuals of a similar background. While he was certainly not the only sociologist to use the concept, it is his work that has been most widely applied to education research. He saw habitus – along with the related concepts of capital and field – as helping us to understand and explain how social inequalities persist through the thoughts and actions of individuals, and how institutions such as the education system contribute to this process.

In examining social class, for example, we saw that the individualistic, 'aspirational' middle-class habitus may be more in tune with – and more likely to be rewarded by – the rules and values of our education system than the working-class habitus. Similarly, in relation to ethnicity, we saw that schools often present an unfamiliar or unwelcoming cultural 'field' to the habitus of the migrant or ethnic minority child. Disadvantaged groups may therefore lack the kinds of habitus and capital (e.g. networks, or cultural understanding) to become valued and successful within an education system that has been designed by, and for, more powerful and privileged groups.

Finally, in considering the value of Bourdieu's work to the practical world of education, Nash asks:

> What does the sociology of education, considered as educational research, offer to teachers? It offers explanations. Our core concern must be with the causes of social differences in access to education. What is the contribution of family resources, of income, educational knowledge, and social connections?
>
> (1999: 185)

In relation to such questions, Nash argues that, in spite of its limitations, Bourdieu's work is enlightening, as it helps both teachers and researchers to understand why there is a tendency for people of different backgrounds and social characteristics to experience and perceive education differently. Moreover, its enduring popularity suggests that many writers and practitioners still find the concept of habitus indispensable in explaining how the education system (or field), in concert with the subjective dispositions of the individual, ultimately reproduces wider social inequalities.

Summary points

- The habitus, as developed through the work of Pierre Bourdieu, is a collection of dispositions and attitudes, derived from background experiences, which guide the individual's thoughts, actions, preferences and inclinations. People of similar social backgrounds (e.g. the same social class, or ethnicity) will share a similar habitus.

- The habitus is closely related to social capital (e.g. networks) and cultural capital (e.g. cultural tastes). These are used as resources to maintain and strengthen the advantaged position of privileged groups, which in turn reinforces social inequalities.
- Within education, for example, various writers have argued that the middle-class habitus provides values, attitudes aspirations and access to forms of capital that benefit the middle-class child. In relation to ethnicity, some writers claim that western education systems tend to favour the habitus of the indigenous white child.
- The concept of habitus (and Bourdieu's work more generally) has been highly influential in the study of education, but it has been criticised for lacking a clear definition, for being wrongly applied by some writers, and for failing to escape a deterministic view of social behaviour.

Recommended reading

Bourdieu, P. (1997) The forms of capital. In Halsey, A. H., Lauder, H., Brown, P. and Wells, A. S. (Eds.). *Education: Culture, Economy, Society.* Oxford: Oxford University Press.

Bourdieu, P. (1990) *The Logic of Practice.* Cambridge: Polity Press. (Particularly chapter 3: Structures, *habitus*, practices.)

Davey, G. (2009) Using Bourdieu's concept of habitus to explore narratives of transition. *European Education Research Journal*, **8**(2), pp. 276–284.

Murphy, M. and Costa, C. (2016) Introduction: Bourdieu and education research. In Murphy, M. and Costa C. (Eds.). *Theory as Method in Research: On Bourdieu, Social Theory and Education.* Abingdon: Routledge.

Acknowledgement

The author would like to thank Claire Soper for her helpful comments on an early draft of this chapter.

References

Ball, S. J. and Nikita, D. P. (2014) The global middle class and school choice: A cosmopolitan sociology. *Zeitschrift für Erziehungswissenschaft*, **17**(3), pp. 81–93.

Bourdieu, P. (1985) The social space and the genesis of groups. *Theory and Society*, **14**(6), pp. 723–744.

Bourdieu, P. (1990) *The Logic of Practice.* Cambridge: Polity Press.

Bourdieu, P. and Passeron, J-C. (1977) *Reproduction in Education, Society and Culture.* London: Sage.

Bourdieu, P. and Wacquant, L. (1992) *An Invitation to Reflexive Sociology.* Chicago: University of Chicago Press.

Burke, C. (2015) Habitus and graduate employment: A re/structured structure and the role of biographical research. In Costa, C. and Murphy, M. (Eds.). *Bourdieu, Habitus and Social Research: The Art of Application.* Basingstoke: Palgrave Macmillan.

Chao, X. (2013) Class habitus: Middle-class Chinese immigrant parents. Investment in their newcomer adolescents. Acquisition and social integration. *Anthropology and Education Quarterly*, **44**(1), pp. 58–74.

Costa, C. and Murphy, M. (2015) Bourdieu and the application of habitus across the social sciences. In Costa, C. and Murphy, M. (Eds.). *Bourdieu, Habitus and Social Research: The Art of Application.* Basingstoke: Palgrave Macmillan.

Crossley, N. (2013) Habit and habitus. *Body and Society*, **19**(2-3), pp. 136–161.

Flynn, N. (2013) Encountering migration: English primary school teachers' responses to Polish children. *Pedagogies: An International Journal*, **8**(4), pp. 336–351.

Flynn, N. (2016) Turning a Bourdieuian lens on English teaching in primary schools: Linguistic field, linguistic habitus, and linguistic capital. In Murphy, M. and Costa, C. (Eds.). *Theory as Method in Research: On Bourdieu, Social Theory and Education.* Abingdon: Routledge.

Jenkins, R. (2002) *Pierre Bourdieu*, (2nd ed.). London: Routledge.

Lehmann, W. (2015) Habitus transformation and hidden injuries: Successful working-class university students. *Sociology of Education*, **87**(1), pp. 1–15.

Levine-Rasky, C. (2009) Dynamics of parent involvement at a multicultural school. *British Journal of Sociology of Education*, **30**(3), pp. 331–344.

Maton, K. (2014) Habitus. In M. Grenfell (Ed.). *Pierre Bourdieu: Key Concepts*. Durham: Acumen.

Moskal, M. (2014) Polish migrant youth in Scottish schools: Conflicted identity and family capital. *Journal of Youth Studies*, **17**(2), p. 279.

Mu, G. M. (2016) Negotiating Chineseness through learning Chinese as a heritage language in Australia: The role of habitus. In Murphy, M. and Costa, C. (Eds.). *Theory as Method in Research: On Bourdieu, Social Theory and Education*. Abingdon: Routledge.

Murphy, M. and Costa, C. (2016) Introduction: Bourdieu and education research. In Murphy, M. and Costa, C. (Eds.). *Theory as Method in Research: On Bourdieu, Social Theory and Education*. London: Routledge.

Nash, R. (1999) Bourdieu, habitus and educational research: Is it all worth the candle? *British Journal of Sociology of Education*, **20**(2), pp. 175–187.

Papapolydorou, M. (2016) Inequalities, parental social capital and children's education. In Murphy, M. and Costa, C. (Eds.). *Theory as Method in Research: On Bourdieu, Social Theory and Education*. Abingdon: Routledge.

Reay, D. (2001) Finding or losing yourself? Working-class relationships to education. *Journal of Education Policy*, **16**(4), pp 333–346.

Reay, D. (2004) 'It's all becoming a habitus': Beyond the habitual use of habitus in educational research. *British Journal of Sociology of Education*, **25**(4), pp. 431–444.

Reay, D. and Lucey H. (2004) Stigmatised choices: Social class, social exclusion and secondary school markets in the inner city. *Pedagogy, Culture and Society*, **12**(1): 35–51.

Reay, D., Crozier, G. and Clayton, C. (2009) Strangers in paradise: Working-class students in elite universities. *Sociology*, **43**(6), pp. 1103–1121.

Riddell, R. (2010) *Aspiration, Identity and Self-belief: Snapshots of Social Structure at Work*. Stoke on Trent: Trentham Books.

Stahl, G. (2015) Egalitarian habitus: Narratives of reconstruction in discourses of aspiration and change. In Costa, C. and Murphy, M. (Eds.). *Bourdieu, Habitus and Social Research: The Art of Application*. Basingstoke: Palgrave Macmillan.

Tooley, J. and Darby, D. (1998) *Educational Research: A Critique: A Survey of Published Results*. London: Ofsted.

UN [United Nations] (2017) The International Migration Report 2017 (Highlights). New York: UN Department of Economic and Social Affairs. Available at: http://www.un.org/en/development/desa/population/migration/publications/migrationreport/docs/MigrationReport2017_Highlights.pdf (Accessed 13 December 2018).

3 Education as hegemonic structure

Graham Downes

Introduction

That we have an education system that is both distinctive and relatively fixed in its structure seems reasonably incontestable. But finding reasons why this is the case is complex. One useful way of making sense of this issue is by applying the concept of 'hegemony'. The Agnews provide a simple definition: that hegemony, more than just a synonym for 'empire', refers to the 'enrolment of others in the exercise of your power by convincing, cajoling, and coercing them that they should want what you want' (Agnew and Agnew, 2005: 1–2). But this general definition does not provide an account of the complex debates that have emerged around the concept. In more recent times, the term has been used by Marxist academics to explain the relationships between a dominant capitalist class and an exploited working class (Gramsci, 1971). Such explanations in turn have been the subject of different theoretical approaches and debates. This chapter will focus on the work of one such theorist, Nicos Poulantzas, locating his ideas within the wider debates on the subject of hegemony. Whilst essentially Marxist, Poulantzas focuses on the complex relations that characterise class domination of state governance. Using examples of historical policy text, the chapter will consider the extent to which education policy can be interpreted as part of a hegemonic state structure as defined by Poulantzas. It will conclude by considering the implications of Poulantzas' ideas for education and how we might address issues that arise at a theoretical level.

Why do we need compulsory education? Why does it look the way it does? How is it that so many elements have not changed over the years? These might seem relatively simple questions. But, on closer inspection, education is a curious phenomenon. Principles of meritocracy, wellbeing, moral rectitude and economic prosperity are all reasons given for the importance of education. However, such principles are not easily reducible to a single overarching narrative. It seems we can agree that education is a good thing, but not necessarily why it is a good.

One way we might look at this concept of education is through Marxist approaches that view the state as an essentially repressive instrument that is manipulable exclusively and at will by a single, economically dominant class (Poulantzas, 1965). The reinterpretation of hegemony has featured prominently in Marxist literature. Early Marxist conceptualisations, particularly those of Gramsci, link the formation of states to wider economic arrangements, namely capitalist relations of production: the involuntary socio-economic relationships people enter into so that they can sustain themselves (Gramsci, 1971). As such, modern states can be seen as capitalist and all state governance as arrangements to meet the needs of capital (Jessop, 2002). Such theories are often referred to as 'economic determinism' because they link the economy inextricably to politics: it is the needs of capital that dictate everything that happens in the political sphere (Resnick and Wolff, 1982). However, the approach has been criticised for being too simplistic and for not acknowledging society as a complex structure containing various processes, aspects, instances, levels, moments and so on (Resnick and Wolff, 2006).

Many subsequent theories have, therefore, attempted to provide a more complex account of the relationship between state, economy and society. Nicos Poulantzas' work, in particular, provides us with a more nuanced conceptualisation. Poulantzas was an academic who emerged from the Althusserian Marxist tradition in France (Jessop, 1985). For Poulantzas, the state is distinct from the economic relations within which it exists. It is its own distinctive institution, which reproduces existing class relations. Furthermore, it cannot be seen as singular, representing one group's interests; traditional Marxism would suggest it exists to assert the interests of the capitalist classes. Poulantzas argues that all such interests are forces actualised through the state itself. Of course, none of this answers the question of how forces come into being and establish a dominant (or otherwise) position within the state. Poulantzas adopts an internal/external model to explain these issues and, in so doing, defines the relationship between the state and modes of production. Specifically, the capitalist system is predicated on the separation of individual freedoms from economic arrangements, manifested in relations between production and the forces of surplus value and exchange. By their nature, these interests are oppositional, and it is the role of the state to secure the economic sphere whilst appealing to individual interests (Jessop, 1985). What is significant in Poulantzas' model is the implicit fact that the state cannot always meet the needs of capitalist modes of production because, whilst democratic interests include corporate interests, it is ultimately a universal interest (it is for everyone) including those dominated in relations of production (workers). Furthermore, Poulantzas (1965) argues that the process of domination of state apparatus does not correlate directly between dominant and dominated classes. In his model, the process of domination can happen *within* classes. Thus, those who dominate policy in a context such as education do not represent all the interests of the class they inhabit. It also explains why there is so much political disagreement within education policy contexts.

Poulantzas argues that the specific arrangements between state and a capitalist economy is what leads to hegemony. It is the relatively independent nature of the state (from economic arrangements) that creates uncertainty. And it is from this uncertainty that a need to generate power blocs emerges so that the interests of capital can be secured. But these power blocs cannot be imposed by force because they undermine the universalising interests of the state: the state exists for all, not just corporate interests. The state is therefore essential to the reproduction of capital, but for Poulantzas this is not a simple matter of class domination and coercion. Rather, he asserts that the state mirrors the existing class relations in society and their various political struggles (Poulantzas, 1965). Political practices reflect the wider class practices of the given society. In reality, this necessarily means an asymmetrical set of power relations between the dominant capitalist class and the subordinate working class (as defined through the capitalist relations of production). For Poulantzas, the state serves to manage existing social relationships by reflecting and condensing them: political practices are always class practices (Poulantzas and Martin, 2008). In effect, the state manages existing class contradictions, secures social cohesion and, in so doing, ultimately secures the survival of the capitalist mode of production. Put more simply, the state is a microcosm of society that is simultaneously universalising (everyone is recognised in state practices) and differentiating (because the state universally recognises all existing class relations, the dominance of a particular class is maintained) (Jessop, 1985).

Whilst undeniably a Marxist account of the state (government and governance are inextricably linked to capitalist modes of production), the model of hegemony presented provides a more nuanced and complex account of the relationships and interactions that constitute state governance. Rather than being a direct act of oppression, the state is an internalised and compressed form of wider (capitalist) social relations. It bridges the gap between universality (through democracy) and maintaining the interests of capital through class domination of its governance arrangements. It also provides a complex account of the internal relationships that constitute class: people can have competing interests, even within a class.

The next section of this chapter will consider the appropriateness of Poulantzas' work as a way of explaining social policy (the application of state interests) and, specifically, the context of state provision of education. It will do so by elucidating three themes that have been identified in policy texts since the implementation of compulsory education policy in Britain with the Forster Education Act of 1870. It should be noted that the process of applying such theory to policy contexts involves significant complexity due to the various ontological assumptions that underpin Poulantzas' work. Specifically, the strong link between materialism and theory generally requires a strong level of commitment from those attempting to apply such ideas. However, this chapter serves as an introduction to the idea of hegemony and, where possible, outcomes are presented as possibilities rather than firm claims.

Questions

- What does 'relations of production' mean?
- What is 'material determinism'?
- Why are these concepts important for Marxists?
- To what extent can we say 'relations of production' and 'material determinism' shape our government?

Social policy and education

With reference to Poulantzas, social policy can be seen as a complex entity that entwines different interests, values and conceptualisations of the world. However, this complex arrangement is often predicated on some relatively simple assumptions about the nature and purpose of a given social policy. In effect, a policy can have its own 'DNA' – a set of self-evident truths that act as a 'communion' on a national scale (Anderson, 2006: 6). In the case of education, this 'communion' is relatively well defined: schools are accepted as a necessary part of the state and are constituted by certain necessary elements (e.g. teacher, pupil, classroom and curriculum). In addition, there are also a number of associated practices such as teaching, learning and literacy.

From a Poulantzian perspective of hegemony, the reasons for this consistency in education policy can be attributed to the historical roots of capitalist states. Many have argued that education is both defined by, and essential to, nation-building (Bailyn, 1972; Corrigan and Sayer, 1991). Tracing the historical roots of compulsory education in Europe, Green (2013) argues that, despite romantic notions of education as part of a process towards democratic enlightenment (Rousseau, 1979), the concept of compulsory education actually has its roots in the totalitarian Prussian state of the early nineteenth century. With reference to Green's work, it was the Prussian education system that was the first of its kind in Europe and one that many in England looked to as a model of distinction. This turn of events excludes the possibility of a necessary link between the expansion of the capital processes of production and education: Prussia had not engaged significantly in industrialisation at the point it introduced state education, and England introduced its own system after its industrial revolution. What is consistently evident in the historical roots of education systems across Europe and the United States is that education is used to reinforce and re-impose class relationships, usually at points of perceived social crisis. These crises were often the result of the rapid expansion of urban areas, which resulted in the breakdown in existing social structures such as the family. Ultimately, Green's link between education policy and class relations at an international level has strong resonances with Poulantzian hegemony. In effect, education can be seen as the apotheosis of the idea of internalised class relations: 'universal' because education is open to all and provides access to all, but 'exclusive' because those making the decisions about what education is and how it operates tend to represent the interests of those already in power. To provide a more detailed exposition of the way that hegemonic class relations might operate through education policy, the next section will consider the case of English education.

The Elementary Education Act of 1870 made state schooling available to for five to ten year-olds, and the 1880 Act made schooling statutory in England. Before that, education provision in England had been fragmented and patchy (Chitty, 2009). However, leading up to 1870, two distinct justifications for compulsory education emerged: the need for skills and training made necessary by industrialisation, and the need to educate the masses to ensure they were able to participate in universal suffrage (Gillard, 2011). These justifications manifested themselves in complex ways across class boundaries and social contexts. For example, the old public schools were placed under increasing pressure to 'modernise' their curriculum to reflect new scientific knowledge, whilst the success of 'monitorial schools' – 'the steam engines of the moral world' (Harrison, 1967: 76) – demonstrated the drive towards a moral education for all. These two conceptualisations often acted in conflict with one another: the Church and politicians advocating a wider moral education, whilst those who represented the interests of industry wanted a narrower curriculum that focused on work-based skills, training and the teaching of the good habits of work (Chitty, 2002). Schools also became increasingly recognised in the political system, culminating in the 1870 and 1880 Elementary Education Acts. Despite some variation, there is evidence that the overriding themes relating to productivity and moral rectitude that were evident in 1870 have been manifest ever since. In fact, the 'communion' of education policy from 1870 to the present day can be broken down into distinct, but related, subcategories. The following sections will provide three examples of such categories. These are by no means exhaustive but are certainly significant and fixed within policy texts relating to state provision of education.

1 *The global imperative*

In his speech to parliament prior to the passing of the Education Act of 1870, its proponent William Forster represented compulsory education as both a necessary part of the nation state and one that was alarmingly lacking. For example:

> We must not delay. Upon the speedy provision of elementary education depends our industrial prosperity. It is of no use trying to give technical teaching to our artisans without elementary

education; uneducated labourers – and many of our labourers are utterly uneducated – are for the most part, unskilled labourers, and if we leave our work folk any longer unskilled, notwith-standing their strong sinews and determined energy, they will become over-matched in the competition of the world.

(Forster, 1870)

As far back as 1870, education was thus imagined as a necessary component of the nation state that, in turn, was imagined as an actor within a globally competitive world. The linking of educa-tion with global competition, together with a highly committed style of rhetoric (representing the world with a high level of certainty) are features of many contemporary education policy texts. This aspect of education discourse can be described as a 'global imperative': the sense that there is an alarming deficit in the national education system, that there is no alternative but to educate, that we need to compete globally and that we need to do so immediately. A similar example of this type of rhetoric can be found in an example from 1955 when Winston Churchill stated:

In the last ten years, the soviet higher technical education for mechanical engineering has been developed both in numbers and quality to an extent, which far exceeds anything we have achieved. This is a matter, which needs the immediate attention of Her Majesty's Government… if we are – not to keep abreast – but even to maintain our proportionate place in the world.

(Young, 1958)

Although the context has changed, the rhetorical elements identified in the first extract are still evi-dent: the high level of certainty with reference to abstract concepts ('Soviet education…has been developed both in numbers and quality'); the sense of urgency ('requires immediate attention'); and the threat of global competition to the nation state ('maintain our proportionate place in the world').

A more contemporary text, produced by the Department for Education and Employment (DfEE), provides another example of similar rhetoric:

We are in a new age — the age of information and global competition. Familiar certainties and old ways of doing things are disappearing. The types of jobs we do have changed, as have the industries in which we work and the skills they need. At the same time, new opportunities are opening up as we see the potential of new technologies to change our lives for the better. We have no choice but to prepare for this new age in which the key to success will be the con-tinuous education.

(DfEE, 1998)

Again, we see the same rhetorical features: the high level of commitment ('we *are* in a new age', 'we have no choice but to') contrasted with the extensive use of abstract concepts ('age of information', 'global competition'), and the use of global competition as an imperative ('we have no choice but to prepare for this new age').

Relating these analyses back to the initial theoretical model, the connection between national consciousness and education is made clear. It is only within the context of a nation state, which is in competition with other nation states, that the need for an education system makes sense. Thus, with reference to the notion of hegemony, all justifications for English education policy can be identified as having their roots in the capitalist state and its competitive economic relationships with other nation states.

2 *Meritocracy and the deserving poor*

One aspect of education policy that is distinctively missing from Forster's introduction to the 1870 Education Bill is the issue of social mobility. Forster concludes his remarks to the House of Commons with the following:

> Let us then each of us think of our own homes, of the villages in which we have to live, of the towns in which it is our lot to be busy; and do we not know child after child – boys or girls – growing up to probable crime, to still more probable misery, because badly taught or utterly untaught? Dare we then take on ourselves the responsibility of allowing this ignorance and this weakness to continue one year longer than we can help?
>
> (Forster, 1870: 466)

Here, the legitimation for universal education is couched strongly in moral and causal terms: a lack of teaching is causally linked to crime. It is the duty of 'us' (parliament) to stop 'ignorance' and 'weakness'. This legitimation has strong normative references and relies particularly on a moral justification for the need for compulsory education (Fairclough, 2003). There is also a strong power dynamic in this discourse: parliament is able to evaluate morality, and is thus morally aware; those who are to be acted upon (those not educated properly) are morally ignorant. The strong reference to causality also creates a strong relationship between 'crime' and 'untaught'. In addition, the text creates a relationship between class dynamics and wealth. For example:

> ....we have done well in assisting the benevolent gentlemen who have established schools, yet the result of the State leaving the initiative to volunteers, is, that where State help has been most wanted, State help has been least given, and that where it was desirable that State power should be most felt it was not felt at all. In helping those only who help themselves, or who can get others to help them, we have left un-helped those who most need help. Therefore, not-withstanding the large sums of money we have voted, we find a vast number of children badly taught, or utterly untaught, because there are too few schools and too many bad schools, and because there are large numbers of parents in this country who cannot, or will not, send their children to school.
>
> (Forster, 1870: 442)

Here, there is a significant discrepancy in the agency attributed to the different actors. 'Gentlemen' are associated with 'benevolent', providing them with a privileged position. They are also given agency within the education system: they 'want' help from the government, as opposed to needing or being provided with help. The text also portrays the poor as often helpless but deserving of help: for example, there is a distinction between those 'who help themselves' and 'those who most need help'. A slightly different portrayal of the poor is provided in the final sentence which adds that there are parents who 'cannot, or will not, send their children to school'. Here, there is a distinction between the helpless poor (the deserving) and the disobedient poor (the undeserving) (Romano, 2017). See also Chapter 7.

This discourse needs to be seen within the historical context of class dynamics and attitudes in England. It was not until the emergence of a welfare state after the Second World War that the notion of meritocracy was foregrounded within education policy. Prior to this, the notion of social mobility was focused on the discourse of a 'deserving poor': hardworking people who deserved a little bit more than they had (Chitty, 2002). More recently, the issue of social justice has become more significant in policy texts. Clyde Chitty links a shift towards meritocratic principles with the expansion of the middle-classes after the Second World War. For Chitty, the expansion of secondary education after the war to include modern schools was met with a wide level of frustration by middle-class parents who found opportunities for their children to access a grammar-school education limited. As a consequence, the resulting reforms, which advocated the establishment of comprehensive schools, gave greater prominence to the ideas of social mobility and equal opportunity. However, it is worth noting that this type of social mobility was *for* the middle classes who were already familiar with the language of aspiration. In the ensuing years, a discourse has emerged that merges both the notion of a deserving poor and the notion of middle-class aspiration. The following extract from the 2006 education white paper demonstrates the way both concepts are used interchangeably:

> ...we must deliver for all children, but particularly for those whose family background is most challenging. Education is one of the keys to social mobility, and so we must make sure that a good education is available to every child in every community. This White Paper sets out how we will meet these challenges and build the school system we all want for our children. More than anything it is a White Paper about aspiration. We must have the highest aspirations for every child whatever their talents and ability. And we must have a schools system that can respond to those aspirations.
>
> (DfES, 2005: 5)

As with Forster's text from 1870, the poorest are presented passively: they need and are not able to help themselves. In essence, this is a reference to the deserving poor: those who cannot help themselves but deserve to be helped. In this extract, however, we can see the use of language that was absent from the educational discourse of 1870. Specifically, this is the language associated with meritocracy, namely 'social mobility' and 'aspiration'. However, an interesting conceptual relationship exists in the opening two sentences of this passage. The first sentence refers to the 'most challenging' families; the opening clause of the second sentence states 'education is one of the keys to social mobility'; the second clause of the second sentence states 'and so we must make sure that a good education is available to every child in every community'. The sequence of statements can thus be reduced to:

- We must deliver education to those from the most challenging background;
- Education is the key to social mobility;
- Education should be available to all.

This use of additive logic means the passage can be read in a number of ways. For example, the passage could mean either that *education helps poor people become socially mobile*, or that *all children should have equal opportunities to do well*. This is significant because it means the text can simultaneously appeal to middle-class aspiration whilst also declaring intent to discriminate against them, that is, by giving particular attention to the poor.

This type of rhetoric is perhaps the most indicative example of Poulantzian hegemony in education policy. Here, we can see the universalising tendencies of state governance (meritocracy, equal opportunity) operating as an inclusive state. Education is open to all and provides everyone with opportunities to access wealth and power. However, a plethora of empirical evidence suggests this is not necessarily true (Social Mobility Commission, 2017). Perhaps the clue to why this is so is in the way the example shifts seamlessly between concepts of a deserving poor and social mobility. In using the terms interchangeably, the text enables simultaneous discourses to occur, one universal (meritocracy) and one that differentiates (between the poor and middle class).

3 *Citizenship and community*

As discussed in the opening section of this chapter, Green (2013) makes the point that at a time of significant social change, the discursive link between education and social cohesion was historically significant. This connection is evident in historical texts. For example, Forster's 1870 speech contained strong causal associations between education and political change:

> To its honour, Parliament has lately decided that England shall in future be governed by popular government. I am one of those who would not wait until the people were educated before I would trust them with political power. If we had thus waited we might have waited long for education; but now that we have given them political power we must not wait any longer to give them education.
>
> (Forster, 1870: 465)

Again, the case for education is made in highly committed terms ('we must not wait') but here its role is justified within the context of democratic process: if all have the potential to rule, all must have the ability to rule, that is, they must be educated so that they can rule. The use of pronouns in this passage is significant: 'I' (William Forster) is equivalent to 'we' (parliament), that is, it is used interchangeably (Fairclough, 2003). The agency between these two pronouns and 'them' (the people) is striking: *we* granted *them* power and *we* must give *them* education…*we* should educate *them* before *we* trust *them* with power'.

By contrast, the people are passive: they are given to, they are to be trusted, and they are to be educated. Again, this reflects the order of discourse that has already been established and, again, it uses moral language in its justification (Fairclough, 2003). The use of the word 'trust' reflects a set of values predicated on fear. Again, this is a reflection of the division between the deserving and undeserving poor, where here the emphasis is on those who are undeserving and worthy of fear. Although the tone of the language varies, more contemporary texts continue to reproduce this rhetoric. For example, in a speech given in 2002, Tony Blair said:

> It is completely unacceptable that young people out of control, excluded from school, are left free to roam the streets causing misery and mayhem in local communities… Schools need to know that the Government is on their side and the community is on their side against unruly children and abusive parents… This is not just about education. It is about what kind of country we want to be. We see all around us the consequences if families and communities fail: disaffection, lack of respect, vandalism, drugs, violence. And that is why, when I got together law

enforcement agencies for that meeting on street crime, I didn't just ask the police, the Home Secretary and the Lord Chancellor, but the Ministers responsible for education, for health, for local government, for sport. Because every child denied a place in a good school is more at risk of falling into crime.

(Blair, 2002)

Again, a particular type of rhetoric is evident: a disengaged group (unruly children and abusive parents) capable of disruption (and thus to be feared) on one side; those capable of providing moral guidance (Government, schools and community) on the other side. And there is a strong class dynamic at work here. Abusive parents and unruly children are equated with symptoms of poverty: drugs, violence, crime and poor education. There is also a strong causal logic within the extract: the 'consequences' of 'failing families' is lack of respect, vandalism, drugs and violence. The sequence of statements also serves to extend the logic to include education by inference: children are excluded from school, they are left to roam the streets, they have unruly and abusive parents, they are from failing families, they fall into crime. Although this appears as an additive logical sequence, there is a strong inference that these events are connected, and the moral language is oriented towards good schools and bad parents.

Such texts often work alongside wider moral panics induced by specific social events. For example, following the 'riots' of 2011, Michael Gove delivered a speech in which he said:

For all the advances we have made, and are making in education, we still, every year allow thousands more children to join an educational underclass – they are the lost souls our school system has failed. It is from that underclass that gangs draw their recruits, young offenders institutions find their inmates and prisons replenish their cells. These are young people who, whatever the material circumstances which surround them, grow up in the direst poverty – with a poverty of ambition, a poverty of discipline, a poverty of soul. I recognise that using a word like underclass has potentially controversial connotations. It can seem to divide society into them and us. But I believe there's a merit in plain speaking. I am also haunted by the thought that I might, if circumstances had been different, have been one of them. I was born to a single parent, never knew my biological father and spent my first few months in care.

(Gove, 2011)

The compound noun 'education underclass' is a direct link between education and an undeserving poor. In this extract Gove sets up a relationship between the word 'poverty' and the moral judgements of the poor that have already been described. Firstly, the material reference to poverty is collocated with the thick moral term 'dire' (the direst poverty). In the next sentence poverty itself is used in moral terms: 'poverty of ambition' and 'poverty of soul'. Despite the recognition that such a statement can create a sense of moral order, Gove goes on to give a strong indication that this is the case with his own reference to 'them' ('I could have been one of them'). Again this is a set of statements with strong causal inference: 'I could have been one of them; I was born to a single parent'. Thus, we even know something about who the underclass is.

All of these elements define a discourse of education that positions decision-makers, participants and outsiders. However, there have been two relatively modern developments that have shifted the dynamics of the discursive structure. Firstly, the extent and veracity of judgements that are passed on the education system have increased. Secondly, there has been an increasing trend to link the concept of community with education. With reference to the first, education has increasingly been seen as a domain of politicians and parents, as opposed to exclusively that of educationalists. A key moment in the development of this discursive feature was James Callaghan's Ruskin Speech in 1976, in which he stated:

> There is nothing wrong with non-educationalists, even a prime minister, talking about (education). Everyone is allowed to put his oar in on how to overcome our economic problems, how to put the balance of payments right, how to secure more exports and so on and so on. Very important too. But I venture to say not as important in the long run as preparing future generations for life. RH Tawney, from whom I derived a great deal of my thinking years ago, wrote that the endowment of our children is the most precious of the natural resources of this community. So I do not hesitate to discuss how these endowments should be nurtured…Let me answer that question 'what do we want from the education of our children and young people?' with Tawney's words once more. He said: 'What a wise parent would wish for their children, so the state must wish for all its children'. I take it that no one claims exclusive rights in this field. Public interest is strong and legitimate and will be satisfied.
>
> (Callaghan, 1976)

Here, an equivalence is set up between the words 'community' and 'everyone'. Specific instances of everyone/community are 'prime minister', 'parents' and 'state'. Children are actually represented as belonging to the community through the possessive pronoun 'our' and thus are not equally part of it. There then follows the setting up of a relationship, which can only be described as a rhetorical sleight of hand.

Referencing R.H. Tawney, Callaghan states, 'What a wise parent would wish for their children, so the state must wish for all its children'. Thus, what a wise parent does, the state should do too, where a wise parent goes, the state should follow. In reality, the relationship between 'parents' and 'state' is asymmetric: it is difficult to conceive of parents having as much sway over the apparatus of government as the sway a government can have over parents (Fairclough, 2003; Ranciere and Corcoran, 2010). Callaghan concludes with a reference to 'public interest': 'I take it that no one claims exclusive rights in this field. Public interest is strong and legitimate and will be satisfied'. Here, the equivalence is scaled back up and the original relationship between parent and state is reversed: what is in the interests of parents is in the interests of 'the public'. Thus, parents do not have exclusive rights over how their children are educated.

Conclusion

Three themes have been identified within education policy texts. Economic discourses are clearly evident, particularly globalisation that has been, and continues to be, an important legitimising concept within the education discursive formation. These economic discourses tend to overlap with notions of fairness, particularly social mobility. Productivity and social mobility tend to be used interchangeably (as an equivalence) and where social mobility is developed as a distinctive characteristic of education, it is always presented in a positive causal relationship with productivity. Social cohesion can also form part of this relationship (communities improve productivity).

However, as Green observes, the need for social cohesion has historically been of prime importance in education and the texts used demonstrate the class dimension to the concept, which is often invoked at times of moral panic. The word 'community' has an eminent position within this discourse, allowing for the articulation of shared values and the identification of problem others (those beyond the community, those harming the community). With reference to Poulantzas' theory of hegemony, the examples above reveal important resonances. Firstly, the relatively fixed nature of education policy suggests, at least, the operation of a 'power bloc'. This does not mean that there has been conspiracy based on class relations, but it does mean that certain ways of talking about education have emerged that suit the interests of particular groups. As discussed, the themes of global competition, the deserving poor and community cohesion are consistent themes in the rhetoric used in education policy texts. These are by no means exhaustive in terms of the discursive content of education policy texts, but they do provide interesting exemplars of the social dynamics of education policy and how it interacts with class dynamics. It is also worth pointing out that these themes are not necessarily compatible and, under certain conditions, can be seen to be contradictory. In effect, the themes are examples of metaphorical 'plate spinning': they offer different perspectives on class tensions and the need to secure the valourisation of capital. But, as Poulantzas observes, these perspectives serve the needs of different factions within a capitalist class: some focus more on industrial expansion, others on order and moral conditioning, whilst simultaneously acknowledging the need for a (rhetorical at least) sense of solidarity that is a prerequisite of a universalising democratic state.

It is also worth noting that, whilst potentially contradictory, these themes can be seen to have a unified purpose in terms of capital. In a sense, they can be broken down into two direct purposes: to expand the reach of capital (through increased productivity and global reach) and to condition a potential insubordinate working class (through moral rectitude and community cohesion). In addition, rhetoric around meritocracy and equal opportunity can be seen as a covering principle that serves both to alleviate the oppressive nature of the expansion of capital (it is in all our interests and we are all able to have a say) and to ensure that the existing relations of production are secured (we are all able to become wealthy capitalists, so our existing situation is either our fault or our choice).

So, it is possible to apply Poulantzas' ideas to the education system in England, and this also appears to fit well with accounts of global education systems provided by academics like Andy Green. But such accounts may be too negative for many. It is important to note that, like most Marxists, Poulantzas' work externalises the forces that affect social relations: it is the fundamental nature of capital that dictates the nature of society. If this is true, it would appear diametrically opposed to the goodwill and intentions of most policy-makers and educators whose primary motivation is to help people to achieve more. But we also know that compulsory education has not achieved the meritocratic outcomes that such individuals desire (Feinstein, 2003). If Poulantzas is to be believed this will not be easy to change: education will always internalise the class dynamics evident in wider society. To this extent, education can be seen undeniably as part of a wider hegemonic process. But this is not to say education cannot be a force to the contrary. To make it so, however, requires a more radical approach from educators, one that breaks down the existing assumptions and discourses that underpin education, and one that would, by definition be uncomfortable for those who currently make decisions about what education is and how it should operate.

Questions for discussion:

- To what extent can we say that our government is defined by class domination?
- Do you agree that the examples of policy texts in this chapter demonstrate class domination of education policy?
- Would you change education policy to ensure that one social class does not dominate it?
- To what extent do you think teachers are part of a hegemonic state structure?

Summary

- Theories of hegemony can help us to explain why education structures tend to reproduce themselves.
- Whilst one explanation of hegemony might focus on economic determinism and relations of production, the chapter focuses on the potentially more nuanced account provided by Nicos Poulantzas.
- Poulantzas' theory places individual and economic interests in tension with one another; it is the role of the political system to ameliorate these tensions.
- Power blocs inevitably form to secure the interests of capital through the political system.
- State education can be seen as part of these political arrangements. Whilst seemingly offering universal access, it is simultaneously exclusive because those who are already in power decide what taught.

Recommended reading

Green, A. (2013) *Education and State Formation: Europe, East Asia and the USA*. London: Palgrave Macmillan.
Jessop, B. (1985) *Nicos Poulantzas: Marxist Theory and Political Strategy*. London: Macmillan.
Mayo, P. (2015) *Hegemony and Education Under Neoliberalism: Insights from Gramsci*. Abingdon: Routledge.

References

Agnew, J. A. and Agnew, P. G. J. (2005) *Hegemony: The New Shape of Global Power*. Philadelphia: Temple University Press.
Anderson, B. (2006) *Imagined Communities: Reflections on the Origin and Spread of Nationalism*, (2nd ed.). London: Verso Books.
Bailyn, B. (1972) *Education in the Forming of American Society: Needs and Opportunities for Study*. New York: Norton.
Blair, T. (2002) Speech on education at Abraham Moss High School, Manchester. Available at: http://webarchive.nationalarchives.gov.uk/20061101012618/http://number10.gov.uk/page1706 (Accessed 6 August 2016).
Callaghan, J. (1976) A rational debate based on the facts. Ruskin College Oxford 18 October 1976. Available at: http://www.educationengland.org.uk/documents/speeches/1976ruskin.html. (Accessed July 2019).
Chitty, C. (2002) *Understanding Schools and Schooling*. London: RoutledgeFalmer.
Chitty, C. (2009) *Education Policy in Britain*. Contemporary Political Studies. London: Palgrave Macmillan.
Corrigan, P. and Sayer, D. (1991) *The Great Arch: English State Formation as Cultural Revolution*. Oxford: Blackwell.
DfEE (1998) *The Learning Age: A Renaissance for a New Britain*. London: The Stationery Office.
DfES (2005) *White Paper: Higher Standards, Better Schools for All*. London: DfES. (Forward by Ruth Kelly).

Fairclough, N. (2003) *Analysing Discourse: Textual Analysis for Social Research*. London: Routledge.

Feinstein, L. (2003) Very early cognitive evidence. *CentrePiece Summer 2003*, pp. 24–30.

Forster, W. E. (1870) Elementary education bill, first reading. *Hansard 1803–2005*, **199**: pp. 438–498.

Gillard, D. (2011) Education in England: A brief history. Online. Available at: www.educationengland.org.uk/history (Accessed 3 August 2016).

Gove, M. (2011) Michael Gove to the Durand Academy. Online. Available at: https://www.gov.uk/government/speeches/michael-gove-to-the-durand-academy (Accessed 6 August 2016).

Gramsci, A. (1971) *Selections From the Prison Notebooks*. New York: International Publishers.

Green, A. (2013) *Education and State Formation: Europe, East Asia and the USA*. Basingstoke: Palgrave Macmillan.

Harrison, J. F. C. (1967) 'The Steam Engine of the New Moral World': Owenism and education, 1817-1829. *Journal of British Studies*, **6**(2), pp. 76–98.

Jessop, B. (1985) *Nicos Poulantzas: Marxist Theory and Political Strategy*. London: Macmillan.

Jessop, B. (2002) *The Future of the Capitalist State*. Cambridge: Polity Press.

Poulantzas, N. (1965) Préliminaires a l'étude de l'hegemonie dans l'état'. *Les Temps Modernes*, **234**, pp. 862–96.

Poulantzas, N. A. and Martin, J. (2008) *The Poulantzas Reader: Marxism, Law, and the State*. London: Verso Books.

Ranciere, J. and Corcoran, S. (2010) *Dissensus: On Politics and Aesthetics*. London: Bloomsbury Academic.

Resnick, S. A. and Wolff, R. D. (1982) Marxist epistemology: The critique of economic determinism. *Social Text*, **6**, pp. 31–72.

Resnick, S. A. and Wolff, R. D. (2006) *New Departures in Marxian Theory*. Abingdon: Routledge.

Romano, S. (2017) *Moralising Poverty: The 'Undeserving' Poor in the Public Gaze*. Abingdon: Routledge.

Rousseau, J. J. (1979) *Emile: Or, On Education*. London: Penguin.

Social Mobility Commission (2017) *Time for Change: An Assessment of Government Policies on Social Mobility 1997-2017*. London: Social Mobility Commission

Young, M. (1958) *The Rise of the Meritocracy*. London: Thames and Hudson.

4 Spaces of invisibility and marginalisation in schools

Martin Levinson

Introduction

There is a danger of viewing schools as spatially neutral sites, overlooking the institutional organisation that positions different community members in different places. Drawing on evidence from three separate ethnographic research projects, this chapter reflects on the uses and meanings of space in school settings, exploring the feelings of marginalised students. The chapter highlights ways in which the students in each context acquiesced, resisted or challenged spatial structures and processes that positioned them as outsiders, as well as ways in which they sometimes constructed new meanings for places they did inhabit.

In each of the three projects discussed here, the research focused on students who, for diverse reasons, were struggling to fit into mainstream school settings. Resistance to institutional norms took various forms, including subversive uses of space. However, different understandings can be drawn from each context. In some cases, students were utilising spaces in order to challenge institutional norms. However, in other instances they were simply exploring distinct group identities and allegiances or just emphasising cultural difference.

Given all the demands on teacher time, it is easy to overlook the ways in which cultural environments are changed through the use of space. The pressure of work leaves limited opportunity for reflection on the social production of space (Massey, 1995, 1999). Massey's (2005: 119) portrayal of place as 'a bundle of trajectories' implies the complex inter-relationships that can shift meanings of specific spaces from moment to moment. Within this dynamic framework there is opportunity for manipulation from above and below.

Structures of spatial hierarchy within a school do not operate solely through adult management and organisation. Far from being neutral, spaces in classrooms are hierarchical, gendered, racialised, etc. in ways that can be easily overlooked. Similarly, uses of space outside the classroom reveal parallel and often still more marked patterns. For instance, identifying a link between a sense of belonging in the classroom and a desire to construct and occupy informal spaces around school, Brown (2017) noted that the youngsters in lower 'ability' sets tended to occupy peripheral spaces.

Spatial organisation in school environments

Far from being *neutral*, the spatial organisation of schools constructs boundaries of inclusion/ exclusion while also contributing to the formation of 'technologies of domination' that serve to establish normality (Foucault, 1988). To understand what occurs in schools, it is essential to understand the meanings and uses of space (McGregor, 2004). Despite occasional efforts to explore flexible or alternative uses of space in schools (see e.g. Imms *et al.*, 2017; Woolner *et al.*, 2014), schools retain conventional and fixed spatial patterns.

Considering the experiences of Gypsy Traveller children in schools, and drawing on Lefebvre's (1991) concepts around perceived, conceived and lived spaces, Cudworth (2015) argues that space is not a neutral medium for social action to take place but also a vehicle for the establishment and reproduction of social life itself. Within such a framework, Gypsy youngsters are often left outside the norms, occupying marginal spaces. Nevertheless, Cudworth (2015: 87) contends that, when accepted at the micro level of a school, these youngsters can become 'part of the ideological make up, or geographical consciousness' of lived (representational) spaces. At the same time, and as Cudworth acknowledges, while such communities remain unaccepted by the wider spaces of society, progress towards equality is limited.

In my own ethnographic work with Gypsy communities over the past two decades (see e.g. Levinson and Sparkes, 2004, 2005; Levinson, 2015) I have drawn attention to the ways in which the behaviours of Gypsy youngsters are shaped by contrasting spatial environments in home and school settings. Taking Bourdieu's (1984: 170) notion of habitus – a 'structuring structure' which organises practices and the perception of practices, I have argued that the habitus of Gypsy children is constructed to fit in with a different social space, where they dominate and are dominated in different ways. As distinct from the school context, with its (spatial and temporal) restrictions of movement, social space in the home setting (on sites, outside the trailer, at least) is typically characterised by relative freedom and fluidity. In Bourdieu's view, structures of dominance are challenged when agents recognise them for what they are and refuse to co-operate in their reproduction. I have suggested that the capital brought to the school environment is not recognised and is of limited use there, making the transition from home to school problematic. (See also Chapter 2.)

Similarly, I have drawn attention to the contrast between the communal uses of space, relatively fluid in the home environment, with an emphasis on outdoor spaces and where there are lax boundaries according to age-groups, and the rigidly bounded spatial environment of the school. I have suggested that spatial structures in schools are not only alien but oppressive, noting difficulties of adaptation to individualised spaces, with fixed borders, characterised by competition as opposed to collaboration. Moreover, I have proposed that increasing sedentarism has been associated by participants with assimilation, and that in such a context many Gypsy youngsters perceive schools as potential sites of resistance in which their cultural identities are reaffirmed and those of mainstream society rejected (Levinson and Sparkes, 2005).

Cultural dissonance can also emerge through the growth of counter-cultures unrelated to pre-existing alternative structures and processes. Considering the situation of children who have been excluded from schools (see Levinson and Thompson, 2016), it is evident that a sense of difference is reflected through spatial orientation. In particular, for such youngsters, difficulties often emerged after the transition from the small, relatively cosy setting of primary schools to the larger-scale, harsher and more impersonal environment of secondary institutions.

Schools regulate socio-spatial interaction in overt ways, most obviously through allocation to classes and groups. The underlying rationale is usually about control, and there is not necessarily much consideration of wider social outcomes or of the likely responses. Schools sometimes seek to interrupt socio-spatial practices that replicate the wider patterns of external society, e.g. splitting up Gypsy/Traveller students across different classes. In such cases, the youngsters involved are liable to feel isolated and vulnerable when separated from friends and family members, their classrooms becoming more alienating or menacing. They can react by becoming withdrawn or can resist through opposition and defiance that are likely to lead to exclusion. However, such interference is usually restricted to classroom contexts and out in the playground, students tend to revert to social clusters that mirror external patterns.

Similarly, youngsters who are segregated according to ability, whereby they are positioned within different spatial frameworks, have the choice in acquiescing in a process that often leaves them feeling disadvantaged and/or inferior, or they can resist and challenge such perceptions by claiming new places for their own, attributing different meanings to them (Ralph and Levinson, 2018). Though not a minority in the same way, through the development of in-group codes and symbols, they can develop a similar outcast tribe mentality. Through their collective culture, they demonstrate that they do not necessarily endorse the form in which a school environment is presented to them, and can and do resist prescribed representations (Schmidt, 2013).

Narratives of cultural difference, identity formation and resistance: The studies informing this chapter

This discussion draws on three separate research studies, the rationale being that each study provides a slightly different understanding of resistance to the structuring of space in schools. All the studies involved students who felt marginalised in school settings, and whose spatial behaviours were distinctive in one way or another.

The first study dates back to a three-year, ethnographically informed study (1997–2000) of the interface between Gypsy culture and the educational system. This entailed a two-month initial period in two primary schools in the South West of England, during which time the researcher observed the spatial behaviour of children (aged 8–11), both in the classroom and playground. In a subsequent phase, observations took place in three further primary schools and two secondary schools in the South West of England. In total, 40 days were spent in these schools, eight days in each. During this phase, an additional 33 Gypsy pupils became involved in the study. Finally, 31 children participated in individual, formal and structured interviews that focused on spatial behaviour and how these connected to wider attitudes and values regarding schools. The next phase of the study entailed visits to Gypsy sites, observation of spatial behaviour among the children in the home context, and informal conversations with family members about the meanings of place and the different ways of using space in home and school settings. In all, 20 Gypsy sites were visited in the United Kingdom, with the majority visited being in the South West of England and 12 of these sites were visited on more than one occasion.

The second study informing the chapter was part of a project (2015) with students who had been excluded from schools. The data were supplemented by earlier research that took place over a two-year period (2012–2014) in the same institution. The interviews took place in 'The Centre' (name used by the students), a Pupil Referral Unit (PRU) for excluded youngsters in the South West of England. The Centre takes students across primary and secondary age-groups. The research explored the views of students and staff about reasons for being in Alternative Education settings, the difference in culture between such contexts and those provided by mainstream schools and feelings about reintegration.

Ten youngsters were then selected for in-depth interviews. This group seemed representative of the wider group, while it was also felt that their testimonies were likely to capture the range of attitudes encountered in the first phase.

The interviews with youngsters (all aged 11–16) explored their experiences of mainstream schools and alternative settings. More specifically, they covered experiences at primary school, transitions to secondary education, experiences in secondary schools and feelings about alternative approaches in the PRU. There was also discussion about plans for the future. Students discussed difficulties in adapting to mainstream school environments on account of behaviour policies and issues around structural organisation. The interviews were organised so that all youngsters were interviewed in pairs in order to facilitate an atmosphere of informality and to create more equal power relationships. During each interview there were periods when the students took control, responding to issues raised by their partner. They were set up as conversations with a few prompt topics introduced at certain stages. At times, it seemed as if the presence of an interviewer was forgotten.

There were also interviews with teachers which explored their perspectives on reintegration, the continuities/discontinuities between mainstream schools and alternative provision, and ways of ensuring that liaison could be improved.

The third study referred to in this discussion was an ethnographic study (2012–2015) in an English secondary school in the South of England. The research project investigated student perceptions of the school and spatial behaviours within it. The focus was on place and how the young people taking part in the research went about constructing and subverting the place that they experienced at school.

A total of 20 participants were involved from Years 10 to 11, aged between 14 and 16. The participants were all perceived as low achievers in the school. There was an ongoing dialogue between participants and researcher during the year in which the project took place, with regular (unstructured but focused) conversations in both individual and group contexts, and semi-structured (15–20 minutes) interviews scheduled over four occasions.

The research questions, focusing on the creation of place and the ways in which place was experienced, required methods that neither prioritised the visual nor were reducible to it (Pink, 2009). A variety of methods were chosen in order to collect data and maximise the engagement of these methods with the creation of place. Observations, interviews and walks with the participants were carried out, while participants were also invited to create photographic representations of places and spaces around their school. Photograph elicitation interviews were used to discuss these photographs and to reflect on aspects of their experience that might not normally be considered in interviews (Rose, 2007). This approach is useful in countering the transience of aesthetic and sensory experience.

All three studies highlighted groups of students who spoke of their respective school environments as being oppressive and who felt estranged from the mainstream groups in their institutions and who were utilising spaces in ways that either emphasised their sense of difference or that demonstrated opposition or resistance.

All names used in this chapter are pseudonyms.

Narratives of alienation, helplessness and resistance

In the case of Gypsy Traveller students, schools have been traditionally associated with antagonistic external environments. Part of an alien Gadje (non-Gypsy) world, their landscapes were daunting on both physical and spiritual levels. Apprehensions have often been passed down by older generations and are sometimes confirmed by hostility encountered:

> The first day at school was a strange experience. There we were walking into this big building – you must remember, we wouldn't enter shops or cafes because of fear of the police and the Gadje world.
>
> (Saki, aged 30s)

> People who aren't Travellers can have no idea what it's like. I'll never forget arriving at school the first time. There's this group of Gadje parents standing outside the building, holding up placards saying 'No Gypsies' and that sort of thing.
>
> (Daniel, aged 40s)

> The other children don't want to be our friends. That's why we stick together all the time.
>
> (Ryan, aged 8)

Children reported apprehension and a lack of agency:

> I used to wait in the playground for my cousin to take me to lessons. Then I'd wait in the classroom to be collected. I was afraid to go anywhere on my own.
>
> (Sophie, aged 9)

> Usually, I just hung around by those classrooms over there – (pointing in the direction of the mobiles).
>
> (Eric, aged 12)

With some exceptions, experiences at primary school were described in a positive light. Problems seemed to mount after moving on to secondary institutions. In reflections on the physical environment, participants often revealed a deep and visceral dislike of school spaces. Isaac, for instance, looking back as an adult, noted that the light was 'all wrong', and suggested that 'maybe us Travellers are like plants; we need plenty of light'. Others expressed dread about the size of the buildings, and large staircases, apprehensions that seemed to be confirmed by participant observation. It seemed significant that a number of teachers described these youngsters as either 'wild' and 'uncontrolled' or 'invisible', 'hiding away' and 'overawed'.

There was a strong sense of injustice and incomprehension that spatial organisation should obstruct social relationships. Sue-Ellen (aged 10) was indignant that she was not allowed to visit her sisters or her cousin and best friend, Yola, who were in separate classes. On several occasions she had found herself in trouble for walking out without permission. She remained defiant:

Me: Why did you decide to go and see Yola?
S-E: I just wanted to. Teachers can't stop me if I want to. Anyway, I didn't even get to see her.
Me: Why not?
S-E: She had P.E. I never even went in.
Me: Why not?

S-E: What?

Me: Why didn't you go into her P.E. lesson?

S-E: We've been told not to go in there.

Me: But you said that the teachers couldn't stop you if you wanted to.

S-E: That's different. That's just going to my friend in her room. Can't stop me doing that.

Me: Which rooms would you have gone into to find Yola?

S-E: Her classroom?

Me: What's the difference?

S-E: What do you mean?

Me: Between going into the hall and going into her classroom?

S.E: If she's in her classroom, it's the same as me. It makes no difference her room.

Me: So the hall's not her room – even though she's in it.

S-E: No.

Sue-Ellen's internal map of the school establishes zones of ownership totally disconnected from those imagined by staff. Yola appears to have certain rights to her own classroom to claim it as a social space. The implication is that Sue-Ellen has, in a sense, extended the concept of paying a social visit to her friend in her trailer on the site where they live to the context of school. Her behaviour might be interpreted in the context of site-life, whereby relatives' trailers are often viewed as an extension of home (Kendall, 1997). There are several potential reasons why Sue-Ellen might have had very different feelings about the school hall, where PE was taking place, one of which was that she had been told by her own parents not to participate in PE lessons.

An aversion to spaces such as the school hall was mirrored by many other Gypsy Traveller children, who identified some spaces around school as being safe and others as dangerous. The buses on the way to school were often unsafe; parts of the playground were deemed as menacing, unless they ensured that they were always together. Indeed, such were the difficulties at one school in Cornwall that at one stage Gypsy Traveller youngsters were given separate break times from other pupils.

While the students in the other two research projects reported here did not enter school environments with quite the same misgivings, it seemed significant that they appeared to develop a similar sense of antipathy towards certain places in the school. Once again, they constructed their own imagined borders between places that passed unrecognised by staff in their institutions.

In the PRU, a particularly common observation was on the difficulties encountered after the move from primary to secondary schools. There were differing reasons for dislike of certain spaces, but Sam's account seemed typical:

> Primary school was fine. I was friends with everyone.... Secondary school was a shock – I mean not just the work and rules and everything, but the feel of it. It was so... like big – and I felt really, you know, tiny, and no one helps tell you where to go. They just expect you to follow your friends. And most of my friends had gone to another school and I was all alone. It was horrible. But after a while sometimes I tried to get lost. Didn't want to be there.
>
> (Sam, aged 15)

There was a common feeling that primary school had felt safe and problems had begun after the transition to secondary schools. Two students (aged 11 and 13) connected these feelings to immediate reactions to the spatial environment, saying that their autism caused a fear of large spaces and also of crowds of people moving from one zone to another. One argued that his obvious discomfort had led to teasing and social isolation, so that unsafe spaces became not only those that seemed physically intimidating but those occupied by hostile peers.

Most of the youngsters at the PRU had attended a succession of secondary schools, having been excluded from each. Almost all were dealing with challenging situations in their home lives, and it was evident that none of their schools had provided the kind of emotional sanctuary they needed. Two 15-year-old girls (who selected pseudonyms 'Cinderella' and 'Tinkerbell') came to the following conclusion: 'At (mainstream) secondary schools there is so much space, but nowhere to run away and nowhere to hide'.

The rigid control of space and lack of agency around movement was mentioned by several participants. In Sam's case, he hinted at some reason he preferred not to elaborate on:

> Then the school had been watching me. I couldn't get dressed with the others after sports. I couldn't use the same toilet. I couldn't go to the atrium. Just because of something that had happened at home.
>
> (Sam, aged 15)

Later in the conversation he returned to the injustice of schools trying to control students by deciding which places were off limits:

> I mean people have a right to go where they want, and there shouldn't be places that some kids can go to and others can't. And teachers don't own those places in the school, do they? They're for everyone.
>
> (Sam, aged 15)

Comparing experiences across institutions, two 16 year-olds, Madeleine and Katie, reflected on the contrast between the 'bitchy' and impersonal environments of secondary schools with the more nurturing milieu of the PRU. Specifically, they referred to small classes, in confined and quiet spaces, and then social meeting places, for example a dining area where teachers and students met in the morning for breakfast.

In common with Gypsy Traveller children, students at the PRU spoke about the oppressive culture of fixed and bounded spaces, governed by rigid temporal and spatial rules. The big difference at the PRU was that they were allowed to walk out of rooms when their emotions were rising and seek refuge in safe areas in which they could regain composure away from their classmates.

The shared solution for many Gypsy Traveller youngsters, and for those in the PRU, was to get themselves excluded. Simply walking out of classrooms was often viewed as simpler than getting involved in altercations with staff. At times, there seemed some collusion from teachers who were not unhappy to lose children deemed to be non-compliant or disruptive.

A rather different form of resistance was occurring in the third context, a study with pupils perceived as 'low achievers' in an English secondary school. While the students in that research also viewed themselves as outcasts, they managed to both appropriate marginalised or abandoned spaces and to contest the ownership and use of established spaces.

At the time of the research project the school was undergoing a period of extensive building work. Invited to record their feelings about the school through photographs, the youngsters involved were keen to identify and provide evidence of examples of shoddy building, delighting in exaggerating the dangers of, for instance, unfinished electrical work.

Charlie: Health and safety I'm thinking!!
Brandon: Charlie, that isn't electrical.
Martin: It's coz they ain't finished the fuckin' school.

They proceeded to downgrade the environment through small acts of vandalism. Defacing desks was particularly popular. On one occasion a student was observed screwing a screw into the ghetto blaster's plastic grill protecting the speakers. Struggling with the screw, he picked up an electric screwdriver instead, failing to cause much damage beyond gouging out the label that ran across the speaker grill. Subsequently, he was observed drilling holes into the teacher's desk. Such actions went beyond the purpose of causing damage; it was about the assertion of a unique spatial identity that set him apart and recorded his place in the history of the institution:

> You always know when I've been somewhere coz I've drilled holes. Or stuck a compass in.
>
> (Brandon, aged 15)

The group of Year ten students (aged 14–15) affirmed a group identity through claiming certain territory as their own. Often these were places abandoned or ignored by others. A favourite place was a rubbish skip in one of the playgrounds, and sometimes they would slip out of lessons to hide there and smoke. There they hung around, surrounded by discarded pieces of furniture and smashing bottles, test tubes and bulbs. As subversive spatial acts this may have seemed rather pointless, as the items had already been discarded; however, it served the purpose of establishing ownership. Perhaps, this explained their sense of outrage when they discovered that other groups in the school were also using the skip as a hideout.

Once they progressed into Year 11 their spatial behaviours changed. Now the photographs they captured showed them infiltrating safer spaces such as the drama-studio and the library. They referred to the relative comfort of these places, but also enjoyed hiding there and challenging established uses of those spaces. They enjoyed provoking the teaching assistants in the library through the pretence of reading. This became a game to be observed by others in the group: how obvious could the pretence become without being thrown out? How wound-up could the teaching assistants become before cracking? The group exaggerated tales of cushion fights and jumping on beanbags, but these were largely uncorroborated through observation.

It seemed significant, too, that, while revelling in the perception of themselves as spatial anarchists, several members of the group stated a preference for being in the library due to its reassuring calmness and predictability. Indeed, this seemed a common feature of all three research projects discussed here: the participants involved sought to challenge and disrupt their socio-spatial environments while reaching out for some alternative equilibrium and order.

Conclusion

Viewing schools as socio-spatial landscapes enables us to construct more complex ecological understandings of the behaviour of those who inhabit them. The organisation of space in schools is never neutral. In the view of Lefebvre (1991), space is likely to be organised in a way that will reproduce the social relations of production.

Within schools, territories that are established and boundaried can only be sustained when there is a shared understanding of meanings of spaces, and where inhabitants of the community (both teachers and students) acquiesce. Spatial organisation perceived as oppressive can remain in place despite subversive acts by minorities, so long as resistance does not become widespread. Resistance can be triggered through cultural dissonance or social inequality. Schools can contain it through disciplinary measures or exclusion unless it occurs on a large scale, in which case there will be a need to restructure and reformulate space.

Foucault (1971) proposed the idea of 'heterotopia', spaces that can both mirror and destabilise the outside world. While schools can both reproduce and replicate inequitable spatial structures in wider society, they also constitute their own micro-environments, generated through both their internal structures and cultures and through external circumstances. Spaces are dynamic, open to re-appropriation (Soja, 2010) and liable to change into new and hybrid forms (Bhabha, 2004).

There needs to be awareness of both the mechanics and the intrinsic fluidity of such processes. For instance, within a context of changing orientations towards school and widening aspirations amongst Gypsy-Traveller communities (Hamilton, 2018), it is likely that socio-spatial interactions will take on new forms in inter-group social contexts. In schools, cultural dissonance will be reduced with uses of space outside student norms becoming less conspicuous and activity previously construed as subversive reduced.

In the case of the groups involved in all three of the research contexts described here, a common factor was the impact of the spatial organisation of schools upon students who might be viewed as *marginalised* or as *outsiders*, and this seemed particularly apparent in secondary education contexts. The extent to which the transition from primary to secondary education was the cause of behaviour perceived by teachers and school managers as disruptive or provocative might be disputed, but the number of both Gypsy Traveller and excluded children who referred to this suggests that moving to large, impersonal environments was the cause of anxiety and distress, and this seems something that building planners and designers of sites for secondary education might consider.

An oversight seems to be the lack of reflection by teachers and school managers on themselves as socio-spatial environments that position children in hierarchical strata. A narrow focus on educational attainment is an underlying cause here, with the notion of the child as a person somehow absent from the school environment, and a false separation between the *learning* child and the *feeling* child (Parker and Levinson, 2018). There is, perhaps, also a wider failure of imagination about the potential meanings of educational landscapes.

Such an impoverished perception of school environments is to the detriment not only of students but of staff. The past couple of decades have witnessed the erosion of collective staff social spaces in UK schools (Slawson, 2018). If schools are to retain a sense of themselves as communities, as distinct from examination-grade factories, it is time for teachers as well as students to recognise and resist the ways in which control is exerted through spatial organisation.

Summary

- It is not possible to understand schools without understanding spatial structures and uses.
- Organisation of space reflects power structures.
- For some students, the structuring of school space is particularly oppressive.
- Resistance to norms can have very different meanings.
- The creation of more flexible spaces may have beneficial pedagogical and social outcomes.

Recommended reading

Lefebvre, H. (1991) *The Production of Space*. Oxford: Blackwell.
Massey, D. (2005) *For Space*. London: Sage.
Soja, E. W. (2010) *Seeking Spatial Justice*. Minneapolis: University of Minnesota Press.

References

Bhabha, H. (2004) *The Location of Culture*. Abingdon: Routledge.
Bourdieu, P. (1984) *Distinction: A Social Critique of the Judgement of Taste*. Massachusetts: Harvard University Press.
Brown, C. (2017) 'Favourite places in school' for lower-set 'ability' pupils: School groupings practices and children's spatial orientations. *Children's Geographies*, **15**(4), pp. 399–412.
Cudworth, D. (2015) Schooling, space and social justice. *Power & Education*, **7**(1), pp. 73–89.
Foucault, M. (1971) *The Order of Things*. New York. Vintage.
Foucault, M. (1988) Technologies of the self. In Martin, L. H., Gutman, H. and Hutton, P. H. (Eds.). *Technologies of the Self*. London: Tavistock.
Hamilton, P. (2018) School books or wedding dresses? Examining the cultural dissonance experienced by young Gypsy/Traveller women in secondary education. *Gender and Education*, **30**(7), pp. 829–845.
Imms, W., Mahat, M., Byers, T. and Murphy, D. (2017) *Type and Use of Innovative Learning Environments in Australasian Schools. ILETC Survey 1*. Melbourne: ILETC.
Kendall, S. (1997) Sites of resistance: Places on the margin – the traveller 'homeplace'. In Acton, T. and Hatfield, G. (Eds.). *Gypsy Politics and Traveller Identity*. Hatfield: University of Hertfordshire Press.
Lefebvre, H. (1991) *The Production of Space*. Oxford: Blackwell.
Levinson, M. (2015) 'What's the plan?' 'What plan?' Changing aspirations among Gypsy youngsters, and implications for future cultural identities and group membership. *British Journal of Sociology of Education*, **36**(8), pp. 1149–1169.
Levinson, M. P. and Sparkes, A. C. (2004) Gypsy identity and orientations to space. *Journal of Contemporary Ethnography*, **33**(6), pp. 704–34.
Levinson, M. P. and Sparkes, A. C. (2005) Gypsy children, space and the school environment. *International Journal of Qualitative Studies in Education*, **18**(6), pp. 751–772.
Levinson, M. P. and Thompson, M. (2016) 'I don't need pink hair here': Should we be seeking to reintegrate youngsters without challenging school cultures? *The International Journal on School Disaffection*, **12**(1), pp. 23–44.
Massey D. (1995) Places and their pasts. *History Workshop Journal*, **39**, pp. 182–192.
Massey, D. (1999) *Power Geometries and the Politics of Space-Time*. Heidelberg: University of Heidelberg.
Massey, D. (2005) *For Space*. London: SAGE.
McGregor, J. (2004) Space, power and the classroom. *Forum*, **46**(1), pp. 13–19.
Parker, R. and Levinson, M. P. (2018) Student behaviour, motivation and the potential of attachment-aware schools to redefine the landscape. *British Educational Research Journal*, **44**(5), pp. 875–896.
Pink, S. (2009). *Doing sensory ethnography*. London: SAGE.
Ralph, T. and Levinson, M. P. (2018) Places of conflict, power and resistance in a UK secondary school. In Collins, P., Igreja, V. and Danaher, P. A. (Eds.). *Nexus Among Place, Conflict and Communication in a Globalising World*. Basingstoke: Palgrave Macmillan.
Rose, G. (2007). *Visual Methodologies*, (2nd ed.). London: SAGE.
Schmidt, S. J. (2013) Claiming our turf: Students civic negotiation of the public space of school. *Theory & Research in Social Education*, **41**(4), pp. 535–551.
Slawson, N. (2018) Death of the Staffroom: Lack of space or divide and conquer. *The Guardian,* 13 March 2018. Available at: https://www.theguardian.com/education/2018/mar/13/school-staffroom-england (Accessed 16 March 2019).
Soja, E. W. (2010) *Seeking Spatial Justice*. Minneapolis: University of Minnesota Press.
Woolner, P., Clark, C., Laing K., Thomas, U. and Tiplady, L. (2014) A school tries to change: How leaders and teachers understand changes to space and practices in a UK secondary school. *Improving Schools*, **17**(2), pp. 148–162.

5 Morality, education and social ordering

Catherine A. Simon

Introduction

The sociology of morality is the sociological investigation of the nature, causes and consequences of people's ideas about the good and the right (Abend, 2008: 87). In other words, the sociology of morality considers why different groups of people hold particular moral views and how those views impact human behaviours and interactions, organisations, institutions or structures. Moral judgements affect us all, whether we are making them or on the receiving end of them. Educational contexts are powerful moral domains: they contain many moments where people evaluate each other's identities and actions. These moments can also have a strong effect on the social ordering that is created around educational contexts. The purpose of this chapter is to explore current interest in the sociology of morality, its intellectual antecedents and its relevance to education, with particular reference to the school as an institution of civil society. The chapter begins by outlining understandings of morality and the contribution of a sociological perspective to already established fields of theology, moral philosophy and moral psychology. It then explores the social contexts of schools as both institutions of civil society and the state and microcosms of social structures, groupings and action. The final section considers the impact of neoliberal market mechanisms on state education, using the example of English education policy since 2010. Drawing on models of community engagement, and the ethics of care, the chapter concludes by exploring education and schooling as the locus of social morality and the means of promoting a socially responsible (rather than a merely 'socially just') system of education.

What is morality?

The answer to the question 'what is morality?' is far from straightforward. At its most basic, it has to do with notions of goodness, fairness, right or wrong. Who or what determines that which is good, fair, right or wrong, and in what circumstances, is highly contested. The word morality comes from the Latin word *Moralis* meaning manner, character or proper behaviour. Morality therefore relates to what are, or might be considered to be, universal truths (that murder, stealing or infidelity are wrong) or to a code of conduct or set of standards associated with a particular culture, philosophy or belief system (for example, respecting elders or holding to professional ethics such as the Hippocratic Oath for doctors). All the key academic disciplines – psychology, philosophy, sociology and theology – as well as professions such as medicine and law have an interest in defining morality or identifying moral codes. Many of the disciplines have contributed moral theories to help make sense of human intentions, decisions or actions at the level of the individual, group or society.

Morality is essentially linked to relational behaviours (i.e. how human beings relate to and interact with one another). It follows then that morality operates on a number of levels. It has, for example, an individual dimension causing persons to consider how they should act or respond in human situations. Morality also focuses on the collective, raising questions about what are the social values, institutions and rules that govern a society or a social group. How are the expectations of its members codified via formal and informal rules and conventions? What is the role of the state in preserving or promoting moral values via its key institutions of law and education?

Edmund Burke, considered the 'father of conservatism', subscribed to a political creed that emerged from the seventeenth century conflict in England that culminated in the Glorious Revolution of 1688. His views were closely associated with those of the philosophers of the Scottish Enlightenment such as Adam Ferguson, David Hume and Adam Smith who conceived of society, its complex web of institutions, laws, morals and customs, to be the culmination of a process of development from primitive society to high culture and civilisation: i.e. social progress. In Smith's view, social institutions represented the product of a complex historical process, cultivated through trial and error, and an understanding of the constraints that preserve social order. Writing in the aftermath of the French Revolution, Burke appreciated that the 'common good' was the product of activities that are not, of themselves, directed towards such a goal and therefore cannot necessarily be the outcome of just or virtuous actions on the part of citizens. His argument was such that people are primarily concerned with what is most immediately their own: concern with the general or common good does not come naturally to most people, but must be cultivated. This can be done by stretching and enlarging self-interest as widely as possible. Thus, Burke viewed the purpose of government as staving off the inconvenience of a pre-societal state where men were not well disposed to one another.

Thomas Hobbes writing a century earlier had defined life outside society as 'solitary, poor, nasty, brutish and short' (Hobbes, 1660). Burke's argument was based, not on the rights of man, but on utility. People will not naturally behave rationally or justly towards one another, even if revolution, as in the case of the French Revolution, is for the sake of achieving such high ideals as justice, defined as equality for all. The common good must, therefore, be achieved through the careful manipulation of human nature. To this end, the prudent and wise statesman understands the raw material of politics: people, their passions, reason and habits. It follows, then, that the statesman, i.e. the politician (and therefore the institutions of the state), cannot aim at perfection, but must use whatever is at his disposal for the sake of good public policy (Simon, 2016). It would appear from Burke's argument that government has a role in setting and/or maintaining the moral tone and values of the society it governs.

As social institutions develop, so morals undergo progressive improvement that can be described by 'social laws'. Moral values and a sense of the general good are not, however, the sole domain of government or the institutions of civil society. Johnstone (2018) for example, argues that the moral injunctions and judgements which evolve from individual and collective interactions have certain characteristics, although such injunctions or judgements may vary between individuals, groups and societies. First, they implicate or involve the individual in that they demand a particular course of action. They may also elicit feelings of worthiness, unworthiness or guilt depending on the action taken: *'I am glad I did the right thing', 'I wish I had not said...'; 'If only I had done x* instead of *y*'. Second, moral injunctions are concerned with what ought to be done for its own sake, rather than being in pursuit of a particular goal: for example, being honest and truthful, even when doing so may be costly. In other words, moral injunctions are explicit and categorical; they are unequivocal. Finally, moral judgements present themselves as objective: 'the right thing to do' – as opposed to being expressions of personal preference, inclination or whim. According to Johnstone then, it follows that if morality is personally implicating, categorical, universal and objective these characteristics also describe the way morality is experienced.

This of course does not imply that moral judgements and actions are necessarily straightforward. Theologians, philosophers and psychologists have presented many a moral dilemma to encourage cerebral thought or debate. Consider, for example, the popular 'trolleybus problem'. Five people on an out-of-control trolleybus can only be saved by pulling a lever and directing the trolleybus into the path of an innocent person who will die as a result. Is the death of an innocent man justified in saving the lives of five others? According to McConnell (2018), moral dilemmas such as the trolleybus problem must contain certain components:

- An agent is required to take one of two or more actions to resolve a problem.
- Either course of action is possible, but the agent cannot do both.
- The agent is subject to moral failure – whatever is done is wrong by doing or not doing a particular action.

Criteria for a moral dilemma, however, do not help with determining whether the solution is right or wrong, good or bad.

Thomas Aquinas, one of the early Christian fathers in the thirteenth century, is associated with the Doctrine or Principle of Double Effect. As in the case of the trolleybus problem, it is the *intentions* behind the action that determine whether the action is morally justifiable: killing another in self-defence is not an immoral act, whereas using unnecessary force and thereby killing another in self-defence has moral consequences. The New Catholic Encyclopaedia (cited in McIntyre, 2019) has four rules for the Principle of Double Effect:

- The act itself must be morally good or at least indifferent.
- The agent may not positively will the bad effect but may permit it. If he could attain the good effect without the bad effect he should do so. The bad effect is sometimes said to be indirectly voluntary.
- The good effect must flow from the action at least as immediately (in the order of causality, though not necessarily in the order of time) as the bad effect. In other words, the good effect must be produced directly by the action, not by the bad effect. Otherwise the agent would be using a bad means to a good end, which is never allowed.
- The good effect must be sufficiently desirable to compensate for the allowing of the bad effect.

Making sense of right and wrong

So how do we make sense of what is right or wrong? According to a utilitarian standpoint, morality is based on reasoning: working out whether the *outcome* will bring about the greatest good for the greatest number. If so, the sacrifice of an individual is morally acceptable. The outcome determines whether the action is good or bad, right or wrong. However, utilitarianism is not easily reconciled to notions of justice or individual rights. What happens to the rights of the individual who may be sacrificed for the many? Is it just that an innocent individual should lose his or her life without any say in the matter? An alternative view is offered by deontology – the study of duty or responsibility. Kant's moral philosophy, for example, bases moral reasoning not on outcome or effect but on *universal moral laws* (the Categorical Imperative). There is no requirement to weigh the costs or benefits of an action. Rules are objective and are linked to fulfilling one's duty. In the case of the trolleybus problem then, it is the individual's duty to sacrifice his/her life for the many, whether knowingly or unwittingly.

The role of moral reasoning underpins many of the primary theories of morality (Hardy, 2006: 207). For example, Kohlberg's (1969) stages of moral development suggest that once moral principles are understood they will inherently guide and motivate moral action. Influenced by Piaget's developmental theory, Kohlberg argued that as an individual's capacity for moral reasoning matures so he or she becomes more inclined to use moral principles in making judgements in moral situations. Through the continued development of moral reasoning, individuals are more inclined to act in line with their moral judgements. However, such insights still do not wholly explain why people act the way they do; moral action must have to do with more than the maturing of moral reasoning over time.

Indeed, critics of Kohlberg have suggested that moral actions can take place outside moral reasoning processes, and that moral values other than justice can play their part. The contexts for moral actions are also very important. Linked to psychology, moral motivation theory seeks to explain moral actions. Normative accounts of moral motivation suggest that it produces moral behaviour and is the process through which moral behaviour is reached (Kaplan, 2016). However, as Kaplan argues, moral motivation is a complex and dynamic process. The lack of moral action is not necessarily accounted for by lack of moral motivation, rather 'the meaning and utility of any particular motivation is context-sensitive, based on the context-specific process of adaptation' (Kaplan, 2017: 199). Moral adaptation involves 'the dynamic development of appropriate responses to the demands of both the social-moral world and the intrapsychic world of images, feelings, needs and desires' (Kaplan, 2017: 199). The world of the imagination and real-life situations both have a bearing on how individuals develop and express moral understandings and actions over time. Moral concerns, priorities and judgements are part of being morally motivated.

There are, of course, consequences that derive from moral actions such as the human emotions of guilt or shame, remorse or regret. This 'moral residue' requires some sort of attention and resolution. Moral psychology is one field of study that tries to address this in attempting to understand why emotions of guilt or regret are natural in circumstances where the actions or consequences of a person's action are contrary to a moral norm, whether justifiably so or not. The unintended consequence of a doctor delivering pain relief on an oncology ward may be to overdose a dying patient. He or she will feel remorse and guilt, even though the intentions were wholly laudable.

Whilst morality helps maintain social order via social institutions, identity theory is used to explain the 'inner workings of the self' (Stets and Carter, 2012: 120). Identity theory can serve to explain the diversity of behaviours and moral residue between people as both social and moral actors. The assumption is that individuals undertake goal-centred actions as they interact with the environment and that this is part of a reflective and iterative process guided by their internal identity standard. Identity is verified when a person's perceptions of who they are in situations corresponds to their internal standard. The converse is also true, generating negative emotions. The identity standard is, therefore, the moral standard and linked to the meanings a person associates with being 'moral'. Feelings of justice and care are included here, although are not necessarily definitive. Other factors may include cross-cultural moral dimensions such as autonomy or dimensions of feelings to do with fairness, loyalty, respect and reciprocity. Diversity in moral behaviours and emotions, according to Stets and Carter, can thus be explained by (a) a person's identity standard and (b) a person's inter-pretations of situations as being morally linked to their feeling rules. In other words, if they violate those rules they are more likely to have feelings such as guilt or remorse.

Summary

Morality has to do with notions of right and wrong, good and bad and is represented by cultural codes evidenced in social institutions. In western cultures institutions of government, medicine, education and law codify what is acceptable for society. Moral codes also exist at the level of the community and the individual. This goes some way to explaining variations in people's beliefs and values, actions and reactions to social situations. The key disciplines of theology, philosophy and psychology have attempted to understand what is meant by morality and moral action and have contributed a number of theoretical perspectives over time. The contribution of sociology to the field is explored in the section that follows.

Understanding the sociology of morality

During the latter half of the twentieth century the sociology of morality fell out of favour amongst sociologists but has had a resurgence of interest in more recent years. Traditionally the sociology of morality considers how morality binds people together through a system of common rules and expectations during interactions (Stets and Carter, 2012: 121). Classical sociology has long been interested in explaining morality and understanding moral capacity. Drawing on philosophical ethics and the social philosophy of the Enlightenment, the sociology of morality is interested in analysing morality and its attendant laws. Bykov (2018: 197) recognises the interdisciplinarity of the soci-ology of morality, drawing as it does on understandings from biology and the cognitive and behav-ioural sciences. Each of these approaches offers different theoretical models for understanding morality's functioning in society.

According to Abend (2013) two main paradigms influence the sociology of morality: the Weberian and the Durkheimian. Weber's interest was in the meanings people attach to actions in social situ-ations and the way they interpret the thoughts, actions and responses of others. There are two principles at play here: (a) that moral judgements are not capable of objective truth or falsehood, i.e. they are socially constructed, and (b) that sociology and the sociology of morality should be value-free or at best not influenced by an individual's values. Scientists can investigate individuals' internal meanings about morality and their actions that ensue, but they cannot determine whether such moral beliefs ought to exist. Therefore, this orthodox view of the sociology of morality is challenged by authors such as Etzioni or Wolfe who hold to Durkheimian principles, that there is such a thing as moral truth; it is the principle of moral freedom that is wrong. Morality, for Durkheim, was the outworking of collective social interaction. Each society has its own moral reality which can be studied in positive scientific ways. However, the distinction between moral philosophy and the sociology of morality is also a matter of contention. For Abend (2008) the apparent dichotomy is about a false distinction between 'scientific', 'objective' and 'external' approaches to understanding morality on the one hand, and 'philosophical', 'normative' and 'internal' approaches on the other. What is called for is a new sociology of morality that proceeds on the basis of there being no truths in ethics. Whilst the sociology of morality can be no more value-free than, for example, public philosophy, there should still be a distinction between the project of the sociology of morality – understanding people's moral beliefs, their causes and consequences – and public, normative and moral philosophy that explores notions of right and wrong.

Morality, schools and schooling

The sociology of morality can make a unique contribution to understanding 'organisations, organisational arrangements and social networks; their effects on moral actions, views and society-level outcomes' (Abend, 2013: 580). Applying this optic to education and schooling in England has significant relevance for a system of state education that is undergoing major structural reform in the first quarter of the twenty-first century. In the immediate post-war period, education was conceived as one of the three pillars of the welfare state alongside national insurance and the National Health Service. However, successive governments over the last 40 years have turned away from creating a welfare state for the benefit of society, to promoting a post-welfare society based on neoliberal principles of private enterprise and competitive markets (Tomlinson, 2001: 1). As a consequence of successive neoliberal policies in England, the schooling system has become a 'quasi-market' (Dumay and Dupriez, 2014). This means that schools are subject to certain market principles such as parental choice, school autonomy and competition between schools. At the same time, education is still public, and the price of instruction is generally non-negotiable. One consequence of the quasi-market in English schooling is that state schools no longer reflect the communities in which they are based, but are subject to the same social stratification at work in civil society.

Oakeshott and the notion of 'School'

Although market principles in English state education can be traced back to the 1980s, the current structure of education and schooling in England owes much to liberal conservatism as espoused by David Cameron, Conservative prime minister 2010–2016 and his Education Secretary Michael Gove. The blending of liberal and conservative political thought is not, however, unique. Michael Oakeshott, twentieth-century political theorist and philosopher, was concerned with the complex relationship between liberal ideas and practice and conservative politics and policy. For Oakeshott, the major function of government was to adjudicate, or resolve, the conflicts that occur between citizens. This comes from a consciousness of the world's imperfection. Citizens need protection from themselves. Morality offers a set of constraints and moral behaviour demonstrates agreement to abide by such constraints. Knowing how to behave is a skill. It involves a serious understanding of the end to which one's performance (i.e. behaviour), is directed, as well as understanding one's part in that performance (Grant, 1990: 48). Therefore, 'knowing how' may also include 'knowing that'.

For Oakeshott then, liberal education should be a means of liberating the learner into the realm of the imagination and ideas. 'To be initiated into this world is learning to become human; and to move within it freely is being human, which is an 'historic' not a 'natural' condition' (Oakeshott, 1972: 93).

The role of the school, however, is not merely about facilitating the growth or maturation of its pupils; learning is more than this. Achievements in learning are achievements in becoming the kind of person we are (Fuller, 1989 cited in Williams, 2007). Oakeshott offers an elaborate narrative of what it is to be a learner and to learn (Williams, 2007). An individual's identity is made up of what they have learned to think, feel, imagine and do. In order to learn, the individual must possess reflective consciousness and understanding. The outcome of learning is human conduct. This is distinct from mere behaviour: a non-reflective manifestation of underlying biological or physical processes. Whether acting impulsively or deliberately, human beings respond according to learned responses. Human learning, therefore, requires understanding which, in turn, is predicated on an understanding of the self and of others. This self-understanding cannot be separated from culture, and culture, for Oakeshott, is a 'conversational encounter' that has taken place through the ages, composed of 'feelings, perceptions, ideas, engagements, attitudes and so forth' (Williams, 2007: 100). In this way, human conduct is an exhibition of intelligence.

In the same way, Oakeshott conceives the process of 'School' as entering a conversation. It is about learning to recognise oneself as a human being. Individuals come to recognise themselves as equal members of 'a community of selves' (Oakeshott, 1972: 201). The practical is the mode in which we conduct most of our lives, and practical experience, of course, holds an element of moral conduct. Here, Oakeshott distinguishes between practical and technical knowledge, the former being generated through experience as in the manner of apprenticeship. Practical knowledge is unreflective. It cannot be reduced to rules. These two forms of knowledge are inseparable, yet distinguishable and are the two components of knowledge in every human activity. It is the primary purpose of schooling to explore the modes of experience represented in the forms of knowledge and understanding (Williams, 2007).

Educating, therefore, demands a unique relationship between teacher and learner, one that is distinct from all other formal relationships such as buyer and seller, doctor and patient, lawyer and client. For Oakeshott, education is not merely about learning to do 'this' or 'that' more proficiently but about acquiring an understanding of the human condition in which the 'fact of life' is continually illuminated by the 'quality of life' (Oakeshott, 1972: 26). It is about learning how to be both autonomous and a civilised human being. Consequently, education has a higher goal than merely socialising the student into the prerequisites of the real world. Education should not simply replicate, but should challenge, the norms of society. The burden of creating truly human beings, rests on the whole of education, beginning within the family and extending through formal schooling and beyond. It follows then that the institution of the school, and the process of 'School' according to Oakeshott's philosophical perspective, play a significant role in articulating social morality.

The impact of market mechanisms on schools and schooling: Post-2010 education policy

One of the most tenacious by-products of neoliberal societies is evidenced in a widening diversity and growing inequality amongst the populace. Different levels of wealth-holding determine how well individuals can face risk in terms of both prosperity and knowledge (Crouch, 2013: 72). Wealth, and the knowledge upon which it draws, allows its holders to win the best deals. For Crouch (2013: 190) this is a problem, not of ideology, but the power of globalised capital which operates at national and local levels through the funding of political campaigns, ownership of mass media, resources for lobbying and the ability to purchase the best brains. On this basis, societies in Britain and the USA particularly have become more and more stratified with particular consequences for the state provision of schooling. Ball (1993) argued that the introduction of markets into education represented a 'class strategy' the consequence of which has been the relative reproduction of class (and ethnic) advantage and disadvantage. This he attributed to 'the interplay of three key elements: the self-interest of some producers; the self-interest of some consumers and the control of the performance criteria of market organisations – which in this case lies with the state' (Ball, 1993: 4).

More recently, the ascendency of individualism – a product of neoliberalism – has shifted existing tensions in the relationship between state and the individual. Rooted in notions such as individual rights, agency and self-efficacy, individualism has pervaded a number of domains including the psychological, social, institutional, cultural and economic (Houston, 2016), and has been reflected in policies such as those to do with human rights and equality agendas. 'Top-down imperatives' in the form of social policy directives, and 'bottom-up currents' in the shape of communal movements and voices, meld to reproduce individualism as a *'force majeure'* (Houston, 2016: 533). Schools belong to the social domain. They stand between the state and the informal sphere of the family and community and must navigate the moral spaces that exist between the two.

Houston's critique of individualism suggests both its potential for reflexivity and creativity on the part of the individual such that he/she can have greater agency in shaping a sense of self, less determined by social structures and mores, but also where social structures have become more fluid and prone to alteration; the sense of self becomes a narcissistic project in its own right. The consequent separation from any sense of the 'we' in society has led to various pathologies such as anomie, evidenced for example in the rise in loneliness (Kaiser Family Foundation, 2018) and mental health issues (Siddique, 2018). Furthermore, 'political correctness' and the practice of 'othering' point to a shutting-down rather than the opening-up of dialogue in the public and social spheres about difference, projecting social morality as something equally fluid and relative. It is no wonder then that 'British Values' were introduced into English maintained schools in 2014 to be taught as part of pupils' social, moral, spiritual and cultural development. It is the role of the school to:

- enable students to develop their self-knowledge, self-esteem and self-confidence;
- enable students to distinguish right from wrong and to respect the civil and criminal law of England;
- encourage students to accept responsibility for their behaviour, show initiative, and to understand how they can contribute positively to the lives of those living and working in the locality of the school and to society more widely;
- enable students to acquire a broad general knowledge of and respect for public institutions and services in England;
- further tolerance and harmony between different cultural traditions by enabling students to acquire an appreciation of and respect for their own and other cultures;
- encourage respect for other people; and
- encourage respect for democracy and support for participation in the democratic processes, including respect for the basis on which the law is made and applied in England (DfE, 2014).

Whether it is possible to codify British Values (if such a concept exists) and whether schools should teach these values unquestioningly is not to be debated here. What is significant, however, is the emphasis on self-knowledge, respect, tolerance and personal responsibility. There are clear links in this DfE framework with identity theory, motivation theory and Oakeshott's notion of School as self-actualisation discussed earlier. If morality is to do with relational behaviours then self-actualisation lies at the heart of understanding one's own and other people's identities and actions. Self-actualisation can contribute to self-knowledge; self-esteem and self-confidence can lead to tolerance of difference and ultimately respect for fellow human beings. According to Held (2006), whether people can think and act as if they are independent rests on the network of social relations established since childhood. People are in fact interdependent and relational in 'the moral claim of those dependent upon us for the care they need' (Held, 2006: 10). The emphasis on personal responsibility counters the normative and individualist/relativist view of tolerance and 'leaving each other alone'.

Conclusion

It is, therefore, in revisiting notions of social responsibility, interdependence and connectedness that schooling can become a conduit for social morality and the means of promoting a socially responsible education system. In recognising the bonds that connect individuals together into families, communities and society, education can serve to counter the slippery idealised notion of social justice that dominates – one that obfuscates the virtues of the individual and the common good and expects government to act in order to bring into effect social desires. Rather, through a commitment to respecting and valuing all fellow human beings, utilising schooling to the purpose of supporting pupil self-actualisation and promoting the good of others through collaboration, the school itself becomes the locus of social morality and justice.

Questions for discussion

- What is morality?
- Who should determine right and wrong?
- What role should schools play in teaching morality?
- Should there be a codification of 'British values'?

Summary points

- Morality has to do with notions of right and wrong.
- How morality is defined is complex. Morality is codified in law and cultural norms.
- Understandings of morality are linked to the key academic disciplines and relate to the individual, community and national levels.
- The sociology of morality makes a unique contribution to understandings of organisations, organisational arrangements and social networks, including schools. It helps explain their impact on moral actions, beliefs and social outcomes.

Recommended reading

Bykov, A. (2018) 'Rediscovering the moral: The "old" and "new" sociology of morality in the context of the behavioural sciences'. *Sociology*, 53(1), pp. 192–207.
Hitlin, S. and Vaisey, S. (Eds.) *Handbook of Sociology of Morality*. New York: Springer.
Stets, J. E. and Carter M. J. (2012) A theory of the self in the sociology of morality. *American Sociological Review*, **77**(1), pp. 120–140.

References

Abend, G. (2008) Two main problems in the sociology of morality. *Theory and Society*, **37**(2), pp. 87–125.

Abend, G. (2013) What's new and what's old about the new sociology of morality. In Hitlin, S. and Vaisey, S. (Eds.). *Handbook of Sociology of Morality*. New York: Springer.

Ball, S. J. (1993) Education markets, choice and social class: The market as a class strategy in the UK and the US. *British Journal of Sociology of Education*, **14**(1), pp. 3–19.

Bykov, A. (2018) Rediscovering the moral: The 'old' and 'new' sociology of morality in the context of the behavioural sciences. *Sociology*, **53**(1), pp. 192–207.

Crouch, C. (2013) *Making Capitalism Fit for Society*. Cambridge: Polity Press.

DfE (2014) Promoting fundamental British values as part of SMSC in schools: Departmental advice for maintained schools. Online. Available at: https://assets.publishing.service.gov.uk/government/uploads/system/uploads/attachment_data/file/380595/SMSC_Guidance_Maintained_Schools.pdf (Accessed 23 February 2019).

Dumay, X. and Dupriez, V. (2014) Educational quasi-markets, school effectiveness and social inequalities. *Journal of Education Policy*, **29**(4), pp. 510–531.

Fuller, T. (2001) *The Voice of Liberal Learning: Michael Oakeshott on Education*. New Haven and London: Yale University Press.

Grant, R. (1990) *Oakeshott: Thinkers of Our Time*. University of Michigan: Claridge Press.

Hardy, S. A. (2006) Identity, reasoning, and emotion: An empirical comparison of three sources of moral motivation. *Motivation and Emotion*, **30**, pp. 207–215.

Held, V. (2006) *The Ethics of Care*. Oxford: Oxford University Press.

Hobbes, T. (1660) The Leviathan. Online. Available at: https://www.ttu.ee/public/m/mart-murdvee/EconPsy/6/Hobbes Thomas 1660 The Leviathan.pdf (Accessed 22 June 2018).

Houston, S. (2016) Beyond individualism: Social work and social identity. *British Journal of Social Work*, **46**, pp. 532–548.

Johnstone, A. A. (2018) Why morality? *The Humanistic Psychologist*, **46**(2), pp. 188–203.

Kaiser Family Foundation (2018) Loneliness and social isolation in the United States, the United Kingdom, and Japan: An international survey. Online. Available at: http://files.kff.org/attachment/Report-Loneliness-and-Social-Isolation-in-the-United-States-the-United-Kingdom-and-Japan-An-International-Survey (Accessed 22 March 2019).

Kaplan U. (2016) Moral motivation as a dynamic developmental process: Toward an integrative synthesis. *Journal for the Theory of Social Behaviour*, **47**(2), pp. 195–221.

Kohlberg, L. (1969) Stage and sequence: The cognitive development approach to socialization. In Goslin, D. A. (Ed.). *Handbook of Socialization Theory*. Chicago: Rand McNally.

McConnell, T. (2018) 'Moral Dilemmas'. *Stanford Encyclopedia of Philosophy* (Fall 2018 ed.). Online. Available at: https://plato.stanford.edu/archives/fall2018/entries/moral-dilemmas (Accessed 5 April 2019).

McIntyre, A. (2019) 'Doctrine of Double Effect'. *Stanford Encyclopedia of Philosophy* (Spring 2019 ed.). Online. Available at: https://plato.stanford.edu/archives/spr2019/entries/double-effect (Accessed 5 April 2019).

Oakeshott, M. (1972) Education: The engagement and its frustration. In Fuller, T. (Ed.). *The Voice of Liberal Learning: Michael Oakeshott on Education*. New Haven and London: Yale University Press.

Siddique, H. (2018) What is happening with children's mental health? *Guardian On-Line 22 November* 2018. Online. Available at: www.theguardian.com/society/2018/nov/22/mental-health-disorders-on-rise-among-children-nhs-figures (Accessed 25 January 2019).

Simon, C. A. (2016) *Beyond Every Child Matters: Neoliberal Education and Social Policy in the New Era*. London and New York: Routledge.

Stets, J. E. and Carter, M. J. (2012) A theory of the self in the sociology of morality. *American Sociological Review*, **77**(1), pp. 120–140.

Tomlinson, S. (2001) *Education in a Post-welfare Society*. Buckingham: OUP.

Williams, K. (2007) *Education and the Voice of Michael Oakeshott*. Exeter: Imprint Academic.

6 Turning 'intersectionality' on its head as we navigate our journeys through difficult dialogue

Victoria Showunmi

Introduction

This chapter explores the concepts of black race and identity in Britain through discourses between a mother and her daughters as they embark on a journey of enlightenment and togetherness while navigating everyday incidents of racism and sexism. The methodology is a retrospective analysis and reflection on day-to-day mother–daughter narratives. The study examines what these narratives reveal, not only about racial and gender-based attitudes in contemporary western society, but also how these impinge on the self-image and psychology of black girls.

The focus of the study is the experience of two black girls whose black mother was raised as a 'white girl' in an adoptive white affluent middle-class family. As such, it is positioned in the theories of intersectionality: Critical Race Theory (CRT) and White Studies. Analysis of these mother–daughter dialogues pulls together life-experiences and recognised theories to illustrate and explore some of the issues faced by young black girls growing up in the UK. It reveals the process through which young black girls' awareness and understanding of racism and sexism towards society can be developed and exposed in everyday conversations. It throws light on areas such as identity, loss and transformation. It also shows how a confident mother can help her daughters to come to grips with the causes and impact of racial and sexual discrimination.

Theoretical framework

The theoretical frameworks of CRT, Whiteness Studies and intersectionality are drawn on to explore and better understand the experiences described in the text.

Critical Race Theory

CRT developed from legal studies (Delgado, 1995) and is more commonly applied within the USA, though increasingly evident in the UK: e.g. Gillborn (2008) and the Journal of Race, Ethnicity and Education Special Issue (2012). CRT starts from the premise that race and racism are endemic in society, and both are considered to intersect with other forms of oppression based on gender, class, sexuality, language and culture (Delgado, 1995; Ladson-Billings, 1998). One of the central tenets of CRT is the recognition of the experiential knowledge and voice (stories) of People of Colour. Dixson and Rousseau (2005) assert that the personal and community experience of People of Colour should be acknowledged as important sources of knowledge. Calmore (1995: 321) describes CRT as tending:

> …toward a very personal expression that allows our experiences and lessons, learned as People of Color, to convey the knowledge we possess in a way that is empowering to us, and, it is hoped, ultimately empowering to those on whose behalf we act.

By providing 'counter stories' CRT challenges 'majoritarian [White] stories [that] are not often questioned because people do not see them as stories but as "natural" parts of everyday life' (Solórzano and Yosso, 2002: 28). Added to this, they serve to critique dominant White ideologies and White privilege/supremacy: 'a system of opportunities and benefits conferred upon people simply because they are White' (Solórzano and Yosso, 2002: 27). By creating new knowledge, counter-stories serve to challenge taken-for-granted norms (Ladson-Billings and Donnor, 2005), and at the same time, help us to rethink the 'traditional notion of what counts as [valid] knowledge' (Bernal, 2002: 109). Castro-Salazar and Bagley (2010: 34) observed that CRT 'help[s] the oppressed to create their own shared memory and history which can then be used as a source of strength as they work within a system dominated by a narrative that excludes and minimises their existence'. CRT therefore seeks to be empowering and is committed to achieving social justice for People of Colour.

CRT scholars utilise personal narratives and stories as appropriate forms to provide evidence and challenge the 'number only' approach to the documentation of inequity or discrimination that tends to support and evidence discrimination from a quantitative rather than a qualitative perspective (Parker and Lynn, 2002).

'Whiteness' and Whiteness Studies

Dyer (1997: 10) implies that 'Whiteness is an invisible perspective, a dominant and normative space against which difference is measured'. Interestingly, McIntosh (1988: 155) supports Dyer's definition and takes it to an even deeper level, contending that 'Whiteness is the capacity that Whiteness brings for passing unnoticed, un-harassed, "unbothered" through public space'. According to Leonardo (2004: 139) 'Whiteness' brings with it racial privilege [which] is the notion that White subjects accrue advantages by virtue of being constructed as Whites. Usually, this occurs through the valuation of White skin colour, although this is not the only criterion for racial distinction (Hunter, 2002). He continues with '…hair texture, nose shapes, culture, and language also multiply the privileges of Whites or those who approximate them' (Hunter, 2002: 171–189). Fanon's (1967) work deals with the desire to inhabit Whiteness, while Twine's (1998) study of Brazil indicates that people 'whiten' up in the census to satisfy personal (yet collectively refuted) desires for privilege.

Garner (2006: 257) argues that the notion of 'Whiteness is most effectively conceptualised as both a resource and a contingent hierarchy, and its utility is that it enables collective identities to be examined in a more nuanced way than is allowed for by the hegemonic Black/White, or more accurately, White/non-White paradigms'. Importantly, White privilege is like any social phenomenon: 'it is complex and in a White-supremacist society, all White people have some sort of privilege in some settings. There are general patterns, but such privilege plays out differently depending on context and other aspects of one's identity' (Jensen, 2005: 8). Garner's (2006) work provides a historical timeline which implies that Whiteness Studies follow a pattern that originates in the cultural path of

Black America, which has then been hijacked by radical elements within the dominant 'White' culture. Such thinking can be traced back through the works of Du Bois (1977, 1935), Hughes (1947), Wright (1992), Ellison (1952), Baldwin (1955) and Fanon (1967). A survey conducted by Roediger on Black perspectives in 1999 enables one to focus on the genealogy of, and vernacular setting for, the expression of Whiteness as 'fear' identified by Morrison (1987) and hooks, b (1997).

Understanding the notion of Whiteness is integral to this chapter because the author, while visibly Black, has had the experience of being socialised as White, and the consequent exposure to White privilege, as part of belonging to a White middle-class family.

Intersectionality

The term 'intersectionality' is mostly identified with CRT scholar Kimberle Crenshaw (1990) who, along with others, contributed to and advocated thinking critically about the multidimensional aspect of women's oppression along race, class and gender lines. According to Delgado Bernal (2002: 116) focusing on the intersection of oppression is vital because 'one's identity is not based on the social construction of race but rather is multidimensional and intersects with various experiences'. Many argue that scholars using the 'intersectional approach' will socially locate individuals in the context of their 'real lives' (Weber and Fore, 2007: 123). Intersectional discussions examine how both the formal and informal systems of power are deployed, maintained and reinforced through notions of race, class and gender (Collins, 1998; Weber and Fore, 2007).

Methodological approach

The chapter draws on a conceptual framework that relates to the works of authors who write in the field of CRT along with Whiteness Studies. I use the notion of CRT to tell the story of racism in this study. The CRT movement

> is a collection of activists and scholars interested in studying and transforming the relationship among race, racism and power. The movement considers many of the same issues that conventional civil rights and ethnic studies discourses take up, but places them in a broader perspective that includes economics, history, context, group- and self-interest, and even feelings and the unconscious.
>
> (Delgado and Stefancic, 2001: 102)

The narrative used throughout is a methodological tool to tell the story of racism encountered in everyday life. What is of particular interest is the way in which racism has arisen, and then been discussed, as part of 'everyday parenting'. The landscape changed after the Coalition Government came into power in 2010. The discussion on who was and who was not British became a heated and contested debate that was ripping through the heart of Britain, British families and the wider community.

The methodology incorporates biographical research to help illustrate the complexities of racism and class differences in modern society. Biographical research is an exciting, stimulating and fast-moving field which seeks to understand the changing experiences and outlooks of individuals in their daily lives (Merrill and West, 2009).

I was having an in-depth conversation (by cell phone) with my daughter about aspects of her studies as she was getting onto a bus in the Woodford area of London. I could hear there was a high level of noise in the background. I continued talking, when my daughter said:

'Mum did you hear that?'
I said, 'No – what was I meant to be hearing?'
'Mum! As I got onto the bus a man just said, "Oh look, we have a Zulu getting onto the bus"'.

This comment serves as a reminder that here in the United Kingdom, even though we may believe that things have begun to change throughout the world since Barack Obama's success, there still appears to be no remedy to the pervasive presence of direct racism. My first reaction was for my daughter's safety as I was unable to help, sitting in a comfortable chair in my office while talking to her on the telephone. Now I could hear the man as he continued to spurt out racist comments for at least another 10 minutes, including the use of the word 'nigger'. It took another black woman on the bus to intervene and challenge his behaviour.

Throughout the ordeal, the bus driver was silent and continued to focus on the job at hand, driving the bus. Eventually, he reluctantly found his voice when the man became louder, and stood up in front of the black woman who was defending my daughter. 'Mate, I am going to call the police if you do not stop shouting abuse, so are you getting off now or shall I call the police'. Thankfully the man got off the bus.

The conversation continued with my daughter as I endeavored to establish whether she was OK. I was bracing myself for another one of those difficult conversations. Instead my daughter said: 'Oh mum, yeah I am OK; this is just Woodford. People keep saying that there's no more racism. Obviously, they're not experiencing the same as we do every day'.

Academic writing is usually seen as requiring distance and objectivity from the author. I have chosen to bring our lives into the work because I believe, along with Lea and Helfand (2006), that our scholarship is deeply informed by how we have experienced the world. Working through the various significant events that occur in one's own life, such as the one described above, provides the opportunity to explore and understand, and to build and develop our differing identities. This was very much the case in the dialogue with my daughter concerning the incident on the bus.

Although my daughter appeared to be taking it in her stride, I was troubled by what had just taken place. What had given the man the right to spurt out racial abuse to a young woman who was getting on the bus in an orderly fashion? Was it that his perceived white privilege gave him the power and right to express his views? Did he think that he was on safe territory, and therefore would not be challenged by those around him?

> Race only becomes 'real' as a social force when individuals or groups behave towards each other in ways which either reflect or perpetuate the hegemonic ideology of subordination and the patterns of inequality in daily life.
>
> (Marable, 1993: 114)

The racism that is being displayed here is raw and directed towards a person of colour in order to create the maximum impact for an attention-seeking white male, who, at the time, might himself be feeling marginalised due to rejection or unemployment. It is difficult to apprehend what was actually going through my daughter's mind. Her undisturbed and matter-of-fact comment of 'well that is how it is in Woodford' is difficult for a mother to work through with her daughter on the telephone. There was a need for one of those mother–daughter dialogues to ensure that the day's events were not lost in the midst of the business of life. The incident continued to play on my mind throughout the day, and I found myself telling other colleagues at work about what had happened to my daughter. Some were amazed that she had experienced such direct racism within our diverse society that we 'British' are so proud of being part of. Others just failed to comment.

The way in which events are addressed in our house is through a series of questions. This particular situation was no different. I continued to ask my daughter questions about the day's event while I was returning home from work. 'What happened to the man who called you such awful names? Do you think that he was a local man who was perhaps just unhappy?' There appeared to be no straightforward answer to whatever question I asked. It was apparent that my daughter took the events as part of everyday life. I wondered if this was due to my own lack of emotional engagement. Had this now been passed on to her? Was this the dismissive attribute that I displayed as part of my own 'Englishness'? Should I have asked my daughter how the encounter had made her feel? Had I just been concerned about the happenings that had taken place on the bus with very little acknowledgement of anything broader?

I realised that, in order to ensure that my daughter was sifting through the information at a pace that suited her, I had taken control of the pace and what went into the overall dialogue. There was no rule book: only my beliefs and values for what I thought a 'good' mother should be. How did I know that this would be good enough in the overall scheme of things? As a parent who has an understanding of how gender, race and Whiteness-theory works, talking about racism with a daughter still poses a challenge. How does one apply all such learning to a conversation with a child/young person who is looking for answers? It seems that when a question is asked, a parent has less than a minute to formulate an answer.

When I arrived home, we talked again about the situation that had occurred on the bus. I suggested that it might be good for her to capture her thoughts on a blog, as I was going to include any thoughts that I had into my academic writing. I was taken back by her response:

'So you are going to use my experience for your work?'
'Well, yes, it is something that I had always thought about doing, if the timing had been right'.

The discussion continued with more questions:

'I am not sure that you can just do that without asking me, can you, mum?'
'I suppose I do need to ask whether you would be OK with me using this experience: what do you think?'

My daughter's eventual response was: 'Of course it's OK, I just didn't know that it would be useful'. It was really evident that her experience had not shifted her matter-of-fact attitude at all; perhaps the fact that she is a well-grounded individual helped her to make sense of – and then shrug off – the incident.

All this reminded me of a similar incident that had taken place on a bus two years prior to this one. The difference was that it was with a black woman who felt the need to shower my daughter with racial abuse. The focus of this abuse was on skin shade. My daughter was out with her university friends when they were on the bus home. As they were a large group, they took seats upstairs and were enjoying the ride home until a woman got on and imagined that my daughter had an issue with people being of darker complexion. The woman threatened violence against my daughter, as she had made the assumption that my daughter viewed herself as superior. Interestingly enough, both my older daughters had experienced 'shadism' from the time that they were toddlers, as society appears more ready to accept the lighter version of black. (The term 'shadism' means to judge or be against a person because of their skin tone rather than their race.) As their mother, I taught them to understand that whether you were light or dark you were still black, facing the same obstacles. I never separated the two, as my experience was that it did not matter how much black there was: in most contexts you would still be seen as black from the classification of race.

The difficultly that had emerged from our conversation was the apparent tacit acceptance by my daughter of the routine racism and shadism she encountered in her life. It was as though she felt there were much more important things to discuss than the issue of racism. Racism was always going to be with us and therefore, 'should we not just get used to it, and accept that was just the way life is'. I was aware that, as her mother, it was important that she knew that the notion of acceptance could be viewed as 'giving up'.

My daughter's passive acceptance of racist behavior has been recognised by Delgado and Stefancic (2001: 102–103) who state:

> CRT (Critical Race Theory) begins with a number of basic insights. One is that racism is normal, not aberrant, in American society. Because racism is an ingrained feature of our landscape, it looks ordinary and natural to persons in the culture. Formal equal opportunity – rules and laws that insist on treating blacks and whites (for example) alike – can thus remedy only the more extreme and shocking forms of injustice, the ones that do stand out. It can do little about the business-as-usual forms of racism that people of color confront every day and that account for much misery, alienation, and despair.

I felt angry that routine, everyday acts of racism were remaining untackled. I found myself defending the current UK legislation, particularly the Race Relations Amendment Act 2000 which shows that things are changing and that there is no need to take people's abuse. A man had recently been jailed for eight months for ranting racial abuse at two children in the north of England. In addition to this, other members of the community, including a police officer, have been caught out by the law that now defines racial abuse as a criminal offence. The conversation with my daughter described earlier made me reflect on when racism/sexism may first have begun to impinge on her life (and the life of my other daughter) as she had seemed so unsurprised and unfazed by her experience on the bus. It made me think back on what both my daughters might have faced at school.

In 1990 my other daughter, then six years old, had previously been at school for one year in a rural area where she had experienced no direct racism and had just started at a school in the suburbs of London. She came home with the following question, 'What is a "paki", mummy? Somebody at school called me a paki'. I had less than a split second to decide how the question that had been posed was going to be answered. Indeed, there were at least three things going on here that needed to be addressed. The first was to explain that the use of the word 'paki' was a very mean word that should not be used by children to describe others. The second point was to explain that 'paki' was shortened for Pakistani and that she was not a Pakistani child. Instead her heritage was made up of her father who was of British and Jamaican roots and her Nigerian mother. I suppose, if I am honest, what took me by surprise was the directness of the racism that my daughter experienced.

This took me back to when I had my own first dose of racism within school at the age of four, and how my foster mother dealt with the difficult conversation that was required to ensure that I was OK. We had just moved into a quaint village which had previously made a petition in an attempt to stop my foster parents from buying a house in the village. The villagers appeared to be afraid of the affluent family that had moved in with black children. I can recall my first morning at the village school in the South West of England. The school was surrounded by lush green fields. As we walked up to the school gate I sensed the parents and children looking at me. I was the only black child in the playground with so many eyes watching me. I did not know what to expect as I had been shielded by Whiteness; even though I knew that I was different, I was still very naïve. The worst part of the day was during playtime when children would call out a range of names: blacky, wog and gollywog. It was the time of day that I hated the most and felt most vulnerable. Contrary to what is often believed, evidence (Tizard and Phoenix, 1993) suggests that such insults were much more common in primary than in secondary schools.

There are some white people who may consider such insults as part and parcel of playground life; however, there is no doubt that many children in Tizard and Phoenix's study found the insults to be deeply distressing:

> It was when I was nine or ten, and we moved to X [an outer suburb] and there was no black people up there, and I got called names, blacky, nigger. I couldn't understand it, I mean, I was a person, it's just that the colour of my skin was different…

(pp. 35–7)

There were times when the village children were attempting to make sense of what was going on – as they did not understand why I was different from them. I was bombarded with many questions stemming from the lack of understanding from both the parents and children. Children would come to me and ask, 'Why are you wearing shoes?' Or they would call me various derogatory names. The way my family dealt with the hostility I experienced at school was to hold a public meeting in the school playground. As you can imagine, things only got worse, and I began to question why God had made me this colour at all.

There are certain social survival techniques that white parents just cannot teach their black children, and experiences that they cannot share. Their child will need to look to other black adults or black friends in order to learn these skills. This is not possible for a child cut off from his/her own community.

> The black reared in his own community can at least retreat to his own people for solace when the situation demands it. What of the black child who is defined as an alien in the white community…? Obviously such a child would be under inordinate stress and he would be likely to crumble under tension.

(Gill and Jackson, 1983: 103)

My mother created a poem for me to read out in class, with the aim of making the children less critical. 'I know a little girl called Flo, who was dropped in snow – and that's why she is a little white girl. I am a little girl who was dropped in gravy – and that's why I'm a little brown girl'. My mother was convinced that it was only names, and that 'sticks and stones may break my bones – but names will never hurt you'. However, the children in Tizard and Phoenix's study, when asked whether they thought that name-calling was always racist, or whether they thought it was just 'a bit different', the vast majority saw it as racist.

I was determined that I would do things very differently with my own daughters. Although they appeared to have come to terms with racist language directed at them, I felt concerned that words *could* hurt. Even though they seemed to have accepted this sort of treatment as the norm, I wondered how it might have impinged on their self-esteem and their feelings of identity. I realised that my daughters' sense of identity would be more complex than just exploring the effects of race. They would also be influenced by my own black–white identity issues which I may have passed on to them, adding another intersectional factor and further confusing their self-image. Would my white associations and characteristics get in the way of the development of my daughters? Had I raised them with English stiff-upper-lip repression of emotions? My daughters and I both have white middle-class English accents – which has made things both difficult and easy for all of us in life.

I asked my daughter how she felt about her identity, to which her initial response was: 'I know where I am coming from'. However, further questioning revealed some identity issues. My daughter recalled being told by fellow university students: 'You won't get on in Hackney (an inner London suburb with a sizeable African-Caribbean population) with that accent'. Comments like this had made her reflect on her own identity. She later said to me: 'The way I speak gets in the way for some blacks'. This revealed not necessarily her own identity issues, but confusion in others about her identity. I wondered whether our frequent mother–daughter dialogues had helped her to develop confidence and a strong sense of identity, or whether they might sometimes make her more sensitive to things that had not previously impinged on her. There are very clear distinctions between the classes within the UK and each of them has its own distinctive accent.

It was clear that there was a further intersectional aspect at work in the above dialogue: that of class. My daughter's accent is middle-class English, which is almost as discriminated against as blackness in an area like Hackney (not to mention the additional issue of gender discrimination and its impact on identity, which has been the subject of many dialogues between myself and my daughters – but that is another story).

Finally, when I reflected on other dialogues that I have had with my daughters it occurred to me that it was not only overt racist behavior that may have affected them, but also indirect symbolic messages. My youngest daughter went to the cinema with her older sister to see the long-awaited *Princess and the Frog* where the princess was black. Both of them were excited that this film had been made. My youngest daughter noticed that the black princess in the marketing pictures was wearing a blue dress, and the white princess the pink dress. (Previously princesses would usually be dressed in pink.) She also asked why the white princess was enclosed in a heart shape with a light background, while the black princess had no heart shape and had a dark background. Had my youngest daughter unconsciously perceived a subliminal racial bias? (The only other characters with dark backgrounds were the beasts.)

Conclusion

In summary, this chapter has provided a glimpse from a range of dialogues between a mother and her daughters. It shows us that, in spite the various equality Acts and perceived ideas that discrimination has disappeared, there is not much change from a six year-old girl asking 'what's a Paki…?' to a 24 year-old woman being addressed as a Zulu on the bus. We are still struggling with ways to move the agenda forward so that racism does eventually become something of the past.

In writing this chapter, I have sought to understand the extent to which CRT, Whiteness Studies and intersectionality are useful theoretical/conceptual tools in conceptualising the experiences of a family grappling with 'every-day racism'. Overall, the chapter exposes contradictions in the Black mothers' and daughters' experiences which are not simply explained away by racism, but instead are fuelled by embodied Whiteness. The chapter contends that, while CRT is a useful explanatory framework in understanding experiences underpinned by racism, other theoretical models may also need to be applied. It also suggests that, while the perspectives of CRT and Whiteness Studies cannot neatly be integrated, they are of value in helping to unpack diverse Black academic staff experiences.

Questions for discussion

- How do we ensure that when considering everyday racism gender is also included?
- How can educators develop a social justice lens in the role of leaders?

Summary

- Understanding the notion of race is complex and is evolving through the many different identities.
- Intersectionality is an approach which can be used as a framework to comprehend difference within structural and oppressive organisations.
- Critical conversation on gender, race and class with young people is crucial to the work of social justice.

Recommended reading

Collins, P. H. and Bilge, S. (2016) *Intersectionality*. Cambridge: Polity Press.
Crenshaw, K. (1990) Mapping the margins: Intersectionality, identity politics, and violence against women of color. *Stanford Law Review*, **43**(6), pp. 1241–1299.
Lykke, N. (2010) *Feminist Studies: A Guide to Intersectional Theory, Methodology and Writing*. Abingdon: Routledge.
Showunmi, V. (2017) The role of the "Black Girls' Club": Challenging the status quo. In Martin, J. L., Nickels, A. E. and Sharp-Grier, M. (Eds.). *Feminist Pedagogy, Practice, and Activism: Improving Lives for Girls and Women*. New York: Routledge.

References

Baldwin, J. (1955) *Notes on a Native Son*. Boston: Beacon Books.
Bernal, D. D. (2002). Critical race theory, Latino critical theory, and critical raced-gendered epistemologies: Recognizing students of color as holders and creators of knowledge. *Qualitative Inquiry*, **8**(1), pp. 105–126.
Calmore, J. (1995) Racialized space and the culture of segregation: 'Hewing a stone of hope from a mountain of despair'. *University of Pennsylvania Law Review*, **143**(5), pp. 1233–1273.

Castro-Salazar, R. and Bagley, C. (2010) 'Ni de aqui ni from there'. Navigating between contexts: Counter-narratives of undocumented Mexican students in the United States. *Race Ethnicity and Education*, **13**(1) pp. 23–40.

Collins, P. H. (1998). *Fighting Words: Black Women and the Search for Justice*. Minneapolis: University of Minnesota Press.

Crenshaw, K. (1990). Mapping the margins: Intersectionality, identity politics, and violence against women of color. *Stanford Law Review*, **43**, pp. 1241–1299.

Delgado Bernal, D. (2002). Critical race theory, Latino critical theory, and critical raced-gendered epistemologies: Recognizing students of color as holders and creators of knowledge. *Qualitative Inquiry*, **8**(1), pp. 105–126.

Delgado, R. (Ed.) (1995). *Critical Race Theory: The Cutting Edge*. Philadelphia: Temple University Press.

Delgado, R. and Stefancic, J. (2001). *Critical Race Theory: An Introduction*. New York: New York University Press.

Dixson, A. D. and Rousseau, C. K. (2005) And we are still not saved: Critical race theory in education ten years later. *Race Ethnicity and Education*, **8**(1), pp. 7–27.

Du Bois, W. E. B. (1977 [1935]) *Black Reconstruction in the United States, 1860–1880*. New York: Kraus International.

Dyer, R. (1997) *White*. London: Routledge.

Ellison, R. (1952) *Invisible Man*. New York: Random House.

Fanon, F. (1967). *Black Skin, White Mask*. New York: Grove Press.

Garner, S. (2006) The uses of whiteness: What sociologists working on Europe can draw from US research on whiteness. *Sociology*, **40**(2), pp. 257–275.

Gill, O. and Jackson, B. (1983) *Adoption and Race: Black, Asian and Mixed Race Children in White Families*. London: British Association for Adoption.

Gillborn, D. (2008). *Racism and Education: Coincidence or Conspiracy?* London: Routledge.

hooks, b. (1997) Representing whiteness in black imagination. In Frankenberg, R. (Ed.). *Displacing Whiteness: Essays in Social and Cultural Criticism*. Durham: Duke University Press.

Hughes, L. (1947) *The Ways of White Folks*. New York: Routledge.

Hunter, M. (2002) 'If you're light you're alright': Light skin color as social capital for women of color. *Gender and Society*, **16**(2), pp. 171–189.

Jensen, R. (2005). *The Heart of Whiteness: Confronting Race, Racism, and White Privilege*. San Francisco: City Lights.

Ladson-Billings, G. (1998) Just what is critical race theory and what's it doing in a nice field like education? *International Journal of Qualitative Studies in Education*, **11**(1), pp. 7–24.

Ladson-Billings, G. and Donnor, J. (2005) The moral activist role of critical race theory scholarship. In Denzin, N. F. and Lincoln, Y. S. (Eds.). *The Sage Handbook of Qualitative Research*, (3rd ed.). Thousand Oaks California and London: Sage.

Lea, V. and Helfand, J. (Eds.) (2006). *Identifying Race and Transforming Whiteness in the Classroom*. Oxford: Peter Lang International Academic Publishers.

Leonardo, Z. (2004) The color of supremacy: Beyond the discourse of 'white privilege'. *Educational Philosophy and Theory*, **36**(2), pp. 137–144.

Marable, M. (1993) Beyond identity politics: Towards a liberation theory for multicultural democracy. *Race & Class*, **35**(1), pp. 113–130.

McIntosh, P. (1988) White Privilege: Unpacking the Invisible Knapsack. Available at https://www.racialequitytools.org/resourcefiles/mcintosh.pdf (Accessed 22 November 2019).

Merrill, B. and West, L. (2009) *Using Biographical Methods in Social Research*. London: Sage.

Morrison, T. (1987) Foreword. In Nekola, C. and Rabinowitz, P. *Writing red: An anthology of American women writers, 1930-1940*. New York: Feminist Press at CUNY.

Parker, L. and Lynn, M. (2002) What's race to do with it? Critical race theory's conflicts with and connections to qualitative research methodology and epistemology. *Qualitative Inquiry*, **8**(1), pp. 7–22.

Race, Ethnicity and Education Special Issue (2012) Critical race theory in England. **15**. Available at: https://www.tandfonline.com/loi/cree20?open=15&year=2012&repitition=0#vol_15_2012 (Accessed 19 August 2019).

Solórzano, D. and Yosso, T. (2002) Critical race methodology: Counter-storytelling as an analytical framework for education research. *Qualitative Inquiry*, **8**(1), pp. 23–44.

Tizard, B. and Phoenix, A. (1993). *Black White or Mixed Race*. London: Routledge.

Twine, F.W. (1998) *Racism in a Racial Democracy: The Maintenance of White Supremacy in Brazil*. New Brunswick, N.J: Rutgers University Press.

Weber, L. and Fore, E. (2007) Race, ethnicity, and health: An intersectional approach. *Handbook of the Sociology of Racial and Ethnic Relations*. New York: Springer.

Wright, R. (1992 [1945]) *Black Boy*. New York: Harper Collins.

7   The ever-present discourses in education: Discourse and educational change

Jessie A. Bustillos Morales

Introduction

Education and schooling are at the heart of society with most developed societies channelling, selecting and imparting ways of knowing, learning and understanding through the established institution of the school. How we make sense of what education means, and is for, is deeply bound to how we talk about education and how these ways convey meaning and value in society. These meanings and relevance which education and schooling maintain tend to change over time, influenced by various political, cultural and societal changes. Throughout this chapter, education is explored as characterised by historical discourses which have shaped and changed the way in which education is thought about, and how the purposes of schooling are defined. Education is, therefore, presented and analysed through various discursive formations which are discussed chronologically and linked to the notion of discourse.

The notion of discourse is used as a critically exploratory tool which helps us think about education and what happens in school more critically, and not just as a result of emerging educational policy. Firstly, the chapter will define the notion of discourse in order to set the scene for the theoretical points discussed. Discourses are presented as important norms in which society thinks about its core dynamics; education is a very important dynamic in society, but discourse creates its social meaning and purpose. Secondly, there are critical reflections on one of the common discourses which contributed to the beginnings of education and schooling, *the deserving poor.* This is a common discourse which revolves around education, perhaps more significantly during the rise of mass education in England which coincides with the Industrial Revolution. This discourse is explored historically, and unravelled with a focus on how its effects shaped the purpose of education. Thirdly, the chapter critically explores discourses around education as serving the needs of the economy, from both a historical perspective and as influenced by key political interventions.

The chapter offers a historical analysis of common discourses in education and revisits important developments in education and schooling. The sections will introduce the reader to important historical developments which have created the system of education and schooling as we know it. Education is a complex process which has become ubiquitous in everyday life, and we rarely ask critical questions about it. Thus, the chapter is an opportunity to examine and discuss why our current systems of schooling and education function in the way they do, utilising the notion of discourse as a critical backdrop to isolate some of the effects behind educational change.

Understanding discourse

The French theorist Michel Foucault speaks of discourse as the ways in which a society creates and divides meaning about any object: 'discourse is not simply that which manifests or hides' the object of which we speak, it is also the object itself; 'history constantly teaches us, discourse is not simply that which translates struggles or systems of domination, but is the thing for which and by which there is struggle, discourse is power which is to be seized' (Foucault, 1987: 52–53). This initial definition points to how Foucault thought about discourse and how he focused on how discourse works, rather than what discourse is. For Foucault, discourse is much more than language or narrative, it is more than words and what can be said about something; it is rather more about how those possible statements create and maintain meaning and purpose. Foucault also argues that discourse normally works through, and becomes organised through, institutions in society such as hospitals, the courts and, of course, schools. Discourse allows and disallows the possible meanings and representations of something in society, and societies administer dominant meanings and representations through selected institutions. For instance, think about how the world of law is transacted in courts of law, and similarly how the world of education is transacted in schools. Thus, schooling is an important institution for any society; it is how societies decide to disseminate knowledge, culture and attitudes that society considers of value at a particular time. However, the ways in which as a society we have constructed an understanding of what education is, or is for, changes through time; changes can be explained by using the notion of discourse.

Although discourse is a very tricky notion to define, it is important to lay some basic definitions which give an insight of what discourse is. Hall speaks of discourse as

> a group of statements which provide a language for talking about – i.e. a way of representing – a particular kind of knowledge about a topic. When statements about a topic are made within a particular discourse, the discourse makes it possible to construct the topic in a certain way. It also limits the other ways in which the topic can be constructed.
>
> (Hall, 1992: 201)

Therefore, discourse does not refer to one particular statement, but rather to various, or a series of, statements which give shape to a discursive formation, resulting from the statements. The discursive formation is the intelligible way in which we can talk about a particular theme or topic at any given point in society. Within education and schooling, this chapter argues that there have been many discursive formations which have allowed ways in which education has become intelligible or understood, and which have defined its meaning and purposes. Yet, this does not mean that education can only be what the discursive formation dictates, as there is no truth about education. It is suggested rather that the meanings we know about education are the result of a series of competing discursive formations which tend to change historically, and depending on which historical point we refer to, we encounter dominant discursive formations.

The following sections pursue a historical analysis of education through the notion of discourse, following the understandings previously laid out. If discourse is said to 'govern the way that a topic can be meaningfully talked about and reasoned about' (Hall, 1992: 44), then what could be some of the dominant discourses that have underpinned the development of education in the UK? Also, how have these discursive formations influenced the perceived purposes of education?

Question for reflection

Taking a moment to think about education, write a list of short sentences which often tend to be said about what education is for, or what education should accomplish.

Mass education and the deserving poor

Movement towards a system of mass education began with the rise of the Industrial Revolution in England. The Industrial Revolution provoked social, cultural and economic change; one very important change was the movement of people from the countryside and rural areas to places which became big industrial cities with constantly rising populations. The construction of factories was made possible with the invention of the steam engine and the opening and establishment of railway routes across the country, connecting cities, facilitated the expansion of industry and new communities (Lawson and Silver, 2007). Once factories began operating, they offered more lucrative and diverse types of work which people saw as new opportunities.

The Industrial Revolution is inextricably linked to the rise of mass education because the rapidly expanding cities produced an urban culture marked by rising mortality rates, disease, overcrowded housing and very poor living conditions. Amongst these emerging social problems child labour, child exploitation and child crime were an everyday occurrence, and it was very difficult to address these problems as the new towns and cities were expanding without any meaningful local monitoring or planning. There was a recognition that urban living conditions were very poor; for instance, regular outbreaks of cholera led to the passing of the 1848 Public Health Act, an attempt to understand and mitigate some of the more pressing public health issues facing the populations in cities. (See also Chapter 11.)

The condition in which children lived did not go unnoticed, and whilst the Church of England was the main provider of schooling at this time, they were by no means able to educate most children in society. Education in church schools was a privilege that few could access and the majority of children could actually be found working in factories in dangerous conditions alongside their families, or sometimes on their own. It is perhaps not surprising that one of the earliest government interventions to introduce the idea of education as part of a child's life was the 1833 Factory Act. The Act was introduced as an attempt to reduce child labour; it introduced a minimum of 2 hours daily for schooling and instruction, banned children younger than 9 from working in factories, prohibited children working at night and reduced the working hours to a maximum of 9 for 9 to 13 year-olds and 12 hours for 13 to 18-year-olds (Lawson and Silver, 2007). However, this Act did not eradicate child cruelty and child labour, nor did it offer a systematic educational vision for children; factory owners determined what the instruction should be.

Discourses around poor children at this time construct a need for change in society which began with notions of charity. The notion of charity has been underpinned by the Christian faith; charity is seen as a Christian practice as it involves supporting those in need, but implicitly leads to ideas of those who are to be helped. Considerable amounts of social change have been achieved by appealing to charity and the discursive formation of 'the deserving poor', who are to benefit from charitable donations and work, 'convincing the powerful of the moral good' behind every act of charity (Choules, 2007: 466). The deserving poor are those groups of people in society whom we regard as deserving of public expense and charity since they are not in control or to blame for the conditions in which they live. The deserving poor as a discursive formation shapes the subjects of discourse, in this case, the children during the industrial revolution, as being 'at risk', 'needing protection', 'lacking in morality and in education'. In present times there are still such discourses which help us identify ourselves with certain parts of the deserving poor discourse. A key example in the UK is Comic Relief, which is organised every other year to help charitable projects and initiatives in poor parts of the world, reaching as far as parts of Africa and South East Asia and raising millions of pounds. By collecting and giving money we are positioning ourselves as the powerful and the charitable in the discourse of the deserving poor, whilst those in receipt of the help, besides being helped, are made into the perfect image of the deserving poor, who should in gratitude accept help in any form it might come. Children and the conditions in which they lived in industrial times appealed to society's sense of charity and moral good, and these are ideas deeply bound within systems of education that followed. Yet they were also paternalistic and patronising in what type of education the poor really needed. (See also Chapter 3.)

The notion of schooling and education that forms as a result of the discourse of the deserving poor is characterised by satisfying the needs of the industrial masters and the factory owners, since the poorer sections of society were not seen as being able to benefit from a liberal education (Lawson and Silver, 2007). Instead, the poor needed simple and religious instruction, based around reading, writing, arithmetic and religion, knowledge which could help them participate in industrialised labour and shape their obedience and moral character. The discourse of the deserving poor is important since it is one of the earliest discourses in the foundations of education and schooling, and one which has contributed to the emergence of schools, but also limited the scope of the education received by people. The discourse of the deserving poor also constructed poor people as only being able to benefit from an education which could instill basic skills, religious observance and a good work ethic. Gone from this discourse are critical thinking skills, the needs of the individual and the nourishing of talents that individuals have.

As a discourse in education, the deserving poor can be seen as the imposition of the needs of society over the needs of the individual. Whilst the establishing of schools had a very big impact on children's lives and living conditions, creating an environment where children were educated, safer and better fed, the level of education they had access to came with distinct limitations and classed expectations. To this effect, Marxist social theorist Louis Althusser (1993) argues in *Essays on Ideology* that schooling's primary purpose is to reproduce the principles of capitalism by training a workforce in more than knowledge, but also training them to learn and accept their place in unequal societies. Althusser explains:

> What do children learn at school?... they learn to read, to write and to add...which are directly useful in the different jobs in production... But besides these techniques and knowledges... children also learn the rules of good behaviour, i.e. the attitude that should be observed by every agent in the division of labour, according to the job he is destined for... rules of morality, civic and professional conscience, which actually means rules of respect... for the order established by class domination... the reproduction of labour power requires not only a reproduction of its skills, but also at the same time the reproduction of its submission to the rules of the established order'.
>
> (Althusser, 1993: 6)

Following this critique of education, the discourse of the deserving poor has created a system of education which is associated with the need of subservient workers who will respect the rules, codes of conduct and behaviour necessary for accessing the labour market. Yet, at the same time, workers work for a wage, and accept their lower position in a capitalist system which is offering greater benefits to those who can create and own systems of production. This creates problematising inequalities since it is more difficult for individuals to be creative and critical if they are educated in systems which are already shaped to satisfy the needs of society.

Education and schooling have historically been influenced by class and privilege, with stark differences in the job outcomes of those who are educated in state schools and those who are educated in fee-paying private or public schools. Francis and Wong (2013) argue that the differential in employment outcomes in England and Wales corroborates how the type of school attended has a huge effect on who secures the top jobs in the country. In their research they claim that over 70 per cent of top jobs in the country are secured by people who attended public and independent schools, when only seven per cent of the population attend these types of schools (Francis and Wong, 2013). The education of the deserving poor was in contrast with the education of those who could afford to pay for a more classical education or attend university. The aim of popular education was to create a workforce, whilst the more classical and privileged forms of education aimed to produce leaders. Lawson and Silver (2007: 231) explain how education from its inception was a matter of class, with the poor to be educated to 'work intelligibly and the middle class to govern intelligibly'.

Systems of education and schooling were further influenced by the Forster Act of 1870, the Further Education Act of 1880, and the Butler Act of 1944. These education Acts mark formal government involvement and allocation of public funds towards a system of schooling for England and Wales. Whilst government involvement meant that a significant portion of public funds were to be committed to educating the masses and paying for schools and teachers, it also meant that the education received by the majority of children was primarily to develop basic skills. Education is said to be one of the main ways in which a country enables equality of opportunity and social mobility between different social classes. However, since its inception education has created divisive class differences diminishing its potential (Bathmaker *et al.,* 2016).

The discourse of the deserving poor in education has left a historical trail highlighting the division between the poor and the wealthy. Vast differences still remain. Although education offered access to a better life for many children, bringing important issues to the foreground, such as, child poverty, child mortality and child exploitation, it has not succeeded in improving overall equalities in society. Social mobility is still a significant issue in England and Wales, with stifling trends in recent years, and a system of education which addresses important social problems, but which does not open up enough opportunities for all (Francis and Wong, 2013; Gristy *et al.,* 2019).

Education and the needs of the economy

Examining educational change through political rhetoric and political discourse is a very important way in which we come to understand education (Bustillos Morales and Abegglen, 2018). How we come to know education, both in its nature and in its purpose, is largely influenced by government interventions in schools and in the production of educational policy. Based on Foucault's (1987) understanding of discourse, this chapter suggests that the knowledge we hold on education is permeated by the very discourses that allow us to speak of it in particular ways. One of the ways in which discourse functions is through the 'will to knowledge' (Foucault, 1987). Schools as social institutions carry a responsibility to will (us) to knowledge. For example, schools will (us) to know-ledge Mathematics in a particular way, will (us) to knowledge History in a particular way, will (us) to knowledge Literature in a particular way and through particular literary works. Yet, who wills us to know education? What education is and what it should be for? In this section I discuss how political discourses on education will us to know education in specific ways, influencing how we define a worthwhile or valuable education. Foucault (1987: 48) states that the will to knowledge:

> … comprises a discrete realm of discursive practices … a conceptual terrain in which know-ledge is formed and produced … Discursive practices are characterised by a delimitation of a field of objects, the definition of a legitimate perspective for the agent of knowledge, and the fixing of norms for the elaboration of concepts and theories.

So which are some important historical points in UK politics which have willed the general public to know education? Arguably, all governments produce a set of discourses on education. However, the changes which began during the 1970s and continued in the next two decades are very significant since they have deeply influenced how we perceive education and schooling and the value they bring to society. An important recurrent rhetoric of this time is that of education needing to satisfy the needs of the economy, taking education beyond its social and cultural values and contribution. Let us explore how education and schooling became so closely tied to the changing economic imperatives of our time.

Discourses around education began to be closely tied with the economy and the needs of industry with James Callaghan's speech delivered at Ruskin College, Oxford on 18th October 1976. The speech initiated a great debate in public which called into question the purposes of educa-tion, and it paved the way for later reforms in education and schooling. Education and schooling in the 1970s were characterised by a loose curriculum, informal teaching methods and very little government intervention. Before Callaghan, Prime Ministers were simply not interested in what went on in schools, but with the Callaghan speech a new set of discursive formations took shape around education, those which equated education with satisfying employers' needs, disguised in a discourse pointing to the need to raise standards. Very importantly, the Callaghan speech marked the beginning of significant changes to the educational system which were introduced during the later governments of Margaret Thatcher and John Major. Callaghan set out some of these ideas in his speech by stating:

> I have been concerned to find out that many of our best trained students who have completed the higher levels of education at university or polytechnic have no desire to join industry. Their preferences are to stay in academic life or to find their way into the civil service. There seems to be a need for more technological bias in science teaching that will lead towards practical applications in industry rather than towards academic studies.
>
> (Callaghan cited in Jarvis and Griffin, 2003: 146)

Following an analysis through discourse allows for understanding how the statements that are made about education create a possible set of meanings which become the discursive reality around edu-cation (what it seems possible to say about education). With the Callaghan speech and statements as the ones above, the world of education and schooling became re-interpreted as needing to serve the interests of employers, particularly with an emphasis on technology and the natural sciences. In the case of education, the vision and discursive formations – the statements used to describe what the key purpose of education should be – outlined in the Callaghan speech opened the inner workings of the school to government intervention and monitoring.

Although James Callaghan did not pursue the changes he had proposed for education himself, his speech laid the foundations for significant educational change. The Conservative governments which succeeded Callaghan's focused on opening schools to Hayekian free-market economics which emphasised competition, normally between schools, and choice for parents and students, who were seen as consumers. The changes to education in the decades between 1979 and 1997 centered on the 'weakening and dismantling of local educational authority (LEA) and teacher autonomy … an uneasy combination of centralisation and devolution' (Ball, 2017: 14). The centralisation of power which had resided in local education authorities to run and fund local schools seemed to be coming apart. Instead, schools were granted options to become independent from local authority control and to devise and pursue other ways of funding themselves. The government project during this time aimed to address the perceived inefficiency of the welfare and public service models, with privatisation and independence from public funding highly encouraged. The emerging discourses around education at the time were linked to the Conservative government's distrust of the public sector's autonomy. Education was talked about as needing change and reform, to make teachers and schools accountable and responsible for their own image and success, and that of their students. The changes to come would primarily affect mainstream schooling, that is state schools, not private schools or the old public schools which have historically been exempt from changes brought by government educational policy.

One significant change occurring after the Callaghan speech was the introduction of a prescriptive National Curriculum in 1988. Before this time there was no statutory government control over what was taught in schools. The origins of the Education Act of 1988 are an inevitable consequence of the Callaghan speech which highlighted the importance of 'school autonomy, the response to the economic crisis of 1970s, and the increasing link being made between education and economic needs' (Wyse and Torrance, 2009: 215). The National Curriculum introduced in England and Wales transformed the everyday lives of pupils and teachers. The National Curriculum affected the organisation, the principles and the very knowledge it imposed on teachers and pupils, reproducing ways in which education could be talked about and thought about, and these reflected 'economically rooted norms' (Apple, 2013: 19). Some of these norms point to the need for standardisation and utility of knowledge and subjects, creating a set of useful facts that have value in society. Also was the idea of a standardised pedagogy in which these facts and knowledge should be presented to students, undermining the expertise of teachers. Lastly, the expectation that these facts and knowledge can be learnt by all pupils within a particular timeline, which can also be monitored and tested through standardised assessment to measure educational outcomes for all pupils. The pragmatic changes brought by the introduction of the national curriculum changed what schools viewed as valuable knowledge. The need for standardisation was closely linked to the government's economic-based discourse around education and schooling. Behind curricular change the most distinctive expectation was that teaching and learning in all schools should reflect the needs of the economy, as interpreted by the government of the time. What an education entails then becomes only intelligible through the economic value it brings to the individual and to society. Learning just for the sake of learning becomes a radical discourse in education, since the prevalent and dominant discourses, dictated by political rhetoric, point to securing a job in industry as the primary goal the education system should deliver.

Callaghan's speech can be seen to underscore other discourses which brought more significant change to education. In the 1990s, Prime Minister Tony Blair spoke of education as 'the best economic policy'; he highlighted how education was at the heart of 'economic policy making for the future' by claiming, 'this country will succeed or fail on the basis of how it changes itself, and gears up to this new economy, based on knowledge' (Blair cited in Ball, 2017: 14). Having seen schools and education opened to competition and choice in the 1980s and 1990s, the New Labour government led by Blair focused on 'the role of education as a producer of labour … and of subjectivities, values and sensibilities like enterprise and entrepreneurship' (Ball, 2017: 13). Leading educational change was the idea of responding to economic necessity, responding to the global economy, competing in global markets and helping individuals to take their place in what is referred to as 'the knowledge economy'. This new economy characterised by creativity and high skills is 'an economy that has shifted from one in which physical resources, human and material, are the main inputs to production, to one, in which the most significant and financially valuable activities are knowledge-based or "symbolic"' (Temple, 2013: 1). This economic model thrives on professionalism and knowing individuals who act like experts and entrepreneurs, not just securing a job in the knowledge economy, but also helping to create more jobs. The educational discourses resulting from this era saw education as a business, providing a service, serving consumers who wanted a particular product, a 'good' education, judged 'good' largely on competitive test results.

New Labour continued discourses around education as 'needing improvement', in order to serve economic purposes, but it also enabled the participation of 'new providers outside the public sector in the delivery of education services when public sector organisations were deemed to be failing or underperforming … what is known as outsourcing' (Ball, 2017: 15). Both Conservative and New Labour governments produced educational changes which created a *derisive* discourse around education in the public sector. Schools and teaching in general were continuously constructed as 'lacking' and 'needing reform', school standards were created 'in relation to institutional and international competitiveness', and not the school community and its specific needs (Ball, 2013: 82). These historical changes have willed us to know the institution of the school as harnessed to competitive markets, career pathways and the skills needed in a knowledge economy, very often overlooking the individuality of students and the immediate needs of school communities.

The discourses around education initiated by New Labour sought to change education by forming what Jones (2003: 160) describes as 'new alliances', seeking privatisation in education which were central to New Labour's project of transformation, leaving 'no place in this new system for the forces associated with earlier periods of reform'. The old forces from early periods are those of the local education authorities and the autonomy of teachers in schools; these were seen as preventing innovation in education and schools. Equating the purpose of education to serve the needs of industry has also had other effects which are seldom discussed, such as the undermining of teachers' and education professionals' expertise, and the notion that education is subservient to economic needs.

More recently, discourses around education have been further opened to the private sector with the introduction of the Academies system in England and Wales. In the early 2000s, the Labour government introduced the Academies programme which was continued and expanded under the Coalition government in 2010. Academy Trusts were given funding to help state schools deemed as 'failing' or 'requiring improvement' by Ofsted inspections; state-schools were to become Academies and be managed by Academy Trusts. Many of these Academies are not just sponsored by the government, but by businesses and companies, under charitable status (Hatcher, 2006). The significantly diminished role of LEA and the increase in sponsorships of schools turn Academies into a unique system which is spreading the privatisation of education, but is also turning schools into an opportunity to influence politics (West and Bailey, 2013). The changes Academies have allowed include private individuals and companies to become sponsors of schools, a way in which governments have sought to pay for education through alternative funding, and not just through tax-ation. Whilst sponsoring might be a way to give back to communities, sponsoring schools may also be a means of winning influence with government. This is illustrated by Hatcher (2006: 612) who says that the former UK head of Enron, listed by the Specialist Schools Trust as a specialist school donor, said that 'sponsorship and donations were the best way of getting access to ministers'. The discourse of education as serving the economy and the needs of employers has redefined the role of the state in the provision of education, allowing the state to retrieve its responsibilities.

There are important points to reflect upon when we think about how education and the world of the schools have become so inextricably linked with economic growth and competitiveness. In a world where globalisation and the knowledge economy have been said to be crashing (Pagano and Rossi, 2009) under the new Protectionism of US politics, and unprecedented political events such as the exit of the United Kingdom from the European Union, known as Brexit, what is the new purpose of education? If we have tied our schools' futures so tightly to the fate of the economy, how can we respond in times of such economic and social upheaval? Perhaps the answer to these questions might be found by considering the discourses which have been pushed aside because of the prevalence of the education-for-the-economy discourse. Thinking about the accepted and desired discourses around education inevitably leads us to reflect upon those other discourses which have become derided and undesirable. Learning just for the sake of learning, individuals pur-suing their interests, education as more than securing employment are some of these discourses which are seen as increasingly deviant.

This theorisation of discourse through the will to knowledge allows us to reflect on how the know-ledge produced around the nature and purposes of education has changed. The chapter presents the view that there has been a harnessing of education to competitive markets, career pathways and skills needed in a knowledge economy.

Conclusion

This chapter has discussed educational developments from a critical historical perspective which isolates some of the societal and political discourses we find in education. Throughout the discus-sion many key historical points have been identified as changing discourses around education. Some of these were the deserving poor and the rise of mass schooling, the Callaghan speech and education as coopted by the needs of the economy. Whilst the historical points are illustrative of how education has been changed by political interventions, the notion of discourse helps us to be more critical as to how we have produced accepted ideas regarding the purposes of education. The notion of discourse, then, is a conceptual catalyst with which we can think more critically about the world of education and its ever-changing nature and climate.

Some of the key perspectives developed point to how the discourse of the deserving poor has generated deep-rooted inequalities and divisions in education as a social dynamic. Importantly, the chapter considered how the discourse of the deserving poor has been part of education from its very early beginnings, producing education as a response to society's social problems and inequalities. This is followed by reflections on how political discourse has constructed education as directly tied to economic prosperity and growth. The pairing of education with economic imperatives has established itself, undermining the expertise of teachers and the very specific needs of students and school communities. The importance of political discourse in education is explored with reference to changes occurring during the Thatcherite era, New Labour and more recently, the Coalition and Conservative governments.

Education is not short of changes and interventions, some of which are discussed in this chapter. However, the underlying discourses produced by these changes always remain undetectable or complicit because of their mandatory nature. For instance, the chapter discussed how the introduction of the national curriculum changed the world of schooling, but also how it creates a set of discourses around education, teaching and learning which give education a whole new purpose. It is very easy just to accept these changes as ways in which we have changed our educational systems to be more progressive, or standardised, and these rules have to be followed as they are educational policy. Yet, it is similarly very important to ask critical questions around what these changes do to the endeavour of educating and schooling a population, how they change and fix the discourses around education.

Thinking about the developments that have created the systems of education that we currently know and experience requires us to become more sensitive to how we define the meaning and purpose of education. In this chapter, an exploration around societal and political discourses has presented a few problematic consequences of harnessing education closely with economic demands. In the process of change that education has undergone in the last 30 years, education has been slowly unravelled from the public services sector, incentivising schools to become independent from local control and convert to academies if they want their funding to increase. What is more, education itself is becoming a business opportunity and more aligned with the demands of employers and industry, with big businesses becoming involved in the sponsoring and the running of schools.

As a result of these changes, the chapter has suggested that education continues to be an amalgam of forces and discourses which change historically, either gaining or losing momentum because of changes to educational policy and pressures from different governments. In this current climate, educators and teachers are constructed as subjects of policy, their role understood as implementers of policy and governmental expectations, rather than individuals with expertise and a vocation for teaching and learning. Schools are having to exist within a competitive educational environment where results impact significantly on funding and resources. Consequently, the meaning and the purpose of education is coopted by discourses of competition, selection and accountability which undermine other possible discourses.

Summary

- The development of education is complex and it can be explained by examining historical, political and social imperatives of the time.
- Discourse as a notion can be used to generate a more detailed analysis of how we perceive education in society. Going beyond the normalised acceptance, we have of changes in policy. Discourse produces a deeper and more critical set of questions around educational change.

- Isolating some of the historical and political discourses around education allows us to see how education has been changed to serve the purposes of dominant discourses, such as, the privileging of economic imperatives over schools' or individuals' needs.
- If education is to change and contest some of the prevalent discourses, there needs to be wide critical engagement with how the dominant discourses in education reduce the importance of teaching and learning, student voice and teacher expertise.

Recommended reading

Ball, S. J. (2011) *How Schools Do Policy: Policy Enactments in Secondary Schools.* London: Routledge.
Ball, S. J. (2012) *Foucault and Education.* London: Routledge.
Hall, S., Evans, J. and Nixon, J. (2013) *Representation: Cultural Representations and Signifying Practices.* London: Sage.
Wetherell, M., Taylor, S. and Yates, S. (2004) *Discourse, Theory and Practice: A Reader.* London: Sage.

References

Althusser, L. (1993) *Essays on Ideology.* London: Verso.
Apple, M. (2013) *Education and Power.* London: Routledge.
Ball, S. J. (2013) *Foucault, Power and Education.* Abingdon: Routledge.
Ball, S. J. (2017) *The Education Debate.* Bristol: Policy Press.
Bathmaker, A. M., Ingram, N., Abrahams, J., Hoare, A., Waller, R. and Bradley, H. (2016) *Higher Education, Social Class and Social Mobility.* Basingstoke: Palgrave McMillan.
Bustillos Morales, J. and Abegglen, S. (2018) The co-opting of education: Education and education studies from a political and economic discourse. *EducationalFutures*, **9**(1), pp. 18–30.
Choules, K. (2007) The Shifting Sands of Social Justice Discourse: From situating the problem with "them" and situating it with "us". *Review of Education, Pedagogy and Cultural Studies*, **29**(5), pp. 461–481.
Foucault, M. (1987) The order of discourse. In Young, R. (Ed.). *Untying the Text: A Post-Structuralist Reader.* London: Routledge and Kegan Paul.
Francis, B. and Wong, B. (2013) *What is Preventing Social Mobility? A Review of the Evidence.* Leicester: Association of School and College Leaders.
Gristy, C., Letherby, G. and Watkins, R. (2019) Schooling, selection and social mobility over the last 50 years: An exploration through stories of lifelong learning journeys. *British Journal of Educational Studies*, DOI: 10.1080/00071005.2019.1589416.
Hall, S. (1992) The West and the rest: Discourse and power. In Hall, S. and Gieben, B. (Eds.). *Formations of Modernity.* Cambridge: Polity Press.
Hatcher, R. (2006) Privatization and sponsorship: The re-agenting of the school system in England. *Journal of Education Policy*, **21**(5), pp. 599–619.
Jarvis, P. and Griffin, C. (2003) *Adult and Continuing Education: Major Themes in Education, Liberal Education (part 1).* London: Routledge.
Jones, K. (2003) *Education in Britain.* Cambridge: Polity Press.
Lawson, J. and Silver, H. (2007) *A Social History of Education in England.* Abingdon: Routledge.
Pagano, U. and Rossi, M. A. (2009) The crash of the knowledge economy. *Cambridge Journal of Economics*, **33**(1), pp. 665–683.
Temple, P. (2013) The development of the University's role. In Temple, P. (Ed.). *Universities in the Knowledge Economy: Higher Education Organisation and Global Change.* Abingdon: Routledge.
West, A. and Bailey, E. (2013) The development of the academies programme: 'Privatising' school-based education in England 1986–2013. *British Journal of Educational Studies*, **61**(2), pp. 137–159.
Wyse, D. and Torrance, H. (2009) The development and consequences of National Curriculum Assessment for primary education in England. *Educational Research*, **51**(2), pp. 213–228.

8 A global political economy of education: The origins

Joe Gazdula

Introduction

The growth of education globally recently facilitated by market forces has created the need for a discussion about the conceptual framework in which this has taken place. This expansion has occurred in complex national socio/economic/political environments, often without uniformity, but with some common market-led features which have prompted some observers to suggest that there is now a global political economy of education (Verger *et al.*, 2016). This chapter examines the historical development of a global political economy of education by considering the origins and development of market forces in education as it is seen through different perspectives. Through the nineteenth century the global development of education generally followed the model in England which saw an increasing role for the state and state funding in education, although some countries such as Prussia had a system of free education funded by state which began in the seventeenth century. It considers the ideas that placed education as a state concern in England during the late eighteenth and early nineteenth century and follows the conceptual debate about the role of the state and the place of market forces in providing for it. By following developments in the political economy of education in England and Wales in this and the subsequent chapter to the present day, and by comparing these to educational developments elsewhere, the chapter provides a factual base against which concepts of the global political economy of education can be evaluated.

The conceptual base begins by looking at the classical approaches to political economy from the eighteenth century as it related to education as outlined by classical liberals such as Adam Smith (1776) where education was a commodity to be purchased. It looks at more socially orientated responses to the pure free-market approaches of Smith by J.S. Mill and Karl Marx (1867) through to Keynes and ideas promoted by the Mont Pelerin Society from the 1930s, and the post-modern concepts of political economy as they relate to education to the 1980s. These have been usefully identified by Novelli *et al.* (2014) as: Modernisation Theory (Inkles and Smith, 1974), the Human Capital Approach (Becker, 1962), Dependency Theory (Frank, 1971) and the Neoliberal Political Economy of Development (Bhagwati, 1982). Critiques of the approaches to education come from Marxist and neo-Marxist critical paradigms and more recently critical neoliberal commentaries and new institutionalism to form a broad cultural political theoretical framework with many subjects and perspectives (Robertson *et al.*, 2007). This provides a socio-political theoretical base through which to compare and contrast developments in the modern era of political economy to the 1980s.

From the 1980s the debate on the wider political economy approach to education is dominated by a return to various ideas of classical economic-based market-driven educational reforms, and these are discussed in Chapter 10.

A number of difficult concepts in this chapter do not align easily with education and are discussed, but two need some explanation. 'Political economy' is the relationship between individual, institutions, the market and the state.

> Political economy is a broad and profoundly interdisciplinary area of study that explores the relationship between individuals and institutions, the market, and the state occurring at different interconnections, as well as the specific (policy) outcomes of these relationships.
>
> (Verger *et al.*, 2016: 15)

The term 'Neoliberalism' has become commonly used and can be even more difficult to understand as it is widely used by different authors writing from a variety of perspectives. It is, therefore, best to consider neoliberalism prior to 1980 as a general term *explaining* the use of free markets, while after 1980 Venugopal (2015) states it is rarely used consistently by authors supporting free markets and should therefore be considered as a lens under which education and other public services are critically studied. 'Neoliberal' is therefore used in this chapter to explain new approaches to liberal free-market-based economics as they relate to education, and to compare and contrast the way free markets and free-market systems since 1980 have become intertwined with the provision of education globally.

The origins of political economy and its influences on educational policy

The concept of political economy stems from the recognition in eighteenth century Europe that the distribution of wealth required explanation. This was undertaken by Economists Adam Smith (1776) in the UK in *The Wealth of Nations* which built on Gregory King's (1688) *Estimate of Population and Wealth, England and Wales*, and François Quesnay's *The Grand Tableau* (cited in Eltis, 1996) in France. These began to explain economic interactions between the state and individuals in terms of political, economic and social factors. They emphasised the role of the individual over the state at a time of general servitude and began the examination of the power of individuals and then institutions. While education was not a specific focus of these economists, there was a general recognition that some form of welfare was desirable and they felt this was better dealt with between individuals (Novelli *et al.*, 2014). Education across the globe at this time was sporadic with some states providing a system from primary to university age (mainly for people who could afford to pay), and some none. Lambert (2018) explains that by the eighteenth century, England had a formative system of schooling ranging from benefactor-supported grammar schools, charity schools for 7–11 year olds with Christian education provided by the Society for the Propagation of Christian Knowledge, while public schools such as Harrow, Eton and universities in Cambridge and Oxford existed but were out of reach financially for most of the population. However, over a third of the population of England could read and write at a time when most countries had no formal system of education.

Further contributions to the notion of the political economy came in the nineteenth century from members of the Political Economy Club founded in 1821 by James Mill. One of its leading members was Robert Malthus who, along with David Ricardo, debated the nature of rent in relation to production factors. Rent through land ownership was then a primary source of income. Members of this club included reformers such as Jeremy Bentham and James Mill who were interested in the power of institutions and the nature of capital. In 1848, James Mills' son John Stuart Mill (commonly referred to as J.S.) wrote the *Principles of Political Economy* which '…argued that the distribution of wealth was determined by power asymmetries between the elites and the working classes' (Novelli *et al.*, 2014: 10). J. S. Mill advocated that by reforming institutions the unequal spread of power in society would be reduced, and advocated co-operatives, more rights for women and an end to slavery.

During the mid-nineteenth century further challenges were being made to the classical political economy's individualistic approach to social justice. In 1867, Karl Marx (2011) published the first part of the collection of works commonly known as *Das Kapital: A Critique of Political Economy – The Production Process of Capital.* It examined the relationship between the owners of capital who have power in society and the proletariat, or workers who have little or none. This suggested that inequality in society was a collective rather than individualistic issue. With Marx, Friedrich Engels had previously written a pamphlet called the *Communist Manifesto* (Marx and Engels, 1848) arguing that this split between the owners of capital and the proletariat (workers) caused a tension in society that would eventually see the proletariat rise up and overthrow the owners of capital and create a centrally organised society where the benefits of capital would be shared equally in a communal (communist) society. Education of the proletariat would initially support these tensions as it would help workers understand the controlling power of capital and then be an enabler of the communist system as people recognised the wholistic benefits of a shared wealth system.

At the beginning of the nineteenth century in England the idea of the need for state support for education had gained impetus. From 1833 the government had been giving grants to church schools and over subsequent years these gradually increased. By 1861 state expenditure on Education was £800,000 (Lawson and Silver, 1973). The 1861 *Royal Commission on the State of Popular Education in England* recognised the need for the state to support church schools more formally and brought in funding for exam attainment in reading, writing and arithmetic (Gillard, 2018). In 1870 *The Elementary Education Act* (also known as the Forster Act) provided for local authorities to raise public funds to provide elementary education for 5–12 year-olds in England and Wales. This marked the first real engagement of the 'political economy' with education. Since 1721 there have been 473 Acts passed by the UK Parliament concerned with education, yet until 1870 all schools were privately funded or funded through church or charitable institutions through government donations. By 1870 there was a significant change to the primacy of 'methodological individualism' advocated by Adam Smith and others of the liberal perspective, and the state had taken significant responsibility for educational provision.

Activity 1

- What might be the implications of having only a system of private fee-paying education?
- What were the benefits and drawbacks of funding education through church schools?
- Explain why governments in industrialising societies began to fund education.

The classical liberal political economy and education

Towards the end of the nineteenth century responses to the political economic theory of the mid-part of the century began to appear. In 1871 Menger's *Principles of Economics* proposed that marginal utility, or the satisfaction a person receives for a good, was more important to its value than its cost inputs, while Jevons' *Theory of Political Economy* (1871) attempted to calculate the marginal utility or change in satisfaction of consuming a good. Walras's *Elements of Pure Economics* (1874–1877) attempted to calculate the value of markets by showing that supply and demand in an economy was consistent across all the markets. Marshall's *Principles of Economics* (1890) continued the emphasis on marginal utility and this group began the marginalist revolution (Novelli *et al.*, 2014). This moved the focus of the political economy away from collectivism and towards a more individu- alistic model of political economy as the economic self-interest of producers, suppliers and workers in a competitive marketplace striving for 'equilibrium', where supply meets demand.

The promotion of a more liberal political economy in England during the latter part of the nine- teenth century failed to stem a continuation of a process of increasing state control in the formative school system. The 1870 Elementary Education Act was a watershed for education as it provided for elected school boards, local education authorities and the funding to run schools. Despite strong resistance from the Church of England, these began to give a more secular approach to education. The curriculum was also beginning to interest the state and further Elementary Education Acts were passed in 1873, 1876, 1879 and 1880. The 1880 Act (known as the Mundella Act) was the first to make school attendance compulsory, promoted a curriculum and identified schools as fair, good or excellent. The 1891 Elementary Education Act was the first act to provide a grant for indi- vidual pupil education and to set the process in motion for free education despite the argument of the Church of England that it 'belittled' the working class. The great public (private or independent) schools were exclusively attended by the upper classes (mainly boys) and out of the financial reach of most of the population. However, they were of variable quality and became the subject of a number of reports which resulted in the state making demands for improvement. Endowed schools and grammar schools were not exempt either from the state's drive to reform, and from 1874 a series of Endowed Schools Acts began regulation of financial and academic approaches in the sector. Universities too were beginning to attract the attention of government, and a number of major cities established university colleges and polytechnics. Yet the educational reform during the period still has its critics. West (1994), for example, argues that the 1870 Elementary Education Act suppressed a robust and developing successful private sector structure for education, and failed to provide free compulsory education. However, it can be seen as a major step in integrating the political economy with education in England and Wales for the first time.

The global picture for education in the nineteenth century remained mixed, with most English- speaking countries adopting educational reforms similar to those in England. Most western countries had state-supported educational programmes of some form, and the study of childhood learning in France was well established, facilitated by Rousseau's *Emile*. France had a widespread Catholic- based education system for boys in the eighteenth century. The early part of the nineteenth century saw Napoleonic attempts to bring a more comprehensive state system to France, but this was disrupted by the financial needs of the Napoleonic Wars, and was preceded by a period of school development under the Catholic Church. However, from 1821 the growth of cities saw the number of schools increase due to a demand for skilled labour, with free schools provided at parish level from 1833. The period to 1880 saw the educational landscape dominated by arguments between religious and secular parties until the Jules Ferry Laws in 1881/2 provided national free education, mandatory school attendance and began the process of educational secularisation. Germany, as a collection of regional states until unification in 1871, had a history of developing compulsory free education which had started in Prussia with the introduction of *Volksschule* in the seventeenth century. This underpinned a strong classical and technical education system which developed into a secondary education system administered largely by the state. In the United States, Horace Mann, Secretary of the Massachusetts State Board of Education, established the principle of free education for all (Ellis *et al.*, 2014). However, globally, education remained largely the preserve of the rich and, even after 1870, children in England were still see as units of labour with concern from parents at removing half-term holidays when children could be sent out to earn money. Education was still heavily influenced by notions of self-support and classical liberalism.

Despite western national political economies being dominated by classical liberal influences, the period from 1860 to 1870 saw the political economy of education drawing many of its reforms, improvements and finance from the state, and becoming significantly more state-led. Western states in particular seemed to have accepted they had some responsibility for education, partly through the example of other states such as Prussia, partly to deal with overcoming the need for a relatively educated population to work in more technologically advanced industries, but also due to an element of social concern and meritocratic advancement. With increasing state intervention and control in many western counties from 1870 to 1900, it is worth noting the UK government spending on education increased from a negligible amount in 1850 to almost two per cent of GDP (UK Public Spending, 2018). By 1900 education had cemented a place in the political economies of nations and, while many national approaches were similar, this was a long way from a global political economy of education as many nations had neither the technology nor the finance to provide resources for education, and in England it was still the preserve of the very rich in private institutions or with private tutors. Tensions between responsibility and funding were also still evident in education as states generally followed neo-classical economic policies, even if education was gradually being incorporated into a more state-supported and controlled model.

Activity 2

- Why were children still seen as units of economic production in 1870?
- What do you think the effects of the Volkschules in Prussia had on the Prussian economy?

The political economy of education in the twentieth century

From the 1900s governments in western countries took an increasingly interventionist approach to education, expanding provision and controlling more of what was taught. In the UK by 1960 education spending was over four per cent of GDP and this would rise to over six per cent during the 1980s (UK Public Spending, 2018). It seemed that governments had finally taken responsibility for funding educational provision and for what was taught. While there was still a significant private sector, what was taught was guided by national policies and usually enforced through inspection or assessment.

Running parallel to these seemingly continuous developments in the political economy of education was a varying approach to political economy generally. In the West, liberalism continued to dominate economic policy until the Great Depression resulting from the Wall St. Crash of 1929. This was a result of the markets' failure to return to equilibrium as expected after the crash through the use of tight fiscal controls: classical supply side measures which reduced wages and minimised costs. The principle here was as wages went down workers would be more in demand, but this failed to materialise in lower employment figures. A number of approaches were considered, including the use of free markets with a more socially directed aim. This was the first manifestation of neoliberalism and came from the Ordoliberalist school of thought as a response to the economic problems of the German Weimar Republic (Bonefeld, 2012). In 1936, John Maynard Keynes published *The General Theory of Employment, Interest and Money*. This was a significant departure from the supply side economic approaches which underpinned most forms of liberalism. Keynes (1936) recommended increasing total aggregate demand in an economy by encouraging public spending, by reducing interest rates and by increasing government spending through borrowing if necessary. His ideas began to be applied in western societies from the late 1930s, most notably in stimulating the United States economy under President Roosevelt's 'New Deal.' This broadly became the dominant ideology of political economy in the West until 1979.

Activity 3

What do you think were the main arguments against Keynesianism – increasing public spending to increase demand?

Critiques of classical liberalism

Institutionalism and political economy

Institutional political economy considers the role of institutions in providing necessary stability for markets. Early thoughts on institutionalism, amongst others, were from Hobbes (1588–1679), Locke (1632–1704) and Rousseau (1712–1778) who sought to explain the power of institutions in helping to provide justice, order and freedom. These were necessary to keep markets in equilibrium and working. During the nineteenth and early twentieth centuries, the relationship between states, the power of their political institutions and their constitutional approaches to facilitating order through key institutions, became the focus of keeping the markets in equilibrium (Heywood, 2015). There are also works of note which bring in a social element and identify institutions which provide support and social justice for individuals. Skocpol (1979) addresses issues of development from an institutional perspective and notes institutions can also support the social needs of individuals, for example through educational provision. This new institutionalism provides an alternative to classical political economy by examining the way institutions affect individuals and socio-political outcomes through regulation and policy. This has become known as 'neo-institutionalism'. Without institutions taking some responsibility for social justice and lack of controls, markets are open to corruption and anti-competitive practices, thus removing the main benefits of a market-oriented economy (Novelli *et al.*, 2014).

New critical political economy

This perspective on critical political economy has its foundation in Marxism but applies to broader societal concern and looks into more specific areas of inequality. It includes the critical political economy tradition, but is broader. Novelli *et al.* (2014: 13) note that a:

> Marxist political economy (includes) feminist, post-structuralist and post-colonial critiques of contemporary capitalist development. (It) explores issues such as the gendered nature of contemporary political economy relationships, the role of culture and identity in the production, distribution and consumption of resources, and issues of race, colonialism and ethnicity.

This broadening of Marxian approaches from societal studies to individualistic effects of power structures in society categorised specific areas of inequality. In studies of critical political economy it has proved useful for education studies and offers areas of study where the search for social justice might occur. A foundation in the theoretical concepts of the contrasting theories of political economy is necessary for students of education, and the brief overview covered here is needed to understand the debates which surround the political economy of education as the global movement of capital which began economic globalisation.

Neo-Marxists and education

Neo-Marxist theories of education can be seen in the four parts of Bowles and Gintis' (1976) Correspondence Theory:

  i. Classrooms prepare pupils as subservient, uncritical workers.
 ii. Education teaches acceptance of authority and hierarchical power structures.
iii. Pupils are taught to be motivated by job prospects and good wages rather than the pursuit of pure learning.
 iv. The fragmentation of learning into subjects prepares pupils for specialising in work without an understanding of the whole process of capital maintenance.

If this was the basis of modern neo-communist commentary then gaining an appreciation of the perspectives of writing on neoliberal education might be relatively easy. However, as Livingstone (1995) notes, there is a divergence of commentary on neo-Marxism from the late 1970s as critics noted a similar historical structure of education in pre-industrialised societies (Curtis, 1984), or argued that wider influences such as the alliances between class-based communities (Livingstone, 1983), ethnicity (MacDonald, 1989) and gender (Katznelson *et al.*, 1982) had been ignored by Bowles and Gintis. More recent neo-Marxian considerations of neoliberalism produce a broad spectrum of conceptual topics at which the term Neoliberalism is at the centre. For example, Crouch (2011) discusses the power of large corporations over public life, while Overbeek and Van (2012) consider neoliberalism a political project to restore power to the capitalist class. Livingstone (1995) argues that perhaps with the exception of the theories of cultural capital (Bourdieu, 1984) and linguistics (Bernstein, 1990) few complete conceptual neo-Marxist theories link education and production capital, and this continues today. The fragmentation of neo-Marxist socio-economic thought which guides much of the writing on neoliberalism and education tends to be categorised as topical or regional thinking such as country, race, gender, policy, economic, etc.

Traditional neoliberal economics

Venugopal's (2015) exploration of the term 'neoliberalism' suggests it has been used in two distinct periods. The term begins to appear in the 1930s as an economic concept used by liberal western economists to describe the social free-market economic ideals of Hayek, Freiburg, Stigler and Friedman. They formed the influential Mont Pelerin Society which continues to this day to promote a form of economic liberalism with a social conscience. Along with the Chicago School of economists, they formed arguments to counter the Keynesian economic argument for state intervention in economies. Keynesianism had gained a measure of ascendency over free-market liberalism after the great recession which began in 1929 and led to the introduction of President Franklin D. Roosevelt's 'New Deal' to attempt to deal with the effects of the recession. This 'traditional neoliberalism' formed arguments which persisted until the late 1960s when the term begins to lapse. There is a resurgence of the term during the 1980s, but this time its meaning was more difficult to determine due to the fragmentation of studies using the term, and it is discussed in Chapter 9.

Activity 4

- Explain the role of institutions in creating free market trading conditions.
- Should education prepare pupils for Education?

Education as global human capital

Despite the dominance of Keynesian economics until 1979, there emerged a number of bodies of thought related to education that began once again to link education to the classical political economy. During the 1950s there was a resurgence of studies explaining how society works, rather than what it *should* be. This was part of the functionalist perspective. In the nineteenth century Emile Durkheim (1933; 1858–1917) began to study why society shared experiences, perspectives, values, beliefs and behaviour to form a common purpose. This was continued by later functionalists, notably Talcott Parsons (1951) in *The Social System* and Robert K. Merton (1968: 477), who will be known to many education students for his ideas of the 'Self-Fulfilling Prophecy'. While it is oversimplistic to describe this perspective as supportive of classical ideals, it often gives explanations which can be used to support the power structure in society. The purpose of education is seen as a way for people in society to rise to the top in a meritocratic way which supports order and the progression of society as a whole.

Human Capital Theory

Becker (1994) argued that investment in people's education and skills increased their human capital, and this made them more valuable to society economically and so contributed to economic growth. While this adds to the perception of the value of education, it does not attempt to enter the argument of how education should be managed, funded, developed, delivered and what should be taught or how. According to Becker (1994: 25) the main purpose of Human Capital Theory is '… as I am concerned is to remove a little of the mystery from the economic and social world that we live in'.

Modernisation Theory

Modernisation Theory examines how countries develop their internal structures and attempt to catch up with more developed counterparts, and sees education as an important part of this. Whiles there are a number of viewpoints on Modernisation Theory, it does have implications for educationalists as it argues that people in developing societies should have the 'right values' and 'right skills' (Harbison and Myers, 1964). For Inkles and Smith (1974) education helps to create the conditions for economic growth by creating individual with these traits which help to create economic growth.

Dependency Theory

Critics of Modernisation Theory argued that it provided a highly westernised view of development and failed to account for increasing global trade and development because it focussed on the internal readiness of countries to become modernised as a western-type state, regardless of the attributes, resources, infrastructure and political environment. In 1950 a series of papers known as the Prebisch–Singer Hypothesis argued that nations trading primary goods to manufacturing nations would find the value of primary goods constantly falling due to the power of the more developed nations to control primary good prices. These conditions mean the value within a developing country will constantly fall (Toye and Toye, 2003). This led to further work emanating from two groups, known as the Latin American Structuralists who examined trade between developed and underdeveloped nations typified by Prebisch, Celso Furtado and Anibel Pinto, and the American Marxists, Paul A. Baran, Paul Sweezy and Andre Gunner Frank (Novelli *et al.*, 2014). Dependency Theory considers the power structures of countries' external trading relations and generally concludes that advanced countries have not developed as a result of internal factors such as market-readiness and education, but through the exploitation of underdeveloped nations, an ability to influence the price of resources and to promote the status quo through the education system.

Education systems are seen by dependency theorists as part of the problem, rather than being the solution to underdevelopment, because they create structures and curriculum content which provide a worldview which supports a *status quo*. They argue that it creates a worldview which shows the importance of corporations and international trade, and through conditional development loans and grants prepares people as workers in this unequal trading system (Carnoy, 1974). During the 1970s some developing countries began to form coalitions such as the Organization of Oil Producing Exporting Countries which appeared to have substantial power in the marketplace, and Dependency Theory became less popular. But recent empirical studies (Harvey *et al.*, 2010; Rodney, 2018) continue to argue for theories of dependency.

These three theories have different approaches to the purpose of education, its influence as a process of development globally, and the way it is administered. But they all recognise the importance of the state in leading educational development.

Activity 5

Explain this statement: 'According to supporters of dependency, educational investment in developing countries creates a continuing dependency on developed countries'.

Education in England and Wales in the 1960s – Golden Years?

There are few periods in history where political economies match the utopian visions of education idealists and the philosophical, governmental, power relationships and fiscal conditions that need to be aligned to create the conditions for a truly egalitarian system of education. Gillard (2018) suggests that, during the 1960s, education in England had entered a period known as the 'Golden Years'. The 1960s were a time of rising school populations and rising funding. Between 1960 and 1969 the school population in primary and secondary schools had increased by 700,000 and, for the first time, the British Government spent more on education than defence: £2.3 billion (Gillard, 2018). From the end of the Second World War the tripartite system of education had been established for secondary education based on pupil results in primary schools. This consisted of selective grammar and technical schools for the brightest, and secondary moderns for the rest. But the 1964 Labour Government under Harold Wilson was elected on a manifesto promising to revolutionise education and aimed to introduce a single-tier comprehensive system. There were a number of influential publications on education and equality published during the decade. These included: *The Home and School* (Glass, 1964) which identified a lack of action to remedy inequality in primary schools. *Education and the Working Class* (Jackson and Marsden, 1962) identified class stratification in schools along economic lines. The Robbins Committee on Higher Education Report (1963) into widening higher education provision was a joint report by the Conservatives and Labour which identified the lack of progression to universities by talented working-class children (boys). The Plowden (1967) Report *Children and their Primary Schools* identified regional inequalities and helped pave the way for Education Action Zones and *All Our Futures* (1968). These publications provided a conceptual base against which reforms of education would take place and took education about as far from classical liberal ideas of education as it would go.

Labour aimed to create an egalitarian system of education which would remove selection and provide a system standard comprehensive education for all. The selection process in the form of the 11 plus examination system was seen to favour middle-class children who were able to attend the selective grammar and technical schools, leaving the rest to attend secondary modern schools. As soon as it came to power in 1964 the Labour Government began the process of replacing the tripartite system of selection with a single system of comprehensive schools which would give all children access to grammar school levels of education (Simon, 1991).

As schools were under the control of local authorities, the then Secretary of State for education, Michael Stewart, advised local education authorities to prepare for comprehensivisation. A number of publications known as the *Black Papers* (Cox and Dyson, 1969) came out strongly against the notion that education should promote egalitarianism, but the public response to this was mixed with arguments for and against a single-tier comprehensive system. There were also arguments with the Department for Education and Science, but by the end of 1965 a new Secretary of State for education, Anthony Crosland, issued Circular 10/65 which requested LEAs to produce plans for introducing a comprehensive education system. The request was seen as giving LEAs a choice; some enthusiastically engaged with planning comprehensivisation, but some did not. The opportunity to compel LEAs to introduce a single comprehensive system of education was lost. Despite Labour's second election win in 1966, growing economic problems coupled with a lack by some local authorities to follow the directive led to different approaches by LEAs and the national comprehensive education system never occurred. However, progress had been made in a number of areas to improve schooling.

The 'Golden Age' of education in Britain was probably termed because there was an egalitarian outlook from the government, and these ideas were backed with funding to increase school populations, build new schools, expand teacher training and introduce new approaches in the classroom. A total of 11 new universities were introduced and the Open University with open access for all regardless of age or qualification was opened. However, despite these improvements the comprehensive system was never achieved and the reforms failed to provide the fundamental basis for an open education system. Even today top universities such as Oxford and Cambridge take 40 per cent of their intake from just eight independent schools and fees mean places are still the preserve of the wealthy (Montacute, 2018). It seemed that, even where the conditions of the political economy were favourable to the creation of a conceptually egalitarian education, its attainment proved elusive.

This chapter forms the historical foundation for understanding the complex relationship between social justice, financial considerations, political ideologies and education. In western societies this has been an uneasy relationship and the funding of education has often been dictated by economic necessities. There have been very few times when the need for education has been seen as a pre-requisite for social justice, perhaps only during the 1830s with the altruistic approaches of J.S. Mill and the 1960s with the reforming Labour Government's 'Golden Years'. The notion of a global social political economy of education grew alongside western economic development as nations competed with each other for world resources from about 1750, and the need for evermore technical industries required a more educated labour force. The realisation that society should fund a comprehensive education for all young people through government or 'public' funds is still a relatively modern notion which gained impetus from about 1850. Despite a strong social justice lobby from the 1830s it is unlikely that education was seen as a way to reduce inequality, but rather a way to enhance economic performance so nation states could be competitive.

There are many perspectives which can be included in any discussion of the social political economy of education and, while the ones covered here are key, the continued exploration of perspectives on the subject should be encouraged for all students of education and personal opinions formed. By exploring the historical juxtaposition of education as part of the social, economic and power fabric of the nation state we provide a firm foundation for students of education to enter this complex debate and develop their own critical view on the global political economy of education.

Activity 6

What features of education reform might bring another 'Golden Age' to education in England and Wales?

Summary

- The origins of a distinct political economy of education began with realisation in the 1820s that inequality in society was not a natural state of affairs determined by an act of god or natural selection.
- Socio-political reformers such as James Mill, Robert Malthus and David Ricardo were preceded by other reformers who were more concerned with education such as Rousseau, but they began the formalisation of social political economy by forming the Political Economy Club.
- The Political Economy Club was concerned with wider social reform rather than education, but their debates on social justice and political economy formed the foundation for future considerations of the place of education in helping to create social justice.
- The 1870 Elementary Education Act began the lasting engagement of education with the political economy and can be said to have been the first manifestation of the political economy of education in Great Britain. However, it is important to note that the liberal free-market approach to education had seen Great Britain having higher levels of literacy than most of the world.
- A key debate for educationalist is whether the needs of industry and commerce, the need for social justice, or the needs of individuals has primacy in education. However, the historical position discussed in this chapter is clear. Despite social reform becoming a political consideration during the nineteenth century, the main driver of educational reform during most of this period, with perhaps the exception of a few 'Golden Years' in the 1960s, has been economic, due to the need for an ever more educated internationally competitive workforce.

Recommended reading

Novelli, M., Higgins, S., Ugur, M. and Valiente, O. (2014) *The Political Economy of Education Systems in Conflict-Affected Contexts.* London: DfID.

Robertson, S., Novelli, M., Dale, R., Tikly, L., Dachi, H. and Ndibelema, A. (2007) *Globalisation, Education and Development: Ideas, Actors, Dynamics.* Researching the Issues 68. London: DfID.

Rodney, W. (2018) *How Europe Underdeveloped Africa.* New York: Verso.

Verger, A., Fontdevila, C. and Zancajo, A. (2016) *The Privatization of Education: A Political Economy of Global Education Reform.* New York: Teachers College Press.

References

Becker, G. S. (1962) Investment in human capital: A theoretical perspective. *Journal of Political Economy,* **70**(2), pp. 9–49.

Becker, G. S. (1994) *Human Capital: A Theoretical and Empirical Analysis With Special Reference to Education,* (3rd ed.). Chicago: University of Chicago Press.

Bernstein, B. (1990) *Class, Codes and Control: Volume 3 – Towards a Theory of Educational Transmissions.* London: Routledge & Kegan Paul.

Bhagwati, J. B. (1982) Directly unproductive, profit-seeking (DUP) activities. *Journal of Political Economy,* **90**(5), pp. 988–1002.

Bonefeld, W. (2012) Freedom and the strong state: On German ordoliberalism. *New Political Economy*, 17(5), pp. 1–24.

Bourdieu, P. (1984) *Distinction: A Social Critique of the Judgement of Taste*. London: Routledge & Kegan Paul.

Bowles, S. and Gintis, H. (1976) *Schooling in Capitalist America*. London: Routledge & Kegan Paul.

Carnoy, M. (1974) *Education as Cultural Imperialism*. New York: D McKay.

Cox, B. and Dyson, A. E. (Eds.) (1969) *The Black Papers on Education*. London: Broadwick House.

Crouch, C. (2011) *The Strange Non-Death of Neoliberalism*. Cambridge: Polity Press.

Curtis, B. (1984) Capitalist development and educational reform. *Theory and Society*, **1**, pp. 41–68.

Durkheim, E. (1933) *The Division of Labor in Society*. New York: Macmillan.

Ellis, A., Golz, R. and Mayrhofer, W. (2014) The education systems of Germany and other European countries of the 19th century in the view of American and Russian classics: Horace Mann and Konstantin Ushinsky. International Dialogues of Education: Past and Present. Online. Available at: https://www.ide-journal.org/journal/?issue=2014-volume-1-number-1 (Accessed 2 January 2019).

Eltis, W. (1996) The *Grand Tableau* of François Quesnay's economics. *The European Journal of the History of Economic Thought*, **3**(1), pp. 21–43.

Frank, A. G. (1971) *Capitalism and Underdevelopment in Latin America*. (Revised edition.) Harmondsworth: Penguin.

Gillard, D. (2018) Education in England: A history. Online. Available at: www.educationengland.org.uk/history (Accessed 21 November 2018).

Glass R. (1964) *Aspects of Change*. London: MacGibbon & Kee.

Harbison, F. H. and Myers, C. A. (1964) *Education, Manpower and Economic Growth: Strategies of Human Resource Development*. New York: McGraw-Hill.

Harvey, D. I., Kellard, N. M., Madsen, J. B. and Wohar, M. E. (2010) The Prebisch–Singer hypothesis: Four centuries of evidence. *The Review of Economics and Statistics*, **92**(2), pp. 367–377.

Heywood, A. (2015) *Key Concepts in Politics and International Relations*. Palgrave: Macmillan.

Inkles, A. and Smith D. H. (1974) *Becoming Modern: Individual Change in Six Developing Countries*. Cambridge: Harvard University Press.

Jackson, B. and Marsden, D. (1962) *Education and the Working Class*. London: Routledge and Kegan Paul.

Katznelson, I. I., Gille, G. and Weir, M. (1982) Public schooling and working-class formation: The case of the United States. *American Journal of Education*, **90**(2), pp. 111–143.

Keynes, J. M. (1936) *The General Theory of Employment, Interest and Money*. London, Macmillan.

King, G. (1688). Estimate of population and wealth, England and Wales. Online. Available at: https://www.york.ac.uk/depts/maths/histstat/king.htm (Accessed 2 January 2019).

Lambert, T. (2018) A brief history of education. Online. Available at: http://www.localhistories.org/education.html (Accessed 2 January 2019).

Lawson, J. and Silver, H. (1973) *A Social History of Education in England*. London: Methuen & Co Ltd.

Livingstone, D. (1983) Class, educational ideologies, and mass opinion in capitalist crisis: A Canadian perspective. *Sociology of Education*, **58**(2), pp. 3–20.

Livingstone, D. (1995) Searching for the missing links: Neo-Marxist theories of education. *British Journal of Sociology of Education*, **16**(1), pp. 53–73.

Marx, K. (2011) *Das Kapital: A Critique of Political Economy*. Washington DC: Regnery Publishing.

Marx, K. and Engels, F. (1848) *Communist Manifesto*, (1st ed.). Moscow: Progress Publishers.

MacDonald, I., Bhavnani, R., Khan, L. and John, G. (1989) *Murder in the playground: The report of the MacDonald inquiry into racism and racial violence in Manchester schools*. London: Longsight Press.

Merton, R. K. (1968) *Social Theory and Social Structure*. New York: The Free Press.

Montacute, R. (2018) *Access to Advantage: The Influence of Schools and Place on Admissions to Top Universities*. London: The Sutton Trust.

Novelli, M., Higgins, S., Ugur, M. and Valiente, O. (2014) *The Political Economy of Education Systems in Conflict-Affected Contexts*. London: DfID.

Overbeek, H. and Van Apeldorn (2012) *Neoliberalism in Crisis*. Basingstoke: Palgrave Macmillan.

Parsons, T. (1951) *The Social System*. New York: The Free Press.

Plowden, B. (1967) *Children and their Primary Schools. Report of the Central Advisory Council for Education (England)*. London: HMSO.

Robbins Committee on Higher Education (1963) Report. London: HMSO.

Robertson, S., Novelli, M., Dale, R., Tikly, L., Dachi, H. and Ndibelema, A. (2007) *Globalisation, Education and Development: Ideas, Actors, Dynamics*. Researching the Issues 68. London: DfID.

Rodney, W. (2018) *How Europe Underdeveloped Africa*. New York: Verso.

Simon, B. (1991) *Education and the Social Order 1940-1990*. London: Lawrence & Wishart.

Skocpol, T. (1979) *States and Social Revolutions: A Comparative Analysis of France, Russia, and China*. New York and Cambridge: Cambridge University Press.

Smith, A. (1776) *An Inquiry into the Nature and Causes of the Wealth of Nations*. London: A. Strahan; T. Cadell.

Toye, J. and Toye, R. (2003) The origins and interpretation of the Prebisch-Singer thesis. *History of Political Economy*, **35**(3), pp. 437–467.

UK Public Spending (2018) UK Education Spending on Education 1900 to 2020. Online. Available at: www.ukpublicspending.co.uk (Accessed 20 November 2018).

Venugopal, R. (2015) Neoliberalism as concept. *Economy and Society*, **44**(2), pp. 165–187.

Verger, A. Fontdevila, C. and Zancajo, A. (2016) *The Privatization of Education: A Political Economy of Global Education Reform*. New York: Teachers College Press.

West, E. G. (1994) *Education and the State: A Study in Political Economy*. London: The Institute of Economic Affairs.

9 The global political economy of education in the twenty-first century

Joe Gazdula

Introduction

The last chapter (8) explained the historical background and the social and economic theories underpinning the global political economy of education. Here, we continue the story with the developments in neoliberal economic thinking at the end of the twentieth century and into recent years. The Labour Prime Minister in the 1960s, Harold Wilson, said 'a week is a long time in politics'. While every effort is made here to analyse recent policy, things change quickly the future is hard to predict.

Education and 'new' neoliberalism

The economic crisis of the 1970s saw a move from the interventionist politics of Keynesianism and a resurgence of free-market approaches to solve the economic problems of the decade. This move towards free-market policies is described by many critical commentators as 'neoliberalism', but was in fact different from the economic forms of neoliberalism which emerged during the early 1930s with the socially conscious free-market ideas of the Ordoliberalist school. During the 1930s Keynesian demand-side economics promoted borrowing and state intervention to stimulate growth. This gained political ascendancy in many western economies to remedy the problems caused by the Great Depression of 1929. However, during the late 1930s, Ordoliberalist ideas were adopted by the influential Mont Pelerin Group, and they and the Chicago School economists during the 1940s began to formulate ideas of a return to more liberal free-trade approaches. This was the first wave of neoliberalism. While Keynesianism remained the dominant political economy approach for many years, a 'new' neoliberalist approach to the political economy began to appear during the late 1970s and early 1980s which began to return political economies to forms of classical liberalism and free-market ideals, sometimes with the social conscience of the Ordoliberalists and sometimes without.

The 'new' neoliberalism, perhaps surprisingly, began in communist China with Deng Xiaoping from 1978 and continued with Paul Volker's installation as head of the US Federal reserve and Margaret Thatcher's election as UK Prime Minister in 1979. Ronald Reagan's election as President of the United States in 1980 continued this impetus (Robertson *et al.*, 2007). These were an attempt to solve the problems of a lack of economic growth during the 1970s and began a worldwide return to liberal free-market economic approaches through de-regulation, privatisation of public services, a reduction in the provision of the welfare state and public spending, and by creating the conditions for finance to operate globally. This was copied by governments across the world. It is against this background that disciplines across the social science spectrum began to use the term 'neoliberalism', but not in a consistent manner, and interestingly, as a general rule, not by economists.

Less evident are the effects of this move on global educational funding through The International Monetary Fund and World Bank loans (Robertson *et al.*, 2007) and *the Third Way*, a neoliberal economic approach with social democratic ideals that were underpinned by new institutionalism to ensure markets provided social responsibility. This approach began emerging during the 1990s and saw a global transfer of public education responsibilities and funding to the private sector. In 2008, Clarke identified what are considered the definitive contexts across which neoliberalism has been used since 1980 and this is shown in Figure 9.1 below.

Because of the conceptual landscape and breadth of contexts in which the use of the term neoliberalism occurs, it is perhaps not surprising that definitions are broad and meanings uncertain. Venugopal (2015: 1) describes the term '...controversial, incoherent, and crisis-ridden even by many of its most influential deployers'. Educationalists using this term need to consider carefully the perspective of authors writing about this 'new' neoliberalism.

In the United Kingdom neoliberalism as a modern concept begins to appear with Margaret Thatcher's 1979 government. Gillard (2018) describes the advent of neoliberalism with Thatcher's first administration in 1979, but it can be traced back further to the establishment of the Institute of Economic Affairs in 1955. This body formulated and promoted right-wing liberal approaches to education and social policy, advocating a return to early nineteenth century free-market principles. A series of *Black Papers* was introduced culminating in one for education in 1977 which advocated a return to free market principles for education and placing choice in the hands of the parents and schools would be allocated funding on the basis of applications (Sexton, 1977: 88–9): there would be 'good schools or they will close', and schools would have a level of self-determination with much less regulation than previously. There would be an independent inspectorate and 'minimum standards and a minimum curriculum' (Sexton, 1977: 86). The 1979 Education Act repealed Labour's 1976 Act and re-introduced local authority selection from the age of 11, ending the comprehensive system of education.

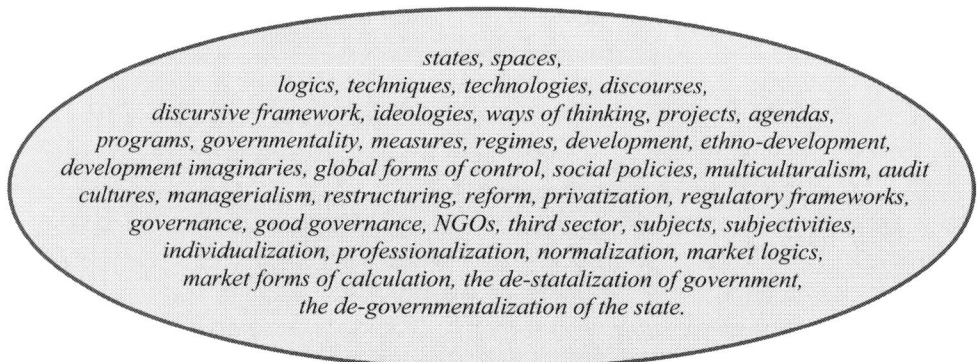

states, spaces,
logics, techniques, technologies, discourses,
discursive framework, ideologies, ways of thinking, projects, agendas,
programs, governmentality, measures, regimes, development, ethno-development,
development imaginaries, global forms of control, social policies, multiculturalism, audit
cultures, managerialism, restructuring, reform, privatization, regulatory frameworks,
governance, good governance, NGOs, third sector, subjects, subjectivities,
individualization, professionalization, normalization, market logics,
market forms of calculation, the de-statalization of government,
the de-governmentalization of the state.

Figure 9.1 Definitive contexts of the term neoliberalism (adapted from Clarke, 2008: 138)

The removal of the aim for a single comprehensive system and the re-introduction of selection and, more importantly, by allowing funding to follow pupils to the school of their choice is where neo-liberalism in education begins in England and Wales. It is distinct from the free-market approaches to education before the 1870 Education Act in that the state is still providing the large majority of funding for compulsory education. However, it begins the marketisation of schooling where education is once again seen as a commodity which can be treated in the same way as other goods and services. It is worth noting that during this Conservative Government administration spending on Education fell for the first time from 6.5 per cent of Gross Domestic Product in 1975–1976 to 4.7 per cent by 1988–1989 (Glennerster and Hills, 1998).

The move towards a more neoliberal approach had begun during this Conservative Government administration, but even within the Conservative Party there were differing and competing perspectives. Chitty (1989) shows that there were those who wished to place emphasis on the free-market economy and termed them 'the neo-liberals', whilst others emphasised the strength of the state and termed them 'neo-conservatives'. This dichotomy is evident in the 1988 Education Reform Act which brought in local management of schools (LMS), began to remove local education authorities from administering schools, and boards of governors and heads of schools were given responsibility for budgets and policy. While this removed the local authority as an intermediary agent, it also devolved many executive responsibilities to school heads, it actually made for greater state control. This was done by the allocation of budgets through pupil recruitment, the beginning of the National Curriculum, and, through the introduction of City Technology Colleges and City Colleges for the Technology of the Arts, broadened selection. Further measures tied schools firmly to government policies such as facilitating employers to sit on curriculum guidance bodies and governing boards, increased individual pupil-funding and a reintroduction of selective grant-maintained schools. This was a long way from the utopian vision of the 'Golden Years' of the 1960s.

The process of 'liberalising' education continued with the John Major's 1992 Government and further National Curriculum reform and the introduction of statutory attainment tests in schools. The 1992 Further and Higher Education Act removed further education colleges from local authority control and established the Further Education Funding Council which was seen as bringing competition into the further education sector.

Activity 1

Consider the following extract from Derek Gillard's *Education in England: A history* (2018)

- For the government, LMS served three purposes:

    i. it was an important element in the creation of an 'education market';
    ii. it took financial control away from the local authorities; and
    iii. it enabled the government to blame the schools for poor management when budgets were cut – as they were from the second year of LMS onwards. Indeed, school budgets were cut in six of the eight years following 1988.

- Which statements might be attributed to the neo-liberal's in Government? Why?
- Which might be attributed to neo-conservatives? Why?

The global neoliberal political economy of education and development

Alongside changes in national political economies, a new global neoliberal paradigm was developing which had significant effects in the way education would be developed. Towards the end of the 1970s and early 1980s a resurgence of neo-classical ideas on the political economy emerged which promoted liberal market reforms as a response to increasing state spending and regulation of markets by governments. They prescribed the way a global interlinked economy could be managed for efficiency and were adopted by a number of key institutions based in Washington DC, including the International Monetary Fund, the United States Treasury and the World Bank. Ten points which would facilitate world development became known as 'the Washington Consensus' (Williamson, 1990).

1. Fiscal discipline to restrict governmental spending
2. Adjustment to public spending patterns to projects offering high economic returns and possibly improve income distribution, such as primary health care, primary education and infrastructure
3. Tax reform to reduce the private tax burden
4. Interest rate competition
5. Market led exchange rates
6. Freeing up world trade markets
7. Encourage inflows of foreign direct investment through reducing regulation
8. Privatisation of public services
9. Market deregulation
10. Firm property rights

The Washington Consensus and was instrumental in guiding developing countries and set conditions under which they received and used loans, grants and other development funding. The principles of these conditions included

> … macroeconomic stabilisation…. through fiscal discipline, structural reforms and trade liberalisation to 'open up' national economies to global competition and foreign direct investment.
>
> (Novelli et al., 2014: 14)

For education in developing countries this meant loans and aid were often tied to a prescriptive approach to market liberalism which generally required a reduction in government education budgets. Robertson et al. (2007) argue that this had a number of implications, including attempting to recover costs for school fees, more community rather than central government financing, allowing private sector access to education and educational services, and the use of human capital theory to prioritise basic (primary and secondary) over higher education. The effect of these 'reforms' is still the subject of much academic research and discussion. They have been critiqued for failing to take into account local economic conditions, using questionable rates of return for promoting basic education over higher education, a lack of appropriate governance and the effects of private education on equality in developing nations (Robertson and Dale, 2013). The progression of these neoliberal approaches was given momentum in the developing world with the debt crisis of the 1990s; they particularly impacted on southern hemisphere countries who sought increased aid and loans.

While much of the theory behind these neoliberal reforms emanates from the United States and was promoted by funding institutions based there, neoliberal reforms in the US found significant opposition to the introduction of such changes. Terzian and Boyd (2004) note that President Ronald Regan's ideas of general freedoms had found some bipartisan support for education. A report, *The Nation at Risk,* published in 1983 contributed to a creation of feeling in the public that the school system in the US was in crisis. A proposed voucher system to widen choice and introduce independent 'charter schools' was found to be a popular approach to improving the situation. Charter schools could be founded through a state-authorised charter by teachers, parents or educational activists and found public support. However, congresses from both sides of the political divide variously opposed their introductions, often for political expediency rather than educational reasons (Verger *et al.*, 2016). Opposition was not always due to the philosophical stance of the Republican or Democratic parties; majority congresses from both side of the political divide turned down legislation to introduce these due to various political arguments. It took until 1997 for a federal bill under Democrat President Bill Clinton to gain bipartisan congressional support and provide the legislation and funding momentum to begin the introduction of charter schools which could be opened and run by interested parties, educators or religious groups (Terzian and Boyd, 2004).

By the beginning of the 1990s these neoliberal approaches to privatisation in education were beginning to align with two main approaches recognisable now: the buying into education or educational services as a provider, usually for profit, and the promotion of a managerial culture oriented toward the achievement of tangible and measurable results.

Activity 2

If you were a schoolteacher in a public-funded school, which educational services might you expect to see privatised under Williamson's 10 points of the Washington Consensus.

A Third Way? The Blair/Brown/Clinton years (1997–2010)

The list of education reforms in the UK during the Blair/Brown years was extensive, and this section highlights certain policies to show the continuing expansion of neoliberal policies in education in the UK and the US as socially democratic governments came to power. In the UK, the Labour Party returned to government under Tony Blair, and Bill Clinton became Democratic President of the United States in 1993, with education featuring as a priority in their election manifestos. Their 'Third Way' has been likened to the Ordoeconomics of the 1930s and is also known as 'the Post-Washington Consensus' (Birdsall, 2011).

In the UK, the soundbite 'Education, education, education' used by Tony Blair during the 1997 election campaign seemed to offer the promise of a 'new golden' era for education (Gillard, 2018). Many expected a return to full comprehensivisation and a local-authority-led system for schools. The Third Way was to harness the power of the markets for social democracy, and many took this to mean social justice. It was adopted by many social democratic parties during the late 1980s and was based on the popular neo-classical notions that individual freedoms and choice could be married to a socially orientated form of neo-classical economics to use market forces for social good. Giddens (1994) argues it was an attempt to use the dynamism of markets to fund social policies, and public–private partnerships were the bedrock of the policy.

However, those expecting a return to a pre-Thatcherite education system were to be disappointed. The 1997 Education (Schools) Act abolished assisted places in private schools; Sure-Start Centres for very young children were introduced and Lifelong Learning initiatives early in the parliament initiatives promised much. However, policies became disparate and tended to move toward more choice, more private finance and the further reduction in the powers of LEAs. The first parental ballot to abolish grammar schools in Ripon, North Yorkshire saw an overwhelming majority of people wishing to keep it. This almost immediately ruled out a return to a fully comprehensive system of education. The privatisation of local education authority services began as Hackney in London received a critical Ofsted report. Private sector companies were invited to bid to run support services such as school advice and finance. The approach was followed in Liverpool and Islington and was a further abandonment of the comprehensive system of education and the encroachment of profit-making services into education.

Other initiatives followed a neoliberal agenda of increasing privatisation in education. In 1998, 25 Education Action Zones were introduced with commercial sponsors, including Kellogg's, British Aerospace, Tate and Lyle, American Express and Brittany Ferries. In 2000, Tony Blair announced the creation of specialist colleges with a promise of special status if they raised £50,000 in sponsorship, and city academies which would be governed by businesses, churches and other groups. City academies would be independent from local authorities in return for a £2m donation towards the capital costs; sponsors would be allowed to rename the school, control the board of governors, influence the curriculum and select up to ten per cent of their pupils. In 2001, the government money was provided for partnerships between grammar schools and comprehensive schools and, in 2002, Education Minister Charles Clarke announced the creation of specialist academies which could be run in partnership with the private sector. Further marketisation was seen to occur with the 1998 Teaching and Higher Education Act which introduced University tuition fees of £3000 and abolished maintenance grants.

The Private Finance Initiative (PFI) introduced by the Labour Government during this administration led to public-private partnerships which saw private capital being introduced into educational infrastructure projects. Private capital was seen as necessary to reverse the lack of investment from the Thatcher years without recourse to public funds. This too was seen by critics of neoliberalism as another encroachment of the 'for profit sector' into education. PFI for schools and other public buildings has been the focus of much criticism for: being more expensive than public funding due to high interest rates, benefits through rental payment for the providers of finance at taxpayers' expense, buildings not meeting or providing the specified criteria or being poorly designed. The element of risk in these projects was also underestimated and, in 2018, the collapse of Carillion, one of the largest managing agents of PFI initiatives, left many public projects unfinished or unmanaged.

Under the Blair/Brown Labour Government, Chitty (2013: 93) notes the following fragmentation of education under plethora of different types of schools including:

- independent (fee-paying) schools
- city technology colleges
- city academies

- grammar schools
- foundation specialist schools
- voluntary specialist schools
- community specialist schools
- beacon schools
- foundation schools
- voluntary aided schools
- voluntary controlled schools
- community schools
- community special schools
- pupil referral units

Blair resigned as prime minister in 2007. Throughout the Blair years, educational policy-makers continued to engage with private sector initiatives, although, unlike in the US, no single policy was followed. While it is difficult to quantify the amount of private capital put into education, school budgets from central government increased by an average of 5.4 per cent per year (Gillard, 2018) and there are generally accepted improvements in the classroom in terms of resourcing, technology and facilities. Curtis (2009) also reported an improvement in attainment: pupils getting five or more GCSEs including English and Mathematics, rose from 40.7 per cent in 2000 to 47.3 per cent in 2008. There were, however, many criticisms of education policy during this period. Wrigley (2014) argues that the curriculum became increasingly dominated by literacy and numeracy, generic employment skills and an earlier preparation for work at 14. Academies were controversial as a means of improving education: some continued to cause controversy, some improved results, some stayed the same and a number gained worse results than the school they replaced. Attainment results improved overall during this period, but some schools were left behind, often in poorer areas. A report by the Sutton Trust (2016) showed that schools in working-class white areas were left behind, with poorer white children the most disadvantaged as only 24 per cent of boys and 32 per cent of girls obtain five good GCSEs. This was well behind all students in other areas.

As Gordon Brown became Prime Minister the financial crash of 2008 occurred, causing an economic recession and a global downturn. Lack of public funds limited education initiatives, but two government acts further linked education firmly with work. This period was unremarkable, but in 2008 the Education and Skills Act required people to be in education or training to age 17, effectively increasing the statutory leaving age. The 2009 Apprenticeships, Skills, Children and Learning Act was a major piece of legislation, but drew criticism due to a number of its sections dealing with classroom behaviour.

In the United States, the Clinton administration promoted charter schools which were finally voted for by congress as bipartisan legislation (written by both Republicans and Democrats) in 1997, and increased options for pupils by allowing attendance through choice rather by allocation. The 'charter' is the promises made by the school to their attendees. The charter school approach is regarded by many in the political spectrum as satisfying both sides and enjoys bipartisan political support (Verger *et al.*, 2016). Although seen as ideologically desirable by many across the political spectrum, privatisation in the United States has been slow due to the political system. Freedom of choice as represented by the voucher system has never become fully accepted and appears to be losing popularity. Another bipartisan bill, the No Child Left Behind Act in 2001, strengthened the elementary system by introducing common core state standards of attainment with testing, and gave pupils options to move schools if theirs was not achieving the required results. This act became unpopular as it provided little support for gifted children, relied too much on contested standards to show improvements and caused accusations of 'gaming the system'. The lack of a full funding model placed a strain on state budgets.

With the election of Barack Obama in 2009 little changed in US educational policy. *No Child Left Behind* was replaced with *Race to the Top* which was given impetus through the fiscal stimulus after the 2007 financial crash as the American Recovery and Reinvestment Act (2009) provided $4.35 billion for charter schools, but also introduced standards for teachers and teacher-monitoring through student results. High-school graduation reached an all-time high and an income-based support system for student loans saw the student financial burden drop considerably. In one of the biggest financial commitments in the US, the government put $50 billion into Pell Grants for low income students, and reduced student diversity debt as fees had become an unsustainable burden.

Activity 3

• Write your own definition of neoliberalism.
• Are student university fees in the UK seen as a result of neoliberal policies?
• Outline the arguments for and against student university fees.

Trends in the political economy of education in developing nations

While this chapter has focussed on the dominant political economies of western education and the influences of western institutions on education in developing nations, it is important to consider what have been held up as successful examples of education in developing nations. This section considers Local Fee-Paying Schools (LFPS), considered by some to be outside the global political economy and the privatisation of a school system in Chile.

In developing nations there is often a policy vacuum. This occurs for various reasons: economic, conflictual, financial, administrative and through natural crises. Educational developments occur '…by default' (Verger *et al.*, 2016: 89) to fill the vacuum and often centre on private fee-paying schools. There is much debate about the scope and nature of these schools, but Verger describes them specifically as '…low-fee private schools (LFPSs) …set up and owned by an individual or group of individuals for the purpose of making a profit, and for low income families'. These schools are mainly in the primary sector and popular in South East Asia (India and Pakistan), Latin America and some sub-Sharan African countries (Malawi, Nigeria, Kenya, and Ghana), and little information exists on them beyond the primary sector (Ashley *et al.*, 2014). The growth in admissions to LFPSs has been more than double the admissions to more expensive schools for middle-class students (*The Economist*, 2015), although in terms of numbers, size and distribution, and even categorisation, makes the extent of schooling in LFPSs contentious because many are unregistered or unrecorded in national statistics. However, their place outside the political economic systems of nations makes them worthy of consideration.

LFPSs can be run by non-governmental organisations, but are more likely to be run for the poor by social, community or religious organisations where profit is not the main motive. In regions where there are free public schools some consideration is needed of why the poorest in society will forego free child education and opt to pay fees. Ashley *et al.* (2014: 2) find there is a perception of '…better quality …(in terms of teaching, teacher attendance, school performance, small class size, discipline) compared with state schools', while parents also value English language teaching and better employability prospects. Whether or not LFPSs do actually give better educational attainment, as advocated by Tooley (2004), is open to debate. Ashley (2014) finds the evidence for better attainment inconclusive, but teacher presence, attendance and teaching activity is better than in comparable state-sector schools.

In terms of the political economy of education, LFPSs appear to sit outside government systems and their purpose seems to be generally altruistic. However, a deeper exploration for the reasons for their growth indicates that they may be a symptom of local and global political economic influences. Härma (2011) finds they may be a reaction to their local political economies; public free schools in some regions are overcrowded and with such poor resources that parents may feel they have no choice but to pay for education. Their relative success may also be due to having students from slightly higher socio-economic backgrounds, with a resultant advantageous cultural approach to education, a factor which is neglected by advocates such as Tooley (2004). The growth of LFPS too seem to have begun to take on aspects of globalisation as donors, entrepreneurs and international organisations are increasingly involved in their operations.

From 1973, difficult economic conditions resulted in Chile reforming its education system by undertaking a programme of privatisation through student vouchers redeemable for a set government fee. This pre-dated the US system by a number of years, but similarly allowed choice of public or private schools through vouchers and began a transfer of public resources to the private sector. In 1990, the military junta gave way to a democratic government and the system continued. This voucher system now funds 90 per cent of primary and secondary education with about ten per cent in independent schools.

This approach in some ways was quite different from the LFPS approach, but in some respects there were similarities, on the surface at least. State schools were places under the control of a local authority through a process of municipalisation. This seems similar to the LFPS approach, but there were differences. A school performance management system based on results was put in place to inform parental choice, along with results-based teacher incentives, although the results were never released while Chile was a military dictatorship. A programme of deregulation of the teaching profession caused an overall fall in salaries. However, adjustments followed the neoliberal economy of education advocated by the Washington Institutions and Chicago School of economics, and educational and economics benefits should have subsequently followed. However, in Chile municipal authorities are disparate regionally and diverse in terms of wealth. While there was a small reduction in administrative costs, this policy had a tendency to leave more wealthy areas with well-staffed and well-resourced schools and good attainment, while more rural schools fell behind in every aspect. This was exacerbated when better schools were allowed to charge extra fees, thus segregating the school population further along the lines of rich and poor. The expansion of the rapid increase in private sector education did not appear to be having any effect on the overall educational outcomes of Chile (Parry, 1997).

Both of these education systems are a reaction to difficult economic conditions which limited government support for education (Verger *et al.*, 2016). On the surface there are similarities in the approaches taken by countries where LFPSs filled the educational gap, and Chile where, despite the perception of a neoliberal approach, government or local governments funded schools through vouchers and still had a say in schools through the municipalities. In both cases the introduction of finance and markets to the education system, however limited, provided a system of education for poorer people, but of a non-uniform quality. In both cases, where people could pay more, the quality of education, as might be expected improved. But where the lowest fees exist, either through payment by fees, or payment by vouchers, improvements were much more contestable.

Activity 4

Outline the differences and similarities between voucher-based education schemes and LFPSs.

UK education from Gove: Austerity and the rise of populism

The financial crisis of 2007 and subsequent recession had a profound effect on government spending around the world, with lasting effects to all budgets including education. In the UK, the return of a Conservative government under David Cameron in 2010, in coalition with Nick Clegg's Liberal Democrats, began a period of austerity in the form of reduced government spending in all public social services. Michael Gove became the Conservative Secretary of State for Education and continued reforms on neoliberal lines, but also promoted a 'traditional' teaching philosophy which advocated rote learning approaches (Gillard, 2018). Labour policy had been to make academies of the failing inner-city schools, known as 'sponsored academies'. Gove's 2010 Academies Act was intended to remove all schools from local authority control into 'converted academies'. Gove went on to promote 'free schools', which were funded by government but could be instigated and run by parents, universities or private companies. By January 2018, 72 per cent of secondary schools and 27 per cent of primary schools were either academies or free schools (National Audit Office, 2018).

Under Gove a range of education budget cuts were implemented with some £8.5 billion removed from the mainstream education budget and funding diverted to opening free schools, often in areas where additional schooling was not required. The 2011 Education Act removed a number of the agencies concerned with education such as the General Teaching Council for England. Gove also introduced a new National Curriculum with a substantial results-based performance system.

From 2010, education began to lose its place in the priorities of global political economies. In the UK the Coalition and Conservative Governments pursued a strict fiscal policy aimed at reducing the budget deficit incurred after the 2008 financial crash. This led to a rise in anti-European sentiment and the populist United Kingdom Independence Party(UKIP) making substantial gains in local and European elections, causing the Conservative Government under David Cameron to hold a referendum on European Union Membership in 2016 which resulted in the UK leaving the EU.

Parliamentary time in the UK after the referendum saw almost no debates on education as Brexit discussions took precedence.

In Europe, serious financial problems in Greece let to a huge bailout by the rest of the Eurozone countries. A run on banks in Portugal, Spain, Ireland and Italy caused similar national financial problems, and more bailouts occurred to keep their countries' banking systems operational. Large-scale migration across the Mediterranean from Africa and over the Bospherous from Syria, Iraq and Afghanistan also caused a rise in populist parties in Europe, and there too education became less of an immediate priority. The USA, too, experienced banking and financial problems; migration from South American countries through Mexico began to play a part in political debates, leading to a populist Republican president, Donald Trump, gaining power in the Oval Office. It would seem unlikely that any significant change in policy here will occur as efforts to stimulate the internal US economy and migration control measure take precedence in political debates.

As education has become less prioritised in the global political economies of the world, one can only outline general expectations for the direction of educational policy. It would seem likely that, with the rise of populism in the UK, across Europe and in the US, the continuing progression of neo-classical solutions to educational problems will continue. However, this may not be a lasting phenomenon as politics since 2010 has generally been shown to be volatile and subject to significant swings in public opinion. At the time of writing (May 2019) in the UK as Brexit stalled and all other political economic business with it, reactions became polarised. A rise in Jeremy Corbyn's opposition Labour Party and a better-than-expected election result in 2017 left a precarious Conservative majority in parliament. In the US, President Donald Trump saw record post-election popularity lows, and in France the *Mouvement des gilets jaunes*, or yellow-vest movement, caused significant disruption, protesting against a continuation of the neo-classical economic policies of previous governments. However, the continuing encroachment of global neoliberal policies in education appear to be continuing unabated.

The conceptual bases

Together with Chapter 8, this chapter has explored the development of the political economy of education and highlights some of the main ways it has developed from the recognition that the distribution of wealth required explanation in the eighteenth century. Education from the middle ages was something solely for the concern of the individual with various interventions by religious bodies and a few altruistic societies to a recognition of its place as a central function of governments and supported by government funding. The developmental path to understanding this is often made difficult due to the ever-broadening, and sometimes bewildering, number of conceptual models, often written from individual perspectives which consider the political economy of education. Table 9.1 below offers an overview of the ones used here and provides a contextual for students of educational studies.

While there is little to suggest that some of the more practical aspects to education in terms of policy, direction or funding is global, there are nevertheless some features of educational development which are widespread enough to be called global features of a political economy of education.

Table 9.1 A conceptual base for understanding the development of a global political economy of education

Conceptual term	Features	Origins
Classical liberal economics	Liberal or Free Market Mercantile System. Supply and demand adjust to keep markets in equilibrium. Social democratic ideas of self. Education as a commodity to be paid for.	Adam Smith, *Wealth of Nations* (1776)
Institutionalism	Institutions (Courts Parliament, Councils etc.) provide features to make markets work e. g. law, order, money, some regulation of markets.	Hobbes (1588–1679), Locke (1632–1704) Rousseau (1712–1778),
Principles of political economy (The beginnings of Institutionalism)	Reforming institutions to reduce inequality, introduce co-operatives, rights for women, end slavery.	J. S. Mill *Principles of Political Economy* (1848)
Communism (beginnings of critical political economy)	Overthrow of the owners of capital by the proletariat, sharing society's resources, communal societal living, education as an enabler.	Karl Marx, *Das Kapital: A Critique of Political Economy - The Production Process of Capital,* (1867) Karl Marx and Fredrich Engels *Communist Manifesto,* (1848)
Keynesian economics	A move from the liberal free market supply side economics to demand side economics advocating increased public spending through borrowing to beat recession.	John Maynard Keynes, *The General Theory of Employment, Interest and Money (1936)*
Neoliberal economics (Ordo-Liberalism)	An approach to explain how markets work from the 1920's to 1930's. Free market approach but with a more social outlook similar to the 'Third Way.'	Walter Eucken, Franz Böhm, Alexander Rüstow, Wilhelm Röpke and Alfred Müller-Armack (1920' – early 1930's but with lasting influence.
Human capital theory	Society as a working meritocracy with education as a key enabler, a sit creates human capital or value in society.	Becker (1962, 1994)
Global human capital	Society as a working meritocracy which add to the global human capital.	Robert Merton Theory of Social Structure (1949, 1957 and 1968)

(Continued)

Table 9.1 A conceptual base for understanding the development of a global political economy of education (*Continued*)

Conceptual term	Features	Origins
Modernisation theory	Developing society must have the 'right values' and 'right skills' with education to provide these for economic growth.	Harbison and Myers (1964)
Dependency theory	As the value of primary goods constantly falls due to the power of the more developed nations to control primary good prices developing nations will always be dependent on them.	Prebisch–Singer Hypothesis (from 1950)
The Golden Years	The term used by observers to describe the Labour Government years during the 1960's when education funding was seen to be good.	Gillard (2018)
The Chicago School of Economists	A group of free market Neo-classical Economists typified by Milton Friedman who paved the way for monetarism.	Milton Friedman *Free to Choose* (1980)
Washington Consensus	Key institutions based in Washington DC including the International Monetary Fund, United States Treasury and World Bank who issued a ten-point plan for world development.	John Williamson (1990)
Neo-Institutionalism/ The Third Way	Institutions as enablers and protection of social democracy from free markets.	Skocpol (1979) and Heywood (2015)
New critical political economy	A divergence of Marxist thinking to a broad spectrum of individualistic topics including feminist, post-structuralist and post-colonial critiques (Livingstone, 1995).	Examples: Education (Bowles and Gintis,1976), ethnicity (MacDonald), 1981) and gender (Katznelson et al., 1982)
Post Washington Consensus/The Third Way	Re-vitalised and powerful institutions to control unfettered markets to create social democratic equality.	Birdsall (2011)
Neoliberalism	A return to the free market ideals as a way of overcoming economic failure. Used to describe many aspects of the way neoliberal economics affect.	Bhagwati (1982) Venugopal (2015)

Conclusion

There are many criticisms of neoliberal approaches to education. In England and Wales the attempt to harness the markets to improve schools under Margaret Thatcher's Conservatives and under Tony Blair's New Labour led to a fragmented approach to education with many different types of schools and educational institutions with different approaches to funding, all competing with each other for pupils and leaving some schools with poorer students and no choice. Further neoliberal reforms by Michael Gove led to a situation where, Gillard (2018) argues, the governance system of schools became a mess. The Sutton Trust (2016) show that white pupils in poorer areas have been consistently 'left behind'.

Globally the formal recognition by almost all governments of the world that education was beneficial to all was given impetus in the 1948 United Nations Declaration of Human Rights which gave everyone the right to education. However, this has been difficult to achieve and developing nations have often found funding difficult. Many turned to richer western nations and organisations to help fund their educational programmes and became tied to conditions of loans and grants. The Washington Consensus in 1990 (Williamson, 1990) ensured these conditions were based on investment conditions and affected how the money would be used and education systems set up. It resulted in a transfer of government funding and assets to the private sector through grant and loan conditions which have affected the educational policies, practices and curriculum of developing nations. The rigorous literature review on a broad range of developing countries by Kingdon *et al.* (2014: 3) indicates there is evidence that:

- Teaching is better in private schools in terms of presence, activity and there is evidence of better learner outcomes.
- The cost of delivery is lower, although private education costs are difficult to ascertain.
- There is a perceived better quality in private schools (in terms of teaching, teacher attendance, school performance, small class size, discipline).
- More boys than girls attend independent schools.
- Parents in independent schools have an effect on the pupils' education.
- It is difficult for states in developing countries to regain management and control of independent schools.

There was little to support the following claims:

- Research cautions against assuming this means they (private schools) are reaching the poor.
- There is a small but consistent evidence base that independent schools are more expensive than state schools in terms of both school fees and hidden costs such as uniforms and books.
- The evidence on whether the poor are able to pay private school fees is ambiguous.
- The evidence base on whether private schools complement or compete with government school provision is very small.
- Evidence that private school competition drives up standards overall is small and contested.

While the effects of the success of neoliberal educational policies are debatable, there can be little doubt that there has been a consistent transfer of public funding to the private sector. In the West, this transition was facilitated through political ideologies. In developing countries by the economic necessity through the need for grants and loans and the conditions tied to them. However, any beneficial effect on education and educational systems is still being debated.

Activity 5

Discuss the pros and cons for the argument there is now a global political economy of education.

Summary

- There are two approaches to neoliberalism. The first emanates from the Ordoliberalist economists in Germany in the 1930s who were seeking to remedy the economic ills of the Weimar Republic through a liberal free-trade economic approach with a social conscience.
- The Mont Pelerin and Chicago Schools of economists began to advocate a similar neoliberal economic approach to the Ordoliberals during the 1930s as a response to Keynesian demand-side economics which promoted state borrowing and intervention.
- Keynesian economic approaches maintained an ascendancy in western political economies until the 1980s, during which time educational spending continued to increase.
- A return to liberal free-market economic policies began from 1979 and was followed by many western countries. While these were not a return to the complete free market approach of Adam Smith and owed more to Ordoliberalism, they nevertheless began the process of moving education and educational resources to the private sector. In the UK and the US, the Third Way of the Blair and Clinton/Obama administrations increased the involvement of the private sector in education and tried to ensure that liberal economics had a social consciousness through regulation by institutions.
- From the 1930s 'neoliberal' was a term used by economists and few others. From 1980 the term neoliberal has been used mainly by its critics from various perspectives, but not by economist, suggesting that its meaning has changed from a descriptive to a critical term.

Recommended reading

Ashley, L. D., Mcloughlin, C., Aslam, M., Engel, J., Wales, J., Rawal, S., Batley, R., Kingdon, G., Nicolai, S. and Rose, P. (2014) *The Role and Impact of Private Schools in Developing Countries*. London: DfID.

Chitty, C. (2013) *New Labour and Secondary Education, 1994-2010*. London: Palgrave Macmillan.

Kingdon, G., Little, A., Aslam, M., Rawal, S., Moe, T., Patrinos, H., Beteille, T., Banerji, R., Parton, B. and Sharma, S. K. (2014) *A Rigorous Review of the Political Economy of Education Systems in Developing Countries*. Final report. Education Rigorous Literature Review. London: DfID, EPPI-Centre ref. 2203.

Venugopal, R. (2015) Neoliberalism as concept. *Economy and Society*, **44**(2), pp. 165–187.

West, A. and Currie, P. (2008) The role of the private sector in publicly funded schooling in England: Finance, delivery and decision making. *Policy & Politics*, **36**(2), pp. 191–207.

References

Ashley, L. D., Mcloughlin, C., Aslam, M., Engel, J., Wales, J., Rawal, S., Batley, R., Kingdon, G., Nicolai, S. and Rose, P. (2014) *The Role and Impact of Private Schools in Developing Countries*. London: DfID.

Bhagwati, J. B. (1982) Directly unproductive, profit-seeking (DUP) activities. *Journal of Political Economy*, **90**(5), pp. 988–1002.

Birdsall, N. (2011) The Post-Washington Consensus: Development after the crisis – Working Papers from Center for Global Development. Working Paper 244.

Chitty, C. (1989) *Towards a New Education System: The Victory of the New Right.* Lewes: Falmer Press.

Chitty, C. (2013) *New Labour and Secondary Education, 1994–2010.* London: Palgrave Macmillan.

Clarke, J. (2008) Living with/in and without Neo-liberalism. *Focaal*, **51**, pp. 135–147.

Curtis, P. (2009) The end of the 'bog-standard' comprehensive. *The Guardian*, 8 December 2009. Available at: https://www.theguardian.com/education/2009/dec/08/education-policy-schools-labour (Accessed 20 August 2019).

Economist (2015) Low-cost private schools: Learning unleashed. 1 August 2015. Online. Available at: https://www.economist.com/briefing/2015/08/01/learning-unleashed (Accessed 2 January 2019).

Giddens, A. (1994) *Beyond Left and Right: The Future of Radical Politics.* Oxford: Polity Press.

Gillard, D. (2018) Education in England: A history. Available at: www.educationengland.org.uk/history (Accessed 21 November 2018).

Glennerster, H. and Hills, J. (1998) *The State of Welfare: The Economics of Social Spending*, (2nd ed.). Oxford: Oxford University Press.

Härma, J. (2011) Low-cost private schooling in India: Is it pro poor and equitable? *International Journal of Educational Development*, **31**(4), pp. 350–356.

Kingdon, G., Little, A., Aslam, M., Rawal, S., Moe, T., Patrinos, H., Beteille, T., Banerji, R., Parton, B. and Sharma, S. K. (2014) *A Rigorous Review of the Political Economy of Education Systems in Developing Countries.* Final report. Education Rigorous Literature Review. London: DfID, EPPI-Centre ref. 2203.

National Audit Office (2018) *Converting Maintained Schools to Academies.* London: National Audit Office.

Novelli, M., Higgins, S., Ugur, M. and Valiente, O. (2014) *The Political Economy of Education Systems in Conflict-affected Contexts.* London: DfID.

Parry, T. R. (1997) Decentralization and privatization: Education policy in Chile. *Journal of Public Policy*, **17**(1), pp. 107–133.

Robertson, S. L., Novelli, M., Dale, R., Tikly, L., Dachi, H. and Ndibelema, A. (2007) *Globalisation, Education and Development: Ideas, Actors, Dynamics.* Researching the Issues 68. London: DfID.

Robertson, S. L. and Dale, R. (2013) The social justice implications of privatisation in education governance frameworks: A relational account. *Oxford Review of Education*, **39**(4), pp. 426–445.

Sexton, S. (1977) Evolution by choice. In Cox, C. B. and Boyson, R. (Eds.). *Black Papers 1977.* London: Temple Smith.

Sutton Trust (2016) *Improving Social Mobility.* London: Sutton Trust.

Terzian, S. G. and Boyd, D. C. (2004) Federal precedents and the origins of the charter school movement in Florida, USA, 1981–1996. *Journal of Educational Administration and History*, **36**(2), pp. 135–144.

Tooley, J. (2004) Private education and education for all. *Economic Affairs*, **24**(4), pp. 4–7.

Venugopal, R. (2015) Neoliberalism as concept. *Economy and Society*, **44**(2), pp. 165–187.

Verger, A., Fontdevila, C. and Zancajo, A. (2016) *The Privatization of Education: A Political Economy of Global Education Reform.* New York: Teachers College Press.

Williamson, J. (1990) The Washington Consensus as Policy Prescription for Development. Online. Available at: https://www.piie.com/publications/papers/williamson0204.pdf (Accessed 17 August 2019).

Wrigley, T. (2014) *The Politics of Curriculum in Schools.* London: Centre for Labour and Social Studies.

10 Rethinking 'international perspective' in Education Studies: 'Knowing' education in the global era

Tingting Yuan

Introduction

This chapter explores the knowledge of 'education' at an international level. It becomes a challenging epistemic and methodological process when we need to know how education crosses territorial boundaries, geographical locations, cultures and religions. The concept of 'education' is becoming increasingly complex in the context of modernisation (Rostow, 1960) and globalisation (Giddens, 1990; Rosenau, 1990). Related research areas in such contexts as 'comparative and international education' are facing challenges in the context of changing international relations and increasing voices regarding alternative approaches to development. This includes a broader understanding of 'education' itself, and a more careful and contextual consideration of related research methodologies.

It is necessary to begin the discussion from reasoning the 'international perspective': why do we need to know 'education' from such a perspective? Before this question is answered, it is essential to recognise that the current 'international context' is not only about education crossing countries (i.e. education in a 'flat' world), but also education within global complexities which have been gradually formed and transformed (i.e. education in international history), and especially power relations (i.e. education in the global hierarchy). There are, therefore, three meaningful reasons for the exploration of education in 'global society' (if there is any):

- First, the development agenda has shifted from a 'multi-lateral agency approach' to a 'global agency approach' – targeting global problems (e.g. poverty) which can only be solved globally (Robertson *et al.*, 2007: 101); educational development and education policies are also involved, meaning a growing interdependence among nation states with the pursuit towards global targets.
- Second, among the various 'influences' on education, aid conditionality (IMF, 2019), which is in many cases via foreign assistance structurally, influences the nature of education and, in particular, promotes the marketisation of education. This has resulted in a need for the serious consideration of social justice as well as global justice in education.
- Third, there is also a trend of increasing international cooperation in education, partly among the global North and South, although also among developing countries themselves. New collaborative models (such as the 20+20 China and Africa higher educational cooperation programme) are challenging the traditional roles in international development, including the orthodox ways of promoting educational development (King, 2014). New roles, assuming emerging powers, provide global society with thoughts on 'alternatives'.

For these reasons, this chapter starts with a historical review of the changing international contexts and how education has been involved and embedded; this is followed by a reflection on 'what we need to know about education' in the global context today. The chapter concludes with some methodological reflections on conducting research in international education based on such understandings.

Modernisation to globalisation: Some conceptualisation

If 'what education looks like in different countries' is the x-axis of international education, then the y-axis may refer to the role that education has played in the changing discourse and practice of international development, especially in the process of developing countries pursuing modernisation. This can be traced back to the 1960s that were labelled the 'development decade' by the United Nations, where such a label corresponded to the 'departing of colonialism' (United Nations, 1961: 17). The concept 'decolonisation' refers to the achievement of independence by former Western colonies in Africa, and the protectorates in Asia following the Second World War. During these transitions from colony to nation-state, the theory of modernisation began to play a key role in international development (Berger, 2003).

Originating in Western developed countries, modernisation theory contends that 'low-income countries could improve the living condition of their populations by a set of prescriptive policies to encourage economic 'taking off' (Robertson *et al.*, 2007: 11). The American economist, Walt Whitman Rostow, introduced five stages of economic growth experienced by countries with investment, consumption and social trends at each stage. During the process of modernisation, he argued that most important is the 'taking off' stage. This has been called the 'Rostovian take-off model', and certain concepts developed by him have become central to modernisation theory (Rostow, 1960). The idea that all countries could become 'modern' and 'catch up' with the West if they followed the same stages as Western countries, can be seen as both a theory and a prescription (Dale, 1982). This logic has provided the basis for the Western model of development.

Education is considered to be important within the context of modernisation theory (Robertson *et al.*, 2007). This is evident in Schultz's (1961) human capital theory which considers the capital produced by investing in knowledge. Human capital theory suggests that education or training raises the productivity of workers by imparting useful knowledge and skills, and thereafter raises the future income of these workers by increasing their lifetime earnings (Becker, 1964). Education, therefore, plays the role of creating 'modern' individuals and 'unlocks the door to modernisation' (Harbison and Myers, 1964: 3). This role of education, as well as the close relationship between education and economic growth, has been rooted in western societies and has spread globally since the 1970s. It is reinforced in the neoliberal agenda through aid and other types of development partnerships from the Latin American debt crisis to the current internationalisation of education.

Contrasted with modernisation theory (a theory based on the economic development of nation states and state intervention) which was formed as protection against the workings of the market, was neoliberalism. This theory arose within the contemporary economic globalisation context based upon the philosophy of a free-capital market. It held 'a strong preference for markets as the mechanism through which production, distribution and consumption within an international economy should be efficiency managed' (Robertson *et al.*, 2007: 13). John Williamson, an economist from the Institute for International Economics, first presented the concept of a 'Washington Consensus' in 1989, listing ten broad sets of recommendations for aid, including financial liberalisation, trade liberalisationand privatisation to globally promote a market-based economy. The key points are liberalisation, privatisation and marketisation, which come from the western liberalism tradition (Williamson, 2004: 3). In the area of education, these recommendations have enhanced the notion of human capital and led to the trend of marketisation and privatisation of education. Education has become 'a global industry' in which the market logic plays a central role (Rose, 2003).

The Washington Consensus and its radical economic reform strategies were replaced by the post-Washington Consensus (Stiglitz, 1998, 2002), which was concerned more with governance and the social factors of the development, with a central agenda based on Poverty Reduction Strategy Papers (PRSPs). It aimed at strategies that are results-oriented, country-driven, participatory and based on a partnership between the governments and other actors. Education is one major element of PRSPs (UNESCO, 2004). Critics see such a commitment to reducing poverty as an international agenda that consists only of the process of integration into the international capitalist economy (Mittelman, 2000). Despite this, certain ideas relating to social capital (i.e. benefiting the poor, searching for a more participatory, bottom-up model of development, as well as the equity issues from the Post-Washington Consensus 'paradigm') have had important effects on the strategy of aid and the goals for educational development globally. In September 2000, building upon a decade of major United Nations conferences and summits, world leaders gathered in New York to adopt the United Nations Millennium Declaration, 'committing their nations to a new global partnership to reduce extreme poverty and setting out a series of time-bound targets – with a deadline of 2015 – that have become known as the Millennium Development Goals (MDGs)'.

At the same time, the neoliberal agenda has not lessened within ongoing globalisation, but now takes various forms and is presented as an antidote to the worldwide problem of poverty. It can be said that the most significant feature of this global era is the neoliberal policies based on economic globalisation. A typical definition from Giddens (1990) describes globalisation as 'a central driving force behind the rapid social, political and economic changes that are reshaping modern societies and world order' (cited in Held et al., 1999: 7). It is also worth introducing the 'transformationists' who claim that we are seeking the interaction of powers and their causal relationships within a 'highly differentiated' transformation. The world is in transformation, which means there is 'no longer a clear distinction between international and domestic, external and internal affairs' (Rosenau, 1990, cited in Held et al., 1999: 7). Furthermore, the transformationists believe that globalisation is a historically unprecedented process requiring governments and societies to make transformations to cope with this new global situation. However, we are not sure about the directions and the trajectory of this process given that the effects are always uneven and contradictory. Therefore, one of the approaches to understanding globalisation is to focus on its 'multi-centric, multi-scalar, multi-temporal, multi-form, and multi-causal' features (Jessop, 2008: 178). Education is under transformation in such a complex context.

The process of globalisation is becoming not only economic, but also political. Looking into the politics of globalisation helps us to capture 'the stretching of political relations across space and time; the extension of political power and political activity across the boundaries of the modern nation-state' (Held et al., 1999: 49). In fact, the concept of globalisation cannot be easily divided into economic and political realms, as the economy is becoming a 'political economy' and politics is becoming 'economic politics'. It is necessary always to consider the 'political economy' which looks at the interactions between political institutions and economic institutions and how this relationship shapes the balance between freedom and equality (O'Neil, 2007). This also applies to education. The global political economy, having modernisation as a fundamental logic for development and current globalisation, and as the accelerator for increasing international connections as well as related complexities, can be defined as the context for our contemporary knowledge about 'education'. In this context, the next section of this chapter will continue to explore the three dimensions 'knowing' education at an international level.

Questions for discussion

- What do we need to consider when education is located within a global context?
- What are the core ideas of modernisation theory and how do these affect the purpose of education?
- What are the relationships between globalisation and neoliberalism?
- How does the neoliberal agenda influence education?

Understanding 'education' in the global context: Three dimensions

Education is based on re-thinking and re-examining in the international context above. It is about how educational discourse and practice cannot be understood simply in the realm of 'education', or as the educational phenomena that have been observed. This chapter suggests that education be understood in a global context based on how nation states and international institutions look at the role of education, and therefore from the following three dimensions: education in individual societies, education in bilateral relations and education in a globally structured agenda.

The function of global citizenship – individual societies

For most of the sociological discussion about education, it is essential to start the study by asking 'what the purpose of education is'. A functionalist focuses on how education contributes to an individual's socialisation, while a conflict theorist criticises the dominant power and its impact on the function of education. Therefore, a functionalist view always represents the 'mainstream' logic on the role of education. From this perspective, education is defined as an agent of socialisation in individual societies. Educational discourse and practice are closely connected to a nation state's specific cultural, economic and political status. Individuals 'develop our "selves" as we learn what we need to know to live and operate with others in social groups' (Bartlett and Burton, 2012: 16). This role of education functionally serves a society's 'culture, norms and values' (ibid), and, at an international level, makes for the creation of 'global citizens'.

An education towards global citizens, ideally, 'would like to think it involves favourable attitudes or beneficial actions towards others in the global community'; and this is not only about 'identity but also about responsibilities' (Bramlett, 2016: 194). Therefore, at an international level, education is not just about individuals' socialisation in one society, but also about individuals' adaptive abilities in the process of modernisation and globalisation. As aforementioned, socialisation emphasises people's adaptation to social norms and adaptation to interpersonal relationships. Adaption towards modernisation emphasises integration into a modern society, mastery of the knowledge and skills needed for modern societies (e.g. modern science and technology), learning and understanding of advanced culture and joining in a process of civilisation. Education, by educating global citizens, plays a key role in globalised modernisation: to modernise individuals in different societies and let them grasp the key knowledge and skills for modern society. This knowledge is related to the existing industrialised and well-developed countries and achieving international targets for certain convergent features in development. Thus, globalisation emphasises the adaptation and integration of international norms, the learning and adaptation of economic and technology globalisation and information societies, as well as an understanding of the global market and the common destiny of the human being. From this perspective, education plays a role, not only for mutual and cross-cultural/inter-cultural understanding, but also for common targets and global convergence. While most of these targets, modern knowledge and advanced culture are promoted by socially advanced groups and classes, it is essential and critical to ask: How would our poverty agenda work for the least advanced groups? What is the purpose of education within the process of 'helping' those people? Is it just to let them live better and participate under current social norms, to let the least developed nation states catch up with the 'advanced societies'? For example, it means training and educating people to understand how they are socialised and classified in well-developed societies in order to be modern and more integrated in the global connection as well as competition? Moreover, should there be a standard definition of the 'global citizen', and is there a global citizen? Does a global citizenship education truly reflect on global justice? These are questions that are more important than how to promote global citizenship via education. It is related to further examination of another two dimensions of understanding education as follows.

Mission for public diplomacy – bilateral relations

Education can be defined as a source of soft power crossing societies, meaning that it can socialise not only people who are educated, but can also influence much broader publics. Education politically and strategically contributes to international relations and public diplomacy (Nye, 2008; Yuan, 2014). This can easily be seen even in many bilateral relations in international politics.

In contrast with hard power (e.g. economic, military power), soft power is more about 'persuasion'. In international relations, soft power is not a new term, but it has become more than persuasion in the current global era; it was used a lot through the media and foreign policies before and during the time of the Cold War (Yuan, 2014). Within these instruments, public diplomacy is used by governments to mobilise resources (culture, political values and foreign policies) to communicate with and attract the publics of other countries, rather than merely their governments (Nye, 2008). Nye brought 'public diplomacy' and 'soft power' together and mentioned the current dimensions of public diplomacy, including 'daily communications', 'strategic communication' and 'lasting relationships' (Nye, 2008: 102). Education and the related cultural exchange play a key role in public diplomacy: for example, higher educational exchange and cooperation. It can be said that education for public diplomacy is a type of 'bilateral socialisation'. It enhances people-to-people connections and exchanges between governments and nation states.

This political function of education is adopted internationally. The US was one of the first to enhance the provision of scholarship in order to attract international students in its foreign strategy decades ago. A practice reflected by the US Secretary of State, Colin Powell, who asserted, 'I can think of no more valuable asset to our country than the friendship of future world leaders who have been educated here' (Nye, 2005: 13). This is practised again by increasing so called 'emerging powers' today, such as China's engagement in the international provision of education, especially tertiary-level training and education. China has sent teachers to African countries since the middle of the last century, and has devoted huge efforts to increasing the number of scholarships for foreign students from all over the world. India also has similar governmental programmes, receiving foreign students from central Asia, Africa and Latin American countries (India.gov.in, 2012). Impressively, these countries, which are mainly faster developing countries in the global South, have naturally and easily established a more equal relationship within their partnerships. The key transformation is argued to be education for developmental experience. In the background paper for the EFA Global Monitoring Report 2015, Reilly (2015: 6) quoted a Chinese expert that, 'China is not really promoting its own approach, but naturally Chinese experts and officials prioritise programs and issues which they think will be useful for developing countries'.

It is therefore interesting to ask, to what extent is the intrinsic value and purpose of education considered when it carries political missions? How can the quality of education for international exchange programmes, international scholarships, teacher secondment, and so on be evaluated? Can knowledge transformation work in a more effective and practical way (including contributing to broader bilateral relations and contributing to a higher level of educational development) when education is provided and exchanged among developing countries themselves? Moreover, are these bilateral exchanges helping to improve education in the poorest areas (or only serving the social elites from two sides). Who are selected to be educated or trained in the various types of international programmes? It may be more meaningful to move to the third dimension so that a fuller picture may be obtained to further question the economic politics of education.

Components of a globally structured agenda – international institutions

How should we 'know' education within the network of various international players, especially the participation of various types of international institutions?

In response to this question, it is necessary to examine international agendas such as Education for All (EFA) and the MDGs as well as their declarations on education. In 1990, UNESCO and the World Bank (the biggest donor for education) set up and coordinated the EFA conference in Jometien, Thailand, which aimed to 'provide quality basic education for all children, youth and adults' (UNESCO, n.d.). This set the context for the educational issues in the MDGs announced in 2000. The MDGs are eight international development goals that range from halving extreme poverty to halting the spread of HIV/AIDS and providing universal primary education (UPE, listed as the second goal), all by the target date of 2015. In 2015 the UN announced its Sustainable Development Goals (SDG), even though the MDGs had not been fully achieved. The SDGs targeted 17 goals, with educational targets listed in Goal 4. More than promising universal primary education in the MDGs and EFA, SDG 4 also targets tertiary education, including higher education and the international scholarship provision for widening access to higher education. Looking at these changing discourses helps us understand how education is embedded in global issues such as poverty, and how nation states are increasingly involved into the 'subscription' of international agendas, including educational provision in this globalisation process.

Although calling for an education for everyone as a basic human right, the role of education is not too different from how it is set out in modernisation theory. Education is working for a 'knowledge economy' (KE) – where 'knowledge' takes over from 'production' as the key driver and basis of economic prosperity (Dale, 2005: 146). Tilak (2002) also states that by the end of the 1980s and the early 1990s, the critical relevance of knowledge – including its production, distribution and utilisation – in the process of economic growth had been widely acknowledged; moreover, knowledge has come to be the most important factor of economic growth.

The World Bank, the largest multilateral donor in education, has been committed to help countries achieve EFA through Education for Knowledge Economy which clearly demonstrated the idea of integrating education into national economic strategies (World Bank, 2009). This has been softened towards more promise on human rights and inclusion in the Bank's post-2015 agenda (World Bank, 2018a). Critiques from Jones and Coleman (2005) argue that the World Bank is consistently promoting firm views of how education policy should relate to the fiscal, economic and social dimensions of public policy. Seen in this light, the bank is both lender and persuader. Such critique has not been reduced in the recent decade. The Bank is still criticised by its promotion of neoliberal policies, in a shifted rhetoric and a continuous engagement in its own perception of 'best practice' in education (Adhikary, 2012; Steiner-Khamsi, G., 2012; Jones, 2006). This can be seen from its current statement on 'human capital through education' within its 'Human Capital Project' launched in 2017 (World Bank, 2018b).

It is therefore essential to ask: Who is globalising education and what is the relationship between education and global justice? Are international institutions promoting the same purpose of education? What might be the divergence and tension among them, and how do these affect education policies in nation states?

Until now, education may be seen as a component of a globally structured agenda accelerated by globalisation. According to Dale (2000) the globally structured educational agenda (GSEA) differs from another approach, the common world educational culture (CWEC), when the effect of globalisation is under discussion. The CWEC argues that the national development of educational systems could be explained by universal education models rather than distinctive national factors that may have been formed through their long histories and social and cultural constructions. In contrast, the GSEA approach examines education by questioning a series of issues related to the actors, mechanisms, conditions and the consequences of education. It has a much broader scope on education than the CWEC approach. The specific methodological approach will be introduced in the next section.

Questions for discussion

- What are the external factors that influence education discourse and practice today?
- What does 'global citizenship' mean for national education? Can there be a global citizenship education?
- What is the relationship between education and the soft power of a country? How does education contribute to international relations?
- Is education demonstrated as a common world culture or located within a globally structured agenda? Can the universal model of education be possible?

Approaching education internationally: Methodological reflection

An IPE/GPE perspective and CCPEE approach

Based on the discussion in this chapter about how education performs on the international stage, this section goes on to reflect on some of the methodological issues in researching education in the global era. First of all, an international/global political economic perspective and Robertson and Dale's (2015) Critical Cultural Political Economy of Education (CCPEE) approach can be useful to allocate education in the global context and the complexities of bilateral/multilateral relationships as well as their power relations. An international political economic (IPE) perspective explores the tensions and interaction between 'state' and 'market' actors (Gilpin, 1987; Strange, 1988) and focuses on economic globalisation and its structural effects. More specifically, the IPE perspective investigates how economic globalisation has shaped national policy and global governance, including the donor–recipient relationship as well as aid conditions created by international institutions such as the World Bank and the International Monetary Fund (Verger *et al.*, 2018).

From an IPE perspective, a CCPEE approach helps to integrate the political economy and takes a cultural turn into an account when globalising education (Robertson and Dale, 2015). The CCPEE approach takes 'the "education ensemble" as the topic of enquiry, whose shifting authoritative, allocative, ideational and feeling structures, properties and practices, emerge from and frame global economic, political and cultural processes' (ibid, 149). The approach is based on a critical realist ontology. In contrast to idealism, realism essentially assumes that the material objects exist externally to us, and independently of our sense experience. The key words of realism are 'independent', 'external' and 'objective'. However, it does not mean that we cannot have true beliefs about objective existence, that the objective (external) world is in principle knowable and can be reflected in our minds, 'and to some extent open to being changed on the basis of such knowledge as we are able to achieve' (Benton and Craib, 2001: 120). It can be argued that one of the key points of realism is the relationship between subjectivity and objectivity. It is about how we can best utilise our subjectivities to approach knowledge, and even make changes to the objective world. The critical realism ontology assumes the reality 'to exist, but to be only imperfectly apprehendable because of basically flawed human intellectual mechanism and the fundamentally intractable nature of phenomena'. So the epistemic rule is 'never fully know', by comparing the findings with pre-existing knowledge (Guba and Lincoln, 1994: 110–11).

This is how the CCPEE approach tries to seek the educational evidence, as well as the mechanism and logic of education, and understand why education looks like this and how it is connected to broader social and power relations. The approach looks at education more than the education which is usually discussed and centred on learning. Methodologically, it specifies four 'moments' within an education ensemble demonstrating the width and depth of the approach: the moment of educational practice which asks 'who is taught what?', the moment of education politics which asks 'how and by whom are these things decided?' the moment of the politics of education which seeks deep political economic and cultural structures of educational discourse and practice, namely, 'the rules of the game', and the moment of outcomes which asks 'how far are the successes of some achieved at the expense of others' (Roberston and Dale, 2015: 156–7). As Robertson and Dale (2015: 150) have explained:

> The use of the concept 'ensemble' reflects the fact that education represents, and is reflected in, crucial, multiple relationships with, and within, societies; it is a complex and variegated agency of social reproduction, broadly conceived. Thus it cannot be reduced to 'a system', or 'an agent' of socialisation and social selection, or indeed a provider of vocational qualifications.

This provides a good and critical reflection upon the aforementioned role of education in individual societies where the 'mainstream' view on education carries a functionalist idea and always simplifies education as a training process. It also echoes the other two dimensions of education mentioned later in this chapter: the public diplomatic role of education and the political economy of education. For example, a 'common world culture' perspective may see international educational exchange as a cultural activity for mutual understanding, or the construction of global society and may focus on the content and quality of the exchange. While the education ensemble of CCPEE may question why this happens, the question is to what extent the two sides interact with each other as governments rather than as educators, and whether this is truly an exchange rather than aid or assistance.

Researching education in a global era: Issues in fieldwork and ethics

Following the above discussion, two methodological issues, fieldwork and research ethics in international Education Studies are discussed in terms of their 'contextualisation' and 'ethnocentricity'.

First, the standardised ethical declaration which is usually set up as a necessary procedure when conducting data collection in western countries may not work under other social contexts, especially in developing countries. There are more issues that need to be considered than the common ones such as confidentiality and anonymity that are listed on a standard ethics form. When approaching participants in another country, the conversation may be influenced not only by the relationship between the researcher and the participants, but also the different culture and politics between the two societies. This requires further consideration and critical reflection of the reliability of data, the broader and potential power relations in the data collection procedure, and approaches to meaningfully anonymising the data, all of which are needed. Among various ethical codes and numerous research bodies across the world, very few standards are agreed in terms of international research ethics (Williams, 2015). A cross-cultural study should not be, and cannot be, regulated only from the researcher's perspective: the researcher has to adjust his/her way of data collection according to the actual situation. This is sometimes also related to the ethnocentrism of a western researcher when they enter less-developed areas, and always have their own assumptions about what is ethical. It is important always to ask, how do we know whether educational research is ethical? Is an approved ethical statement sufficient for international studies in education? What might be the potential ethical dilemmas?

Second, fieldwork should help to reduce ethnocentrism rather than increase it. There is a central question around this issue: Why do we conduct international education research? During fieldwork, are we going to explore, or evaluate educational issues in another country? Are we only going to know what education looks like in another context? This goes back to all of the discussion in the first and second sections of this chapter: education is not just the intrinsic part of education, but very much about how education is located in national and international structures, strategies and agendas. If the nature of education is seen from a critical realist perspective, via a CCPEE approach, then the fieldwork should be an opportunity to truly reflect on the whole power relations, including the relationship between the researcher and the participants. Is there a hierarchy and is there an assumption that already exists before any data is collected? If the fieldwork is aiming to find a way to contribute to knowledge, then this procedure itself should be flexible and self-reflective. It is worth 'keeping in mind that fieldwork is, in many respects, concerned more with uncertainty than with certainty', and it is 'not the kind of research that relies on a "scientific" distance between researcher and research subject or object' (Pole and Hillyard, 2016). More specifically, for instance, in a fieldwork conversation, a focus group seminar may help the conversation gain more depth and 'soften' the interviewer–interviewee relationship in order to achieve more flexible dynamics among the participants and the researcher.

Questions for discussion

- What are the four moments of Dale and Robertson's 'education ensemble'? Can you apply these moments to a case study in education?
- How does a critical realist look at 'education' and educational problems?
- What might be different or need particular attention when we investigate education and collect evidence at an international level?

Conclusion

In this chapter a comprehensive reflection of 'education' from an international perspective with a focus on a 'global context' has been conducted. From a historical review, to a conceptualisation of 'education' from three dimensions, followed by further epistemic and methodological considerations, the chapter emphasises the value of exploring educational practice and discourse under contemporary globalisation and the necessity of updating and extending the knowledge of education beyond educational knowledge in the changing global political economy. However, the dimensions of education here are still limited, and mainly within a political economic framework. The chapter hopes to stimulate further thought about how to understand (theoretically), investigate (through fieldwork) and reform (in social practice) education in the face of current global transformation.

Summary

- Education under the global context is not 'flat': it is embedded in the changing international relations and international development agendas. The current educational targets are still rooted deeply in modernisation theory.
- Neoliberal globalisation accelerates and helps spread the idea of a marketised education, and education is supposed to contribute to knowledge economy.

- Education is not only related to learning procedure and cultural exchange. It is essential to look at the role of education under the global political economy. A critical approach helps not only to look at the evidence on the cultural political and economic aspects of education, but also the interaction, mechanisms and power relations of an education 'ensemble'.
- In order to 'know' education broadly and also in more depth under the global context. It is also worth keeping in mind the ethics of international studies and the features, as well as nature of international fieldwork.

Recommended reading

Robertson, S. and Dale, R. (2015) Towards a critical cultural political economy account of the globalising of education. *Globalisation, Societies and Education*, **13**(1), pp. 149–170.

Verger, A., Novelli, M. and Altinyelken, H. K. (Eds.) (2018) *Global Education Policy and International Development: New Agendas, Issues and Policies*, London: Bloomsbury.

Williams, C. (2015). *Doing International Research: Global and Local Methods*. London: Sage.

References

Adhikary, R. W. (2012) The World Bank's shift away from neoliberal ideology: Real or rhetoric? *Policy Futures in Education*, **10**(2), pp. 191–200.

Bartlett, S. and Burton, D. (2012) *Introduction to Education Studies*, (3rd ed.). London: Sage Publications.

Becker, G. S. (1964) *Human Capital: A Theoretical and Empirical Analysis, with Special Reference to Education*. New York: Columbia University Press.

Benton, T. and Craib, I. (2001) *Philosophy of Social Science: The Philosophical Foundations of Social Thought*. London: Red Globe Press.

Berger, M. T. (2003) Decolonisation, modernisation and nation-building: Political development theory and the appeal of communism in Southeast Asia, 1945-1975. *Journal of Southeast Asian Studies*, **34**(3), pp. 421–448.

Bramlett, B. H. (2016) Age and global citizenship attitudes. In Langran, I. and Birk, T. (Eds.). *Globalization and Global Citizenship: Interdisciplinary Approaches*. Abingdon: Routledge.

Dale, R. (1982) Education and the capitalist state: Contributions and contradictions. In Apple, M. W. (Ed.). *Cultural and Economic Reproduction in Education: Essays on Class, Ideology and the State*. London: Routledge and Kegan Paul.

Dale, R. (2000) Globalisation and education: Demonstrating a 'common world educational culture' or locating a 'globally structured educational agenda'? *Educational Theory*, **50**(4), pp. 427–448.

Dale, R. (2005) Globalisation, knowledge economy and comparative education. *Comparative Education*, **41**(2), pp. 117–149.

Giddens, A. (1990) *The Consequences of Modernity*. Cambridge: Polity in association with Blackwell.

Gilpin, R. (1987) *The Political Economy of International Relations*. Princeton: Princeton University Press.

Guba, E. and Lincoln, Y. (1994) Competing paradigms in qualitative research. In Denzin, N. and Lincoln, Y. (Eds.). *Handbook of Qualitative Research*. Thousand Oaks: Sage.

Harbison, F. H. and Myers, C. A. (1964) *Education, Manpower and Economic Growth*. New York: McGraw-Hill.

Held, D., McGrew, A., Goldblatt, D. and Perraton, J. (1999) *Global Transformations: Politics, Economics and Culture*. Stanford: Stanford University Press.

IMF (2019) Conditionality. Online. Available at: https://www.imf.org/en/About/Factsheets/Sheets/2016/08/02/21/28/IMF-Conditionality (Accessed 6 May 2019).

India.gov.in (2012) Government of India Scholarships for International Students. Online. Available at: https://archive.india.gov.in/overseas/study_india/studyinindia.php?id=10 (Accessed 6 May 2019).

Jessop, B. (2008) *State Power: A Strategic-relational Approach*. Cambridge: Polity.

Jones, P. W. (2006) *Education, Poverty and the World Bank*. Rotterdam: Sense Publishers.

Jones, P. W. and Coleman, D. (2005) *The United Nations and Education: Multilateralism, Development and Globalisation*. London: RoutledgeFalmer.

King, K. (2014) China's engagement with the post-2015 development agenda: The case of education and training. *International Journal of Educational Development*, **39**, pp. 70–77.

Mittelman, J. H. (2000) *The Globalization Syndrome: Transformation and Resistance*. Princeton: Princeton University Press.

Nye, J. (2005) Soft power and higher education. Forum for the Future of Higher Education, 1 January 2005, pp. 11–14.

Nye, J. S. (2008) Public diplomacy and soft power, *The ANNALS of the American Academy of Political and Social Science*, **616**, pp. 94–109.

O'Neil, P. H. (2007) *Essentials of Comparative Politics*, (2nd ed.). New York: W.W. Norton.

Pole, C. and Hillyard, S. (2016) *Doing Fieldwork*. London: Sage.

Reilly, J. (2015) The role of China as an education aid donor. Paper commissioned for the EFA Global Monitoring Report 2015, Education for All 2000-2015: achievements and challenges. Paris: UNESCO.

Robertson, S. and Dale, R. (2015) Towards a critical cultural political economy account of the globalising of education. *Globalisation, Societies and Education*. **13**(1), pp. 149–170.

Robertson, S., Novelli, M., Dale, R., Tikly, L., Dachi, H. and Alphonce, N. (2007) *Globalisation, Education and Development: Ideas, Actors and Dynamics*. London: DfID.

Rose, P. (2003) From the Washington to the Post-Washington Consensus: The influence of international agendas on education policy and practice in Malawi. *Globalisation, Societies and Education*, **1**(1), pp. 67–86.

Rosenau, J. N. (1990) *Turbulence in World Politics: A Theory of Change and Continuity*. London: Harvester Wheatsheaf.

Rostow, W. W. (1960) *The Stages of Economic Growth: A Non-communist Manifesto*. Cambridge: Cambridge University Press.

Schultz, T. W. (1961) Investment in human capital. *American Economic Review*, **51**(1–2), pp. 1–17.

Steiner-Khamsi, G. (2012) For all by all? The World Bank's global framework for education. In Klees, S., Samoff, J. and Stromquist, N. P. (Eds.). *The World Bank and Education*. Rotterdam: Sense Publishers.

Stiglitz, J. E. (1998) *Towards a New Paradigm for Development: Strategies, Policies and Processes*. Geneva: United Nations Conference on Trade and Development.

Stiglitz, J. E. (2002) *Globalization and its Discontents*. New York: Penguin.

Strange, S. (1988) *States and Markets*. London: Pinter.

Tilak, J. B. G. (2002) Knowledge society, education and aid. *Compare: A Journal of Comparative and International Education*, **32**(3), pp. 297–310.

UNESCO (2004) Education and PRSPs: A review of experiences. Online. Available at: https://unesdoc.unesco.org/ark:/48223/pf0000137664 (Accessed 6 May 2019).

UNESCO (n.d.) Education for all movement. Online. Available at: http://www.unesco.org/new/en/archives/education/themes/leading-the-international-agenda/education-for-all/ (Accessed 6 May 2019).

United Nations (1961) United Nations Development Decade: A programme for international economic co-operation (i). General Assembly – Sixteenth session, pp. 17–18.

Verger, A., Novelli, M. and Altinyelken, H. K. (2018) Global education policy and international development: A revised introduction. In Verger, A., Novelli, M. and Altinyelken, H. K. (Eds.). *Global Education Policy and International Development: New Agendas, Issues and Policies*. London: Bloomsbury.

Williams, C. (2015). *Doing International Research: Global and Local Methods*. London: Sage.

Williamson, J. (2004) A short history of the Washington Consensus. Paper presented at the conference: 'From the Washington Consensus towards a new Global Governance', Barcelona, 24–25 September.

World Bank (2009) Education for the knowledge economy. Online. Available at: http://bit.ly/2HC9U71 (Accessed 6 May 2019).

World Bank (2018a) *Education Overview (English)*. Washington, D.C: World Bank Group.

World Bank (2018b) *The Human Capital Project*. Washington, DC: World Bank.

Yuan, T. (2014) Diploma serves diplomacy: China's 'donor logic' in educational aid. *China: An International Journal*, **12**(2), pp. 87–109.

11 Education, urbanisation and the case of 'the child in the city'

David Blundell

From the foldings of its robe, it brought two children; wretched, abject, frightful, hideous, miserable. They knelt down at its feet, and clung upon the outside of its garment.

'Oh, Man! look here. Look, look, down here!' exclaimed the Ghost.

They were a boy and girl. Yellow, meagre, ragged, scowling, wolfish; but prostrate, too, in their humility. Where graceful youth should have filled their features out, and touched them with its freshest tints, a stale and shrivelled hand, like that of age, had pinched, and twisted them, and pulled them into shreds. …

Scrooge started back, appalled. … 'Spirit! are they yours?' Scrooge could say no more.

'They are Man's,' said the Spirit, looking down upon them. 'and they cling to me appealing for their fathers. This boy is Ignorance. This girl is Want. Beware them both, and all of their degree, but most of all beware this boy, for on his brow I see that written which is Doom, unless the writing be erased. Deny it!' cried the Spirit, stretching out its hand towards the city.

(Charles Dickens, *A Christmas Carol*, 1843)

Introduction

In 2007, humans could justifiably be described as a city-dwelling species when for the first time a majority of the world's population was recorded as living in cities and urban environments. This presents challenges on many fronts, not least for education, as we seek to address common futures in which not only do urban ways of life dominate human social organisation, but the actions of urbanised humans impact all aspects of life on planet Earth (Lewis and Maslin, 2018). This chapter examines historical and contemporary evidence for the material experience of children in the city, but also how historically-located constructions of *the child* and *the city* are braided into the complex entanglements that constitute the trope of *the child in the city*. Finally, the chapter reflects on whether these entanglements serve the interests of children inhabiting globalised and trans-national realities, as well as whether they provide a solid platform upon which education to meet the goals of economic and social justice on a planetary scale can be realised.

Industrialisation and the city

As the nineteenth century dawned, Britain was in the throes of changes that were reshaping its economic, social and political landscape at home and across the world. Exploitation of energy stored in fossil fuels allowed the proliferation of power on a hitherto unimagined scale which, along with transport and communications technologies, facilitated transformations in modes of production that drove Britain's population from the land to find work in its booming towns and cities. Whereas in 1801 Britain had a population of around 10 million, with the majority living and working in communities founded on agricultural production and craft skills, by 1914 the figure was close to 40 million, with the majority inhabiting towns and cities. The effect on particular cities was marked, so that between 1770 and 1830 Manchester grew from a population of around 25,000 to over a quarter of a million – a ten-fold increase; similarly, the small port town of Liverpool's population numbered merely 1,210 in 1700, by 1801 it stood at 92,000, but exceeded 286,000 by 1841 and was ranked as the third largest city in Britain (Miles, 2006: 389). In South Wales, Cardiff's population rose from 18,000 to 164,000 over the course of the nineteenth century. London, as metropolitan capital for the British Empire, ranked as the largest city in the world with around 4.5 million inhabitants on the eve of the First World War (plus 2.8 million people inhabiting its suburban 'home counties' and benefiting from rapid rail transport systems), having had half that population in 1851.

Although improvements had been seen in the living conditions of these new urban dwellers by the beginning of the twentieth century, the statistics on infant mortality and life expectancy around the time that Dickens wrote *A Christmas Carol* are truly shocking. Archaeologist David Miles tells us that:

> The big cities, with their open sewers, fetid streets and tenements packed with people and livestock, were killing grounds for their own population and particularly the young. Of the 350,000 deaths in England and Wales in 1842 nearly a quarter were children less than a year old, and 140,000 were children under five years.
>
> (Miles, 2006: 391)

Despite these high levels of mortality, continued migration within Britain and from Ireland meant that the rapid growth of towns and cities continued apace. In consequence, living conditions became overcrowded, squalid and insanitary with epidemic surges in diseases such as typhus, cholera and diphtheria and the ongoing dangers of tuberculosis, venereal disease, violent crime, and industrial injury that stalked life in slums and factories. A German émigré named Friedrich Engels (1820–1895) vividly documented these condition in Manchester and Salford over the autumn and winter of 1844–1845, but only published in English translation as *The Condition of the Working Class in England* in 1887. Engels would subsequently collaborate with Karl Marx as author, editor and funder to produce *The Communist Manifesto* in 1848 and *Das Kapital* in 1867 (Marx 1867, 1848).

Dickens, schooling and the child of the city

Charles Dickens published *A Christmas Carol* in December 1843, and the forlorn figures emerging from the gown of the second ghostly apparition are representative of a concern at the forefront of the author's mind. Earlier in that year Dickens had visited the Field Lane Ragged School in London's Saffron Hill, an area where deep-seated poverty and criminality provided the backdrop for Fagin's den in *Oliver Twist* (Dickens 1837, 1843). Shocked by his visit, Dickens joined titled figures, including Ashley-Cooper, Lord Shaftesbury and Angela, Baroness Burdett-Coutts as public champion for ragged schooling (Blundell, 2012: 85–88).

However, while Dickens championed these schools and approved their 'self-help' ethic, he was also critical of them in ways that prefigure debates about the respective claims of secular and religious interest groups in education. Whereas he could describe the good intentions and moral courage of the teachers as '… beyond all praise', and that 'their office is worthy of the apostles', he was less enthusiastic about their poor skills as teachers and critical of the emphasis on religious instruction in doctrinal niceties that served to 'perplex the minds of these unfortunate creatures with religious mysteries that young people, with the best advantages, can but imperfectly understand' (Collins, 1963: 88–9). Dickens also baulked at the moral naivety of textbooks 'pervaded by a grimly ludicrous pretence that every pupil was childish and innocent'; as Philip Collins adds, 'tough youngsters off the streets were expected to interest themselves in infantile goody-goody stories' (Collins, 1963: 91). Rather, Dickens argued for more practical instruction that would both set children on a path that was neither delinquent nor criminal, as well as for the provision of washing facilities to address the insanitary condition in which they lived.

This fear that debilitating diseases and the insanitary conditions led to moral degradation amongst the children of the urban poor extended beyond ragged schooling and stalked the wider Victorian imagination:

> … the writings of reformers were the products of deeply held and widely debated convictions about the nature of the social order at a time when the middle class was anxious about what it deemed to be the rebellious and aggressive attitudes and behaviour of those young people (and their parents) who frequented the streets of urban areas.
>
> (Hendrick, 2015: p. 38)

Childhood historian Harry Hendrick identifies this as the discourse of 'the delinquent child', wherein the child is held to have acquired a surfeit of experience that was detrimental to the proper condition of childhood innocence. As much as this expresses direct anxiety about the urban poor, its force relies on a growing recognition that childhood should not be like this, thereby signalling the emergence of a widespread ideal sensibility concerning children as a whole.

Dickens' criticism of excessive moralisation in the curriculum places him in the vanguard of this emerging sensibility as opponent to assumptions of children's recondite original sinfulness. They are axiomatic for orthodox Christian doctrine and rooted in the work of the Roman bishop St. Augustine of Hippo. Proceeding from Augustine's assumption that human nature is morally 'fallen' and thus, fatally flawed, Dickens' ragged-school associates were not alone in aligning religious redemption with education and schooling. Mass migration to the industrial cities and the presumed disintegration of traditional family and communal ties conjured up fears about the rise of a youthful heathen populace, untutored in Christian virtue and the orthodoxies of faith. Their response was to establish systems of schooling to address these anxieties, hence the heavy emphasis on points of doctrine and theological knowledge found in the ragged schools. If the non-conformists had the ragged schools from the late eighteenth century on, the would-be Quaker missionary Joseph Lancaster established British Schools in 1798, before the established Church of England followed suit with their system of National Schools in 1811 and, the Catholic Poor School Committee established its own schools following Catholic emancipation in 1827 (see Blundell, 2012).

Dickens' concern to effect practical change rather than spiritual redemption echoes the moral neutrality concerning human nature of English empiricist philosopher John Locke. In *Some Thoughts Concerning Education* Locke (1693) wrote that 'of all the Men we meet with, Nine Parts of Ten are what they are, Good or Evil, useful or not, by their Education' proposed that environment and instruction played a greater part in forming human character than innate sinfulness. Dickens, therefore, advocates a modernising disposition towards childhood, where schooling serves as counterweight to the depravity of the industrial city, and schooling as children's right and proper condition.

Dickens died on 9 June, 1870, two months to the day before the landmark 1870 Elementary Education (or Forster) Act passed into law. With it a framework was established that would see basic schooling as a compulsory, universal norm by the end of the century. As Philip Collins, Dickens' biographer, acknowledges, the plaudits for seeing the general principles and detailed measures of the legislation should go to the educationist Sir James Kay-Shuttleworth, a friend and associate with whom Dickens had collaborated on Ragged School development. But for widespread advocacy of the matter and sympathetic esteem in the public eye, no one had greater influence than Charles Dickens.

Schooling was transformative not only for children and their place in the city, but also contributed to a growing modernising consensus about the meaning of 'a good childhood'. Hendrick outlines the impacts and nature of the transformation succinctly:

> In 1800 the meaning of childhood was ambiguous and not universally in demand. By 1914 the uncertainty had been virtually resolved and the identity largely determined, to the satisfaction of the middle and the respectable working class. A recognizably 'modern' notion of childhood was in place: it was legally, legislatively, socially, medically, psychologically, educationally and politically institutionalized.
>
> (Hendrick, 2015: 30)

This was not merely a break with past ways; it reflected a recognition by state and industry that mass urbanisation had not merely relocated the nation's population, but that with this *modern* society a wholly different set of human circumstances was emerging. However, whilst Locke's empiricist philosophy and John Stuart Mill's utilitarianism influenced the secularised state education system, they were not alone in challenging established convictions about children and childhood. The Lockean emphasis on childhood as a preparation for adulthood – sometimes summarised as a state of 'becoming' – found its complement in Jean Jacques Rousseau's argument for childhood as a state of 'being' in and of itself that was realised through the work of Johann Friedrich Froebel (1782–1852) and his educationist followers. Despite these differences, each embodied attitudes rooted in Enlightenment modernity and shared a confidence in social progress and the possibility that moral improvement could be secured through education. That said, the state's response to these emerging urban social realities was not welcomed by all. Irrespective of debates surrounding childhood as a state of either being or becoming, religious authorities (not least Dickens' allies in the Ragged School Union) objected to what they saw as a creeping secularism in Forster's Elementary Education Act. On a more directly practical level, compulsory schooling imposed economic constraints, and many parents and children resented the loss of vital family income as schooling took the place of paid work (Blundell, 2012; Tomes, 1985).

That said, state involvement and the changes it brought about did catalyse interest in educating the children of the urban poor. Pioneers such as Rachel and Margaret MacMillan in Deptford south-east London addressed urban problems through open-air nurseries and night-camps combining education, gardening and other activities with play and the provision of health care that established a template for nursery education. Its form is echoed in the Children's Centres promoted through the Sure Start and Every Child Matters policy initiatives (Blundell, 2012) at the turn of the last century.

Similarly, in an era without antibiotics when tuberculosis claimed so many children's lives, the first half of the twentieth century saw an enthusiasm for Open-Air Schools in Britain and across Europe, where learning in semi-rural, open-air settings was prescribed (Châtelet, 2008).

These attempts to alleviate the conditions in which the children of the urban poor were growing up frequently relied on scientifically-referenced and medicalised approaches (Foley, 2001); this turn towards science was complemented by developments in social science that sought to understand the city in ways that would support the thinking of policy-makers and practice of urban planners.

Understanding the city: Social science and the Chicago School

The 1887 English translation of Friedrich Engels' survey coincided with the work of social science pioneer Charles Booth (1840–1916) and his enquiries into poverty amongst London's working-class population (Engels, 1887). Over the period from 1886 to 1903, Booth undertook an 'Inquiry into Life and Labour in London' that compiled evidence in 450 notebooks and rendered it through maps in support of his contention that around 35 per cent of London's population lived in a condition of abject poverty. This period also saw a number of initiatives not only to document poverty, but to eliminate it through idealistic, even utopian, urban design. Many of these were isolated acts of philanthropy funded by wealthy industrialists who sought to provide healthier living conditions for their workers, including: Titus Salt (1803–1876) at Saltaire, West Yorkshire; Quakers Richard and George Cadbury who in 1879 established their 'factory in a garden' as a community village named Bournville, and William Hesketh Lever's 'Port Sunlight' model village on the Wirral in 1888. Perhaps the fullest expression can be seen in Ebeneezer Howard and the Garden City Movement that built complete towns, where a combination of urban and rural was intended as antidote to the vicious-ness of industrial cities, beginning with Letchworth Garden City in 1903. Howard's work epitomised the hope that the application of rational planning and design could reform the city and the existing social order.

Booth's poverty maps exerted a particular influence on the emergent discipline of sociology and its concern to understand the social life of the city through scientific methods; in particular, the sociolo-gist Robert E. Park as leading figure in The Chicago School drew inspiration from his work. The sem-inal work of Robert E. Park, Ernest Burgess, Roderick D. McKenzie and Louis Wirth established the Chicago School as the most influential contributor to the twentieth century's understanding of urban sociology and the geography of the city. *The City* (Park et al., 1925) established the terms that shaped subsequent urban sociological study, but extended beyond the academic realm to provide a vocabu-lary and conceptual toolbox that continues to shape ways that cities are imagined and represented by urban planners and developers. Inspired by the intellectual climate surrounding Darwinism and seeking to extend it to address social phenomena, Park *et al.* championed an 'ecological approach' to understanding the city, in which metaphors drawn from the biological sciences, such as 'colony', 'com-munity', 'growth', 'invasion and succession' rendered it as a complex, dynamic, and self-regulating super organism. The Chicago School's primary source of empirical data was Chicago itself as acme for early capitalist industrialisation in the United States and its connectivity as a hub in the rapidly-expanding rail network through which an abundance of raw materials, goods, people and ideas flowed (Allen *et al.*, 1998: 20–41). Burgess' mapping produced a model of Chicago as a series of concentric rings that not only represent locational patterns, but also a dynamic social ecology as individuals and communities sought to improve their location away from the central business district and inner urban areas towards better neighbourhoods found in suburban and satellite cities that best fit their means. Burgess asserted that his model represented '[all] the manifestations of modern life' (p. 47) and expanding rail and other rapid transport systems play a vital role in facilitating this locational mobility. Yet whilst a particularly American self-image as a restless immigrant society can be discerned in its dynamic form and inherent emphasis on growth, the concentric rings model has exerted a wider impact beyond the specific circumstances in which it was produced.

Thus, although Burgess' concentric rings model bears an empirical relationship to the material and social form as well as economic processes that made Chicago, it has had a far wider currency as a research tool with which social scientists approached an understanding of cities. Through his theory Burgess rendered tangible what otherwise appeared disordered and elusively beyond description, thereby providing a language within which planners, architects, students and academic researchers could examine cities as a generalised class. To achieve this Burgess relied on the detachment afforded by 'the view from above' that is vital to the way in which maps work. Being commonplace, it is easy to overlook the ways in which maps manipulate and present data about the world through a near-invisible knowledge technology reliant on a ubiquitous view from above. The high degree of generalisation found in the Burgess model as a large-*scale* map with comprehensive *scope* offered options to control and manage cities as complete worlds (Paddison and McCann, 2014). In this it also reflects a broader intellectual commitment across the social and human sciences to seek rational, universal laws for social phenomena having a status akin to those found in natural sciences such as physics, chemistry and biology. Having begun life as an empirical model of Chicago, Burgess' concentric rings attained an iconic status to become representative of *The City* as an abstract general truth and the detachment of the view from above facilitates this.

Whilst a powerfully influential understanding is facilitated by this approach, its quest for generality requires the detachment of the observer and so risks obscuring important insights into the actuality of people's lives, including what it means to be an inhabitant of a particular city or how differences between social groups are experienced face-to-face within a city as a lived space. Therefore, whilst Burgess' co-worker Robert Park saw the *nomothetic* pursuit of highly generalised laws governing city form and process as necessary, he argued against seeing the city as primarily buildings, streets, traffic, or as its social institutions, but rather that it could be captured in the plenitude of personal interactions through which its *social* fabric is woven and reinforced. Park argued that the industrial city's fabric comprised forms of relationship and interaction that were distinct from those under pre-industrial conditions and were best understood through an *idiographic* or qualitative mode of enquiry. Park's associate Louis Wirth set out a classic exposition of these distinctive urban ways in his essay *Urbanism as a way of life* published in 1938. For Wirth 'urbanism' exhibited distinctive patterns of life and social interaction that follow from the presence of large numbers of people living at high densities and characterised by a diverse heterogeneity as individuals and groups. Wirth is probably best known for his concept of 'anomie', through which the social isolation experienced by urbanised individuals could be explained and understood as a characteristic condition of the modern city's densely population and social heterogeneity.

Armed with the rational methods, scientific theorisation, and powerful iconography of the Chicago School, generations of planners set about enhancing the city and improving the living conditions of urban populations. As accompaniment, the first half of the twentieth century saw a gradual turn towards rational, scientifically-informed approaches to understanding childhood that were founded on the easy access to medical data afforded by universal schooling and the insights of the new field of developmental psychology (Foley, 2001). However, attempts to transform the city did not always sit comfortably alongside emergent ways of seeing childhood, especially in relation to opportunities for the child in the city to realise a developmental need to play that this scientific turn promoted.

Children living, playing and learning in the city

If the nineteenth century concerned itself with the education and welfare of the child in the laissez-faire industrial city, the twentieth century worried about children's experience of childhood in the rationally planned city, and the degree to which this accommodated spaces for them to live, learn and play. Few were more eloquent as a critic of the ways in which the mid twentieth century sought to reconstruct the industrial city than an American public intellectual named Jane Jacobs (1916–2006). Moreover, Jacobs' critique of urban planners and their approach to solving the problems of the city was articulated through the experience of children and the harm wrought by their ultra-rational schemes. Published in 1961, Jacobs' seminal work laid down the gauntlet with the challenging title *The Death and Life of Great American Cities* in which she presented a powerful critique of a cabal comprising planners, politicians and architects that sought to transform cities in ways that curtailed their vitality as humanistic, lived spaces. Jacobs' work contrasts communal spaces in which spontaneous sociability and children's informal play go hand-in-hand with the attempts at social engineering pursued by this detached professional cabal. Jacobs' work indicts the way that the view from above and its mentality of rational detachment from everyday life had come to dominate professional planning. In chapter 4 entitled *The uses of sidewalks: assimilating children*, Jacobs takes to task the planners' conviction that children must be rescued from the perils of the street and afforded bespoke spaces for play, where their physical, mental and social development will be facilitated. Rather, she argues that these rationally-designed and equipped spaces for play failed to match the spontaneous sociality of streets and the multiple possibilities they afford for playing in-step with the ebb and flow of neighbourhood life, as follows:

> A lot of outdoor life for children …. happens in brief intervals. …. They slop in puddles, write with chalk, jump rope, roller skate, shoot marbles, trot out their possessions, converse, trade cards, play stoop ball, walk stilts, decorate soap-box scooters, dismember old baby carriages, climb on railings, run up and down.
>
> (Jacobs, 1961: 112)

Thus Jacobs focused on those aspects of the city that, she maintained, were invisible to the professional imagination and in doing so struck a resonant chord with her many readers. The great American cultural commentator, critic and urban historian Lewis Mumford notes that, armed with this sort of rhetoric, Jacobs' arguments became the focus for dinner-table conversation across the USA. Moreover, he clearly approved Jacobs' impact as she:

> … stepped into prominence at a planners' conference at Harvard. Into the foggy atmosphere of professional jargon that usually envelops such meetings, she blew like a fresh, off-shore breeze to present a picture, dramatic but not distorted, of the results of displacing large neighborhood

populations to facilitate large-scale rebuilding … This able woman had used her eyes and, even more admirably, her heart to assay the human result of large-scale housing, and she was saying, in effect, that these toplofty barracks that now crowd the city's skyline and overshadow its streets were not fit for human habitation.

(Mumford and Miller, 1995: 186)

However, much as he admired Jacobs and the iconoclastic challenge she presented to planning and its overweening rationalities, Mumford was also critical of her arguments. His criticisms revolve around what he sees as a narrowly-drawn set of examples with their reliance on a highly edited and romanticised perception of cramped, ageing, high density and, frequently, insanitary traditional housing that might justifiably be described by others as slum-dwellings. For Mumford, besides her failure to acknowledge that the sidewalk-play she champions exists cheek-by-jowl with the roar and dangerous ravages of traffic, Jacobs overlooks the wider conditions of societal breakdown within which city dwellers lived. Furthermore, that the relationship of children and young people to this breakdown was far from one of passivity, and victimhood was evidenced for him by recent outbreaks of rioting and disorder, that were notable for: '… the presence of roaming bands of children, armed with bottles and stones, taunting and defying the police, smashing windows and looting stores' (page. 239). However, Mumford shares a common cause with Jane Jacobs by placing children's welfare as a bellwether test for the merit and fitness of schemes for urban renewal when he asserts that: '(t)he core of any adequate neighborhood housing program should be, above all, the provision of health, security, education, and the adult care of young children …' (Mumford and Miller, 1995: 239).

In Britain, Jacobs' arguments found an echo in the burgeoning adventure play movement that had origins in Denmark prior to the Second World War (Blundell, 2016; Burns, Abegglen and Blundell, 2019; Kozlovsky, 2008). The 'Junkyard Playground' (changed to 'adventure' in Britain) came to prominence during the Second World War through a belief that the psychological damage wrought by Nazi occupation could be addressed through providing children with opportunities for free play.

If the junkyard playground was seen as offering city-dwelling children opportunities to exorcise their traumatic wartime experience, its learning through play philosophy was also held to afford therapeutic recovery to children traumatised by the experience of recent aerial bombardment in post-war Britain. The key exponent here was a remarkable woman named Lady Marjory Allen of Hurtwood who had visited Denmark and been impressed by the work of the junkyard playgrounds. Writing in 1948 about her experience in the popular periodical *Picture Post* and using her connections with senior politicians and establishment figures, Marjory Allen promoted a number of 'Adventure' playgrounds on bombsites in inner London, Liverpool, Grimsby and Bristol, including one strategically located within walking-distance of the UK Houses of Parliament so that politicians could see the playground for themselves.

Along with the emphasis on psychological rebuilding, Marjory Allen was concerned about the priorities of architects and planners and their systematised and overly rationalistic approach to urban renewal that frequently failed to acknowledge the existence of children and the conditions that made for a healthy childhood. In her autobiography, Allen's sentiments echo those of Jane Jacobs:

The fact has to be faced that modern civilization, with its disregard for the worth of individuals, interferes with a hard and heavy hand in the spontaneous play of children. Most of the vast rebuilding schemes in industrial countries are horrible places, and the surrounding land is laid out with little love or understanding or, indeed, practical sense.

(Allen and Nicholson, 1975: 249)

Marjory Allen's associate Joe Benjamin wrote forcefully to argue for greater recognition of children's spontaneous play in the urban world and championed their active capacity to find ways to play as well as a multitude of opportunities for learning that accompanied it:

> [w]e must stop regarding the streets and similar favourite haunts in the negative way we do. These places can and do provide much more than opportunities for free play; they stimulate the child's need to learn about motor cars, engines, transport, shops and ships; about the lives of bus conductors, factory workers, builders, painters, telephone engineers, shop assistants, policemen and nurses.
>
> (Benjamin, 1974: 88)

Both Benjamin and Lady Allen are credited by the anarchist author and polymathic educator Colin Ward in his influential seminal book *The Child in the City* (1978). Ward's book went on to acquire a near mythic status as a clear-eyed exposition of children's lives in densely urbanised environments that unequivocally champions their agency without lapsing into an unreflective romanticism. In this, Ward challenged policy-makers, educators and academic theorists to see children as active constructors of their worlds, often in spite of the social, economic and material constraints that provide a stage-setting for their lives:

> Every generation assumes that the street games of its youth have been destroyed by the modern city. Yet they survive, changing their form in innumerable adaptations to exploit environmental changes. ... The lifts of the tower block, the trolleys from the supermarket, are incorporated into the repertoire of playthings...
>
> (Ward, 1978: 77)

Ward recognised the importance of embracing children's experience of the environments that surrounded them as the starting point for an environmental education that offered meaningful and active learning experiences. Thus he places the urban world and its affordances centre-stage as a resource to excite curiosity:

> The city is in itself an environmental education, and can be used to provide one, whether we are thinking of learning *through* the city, learning *about* the city, learning to *use* the city, to *control* the city or to *change* the city.
>
> (p. 152).

For Ward and his enthusiastic followers, environmental education was more than another subject on the school timetable; rather it provided a hub around which the whole curriculum could be articulated and rendered meaningful for learners. For our purposes, the everyday experience of being a child in the city was central to, and thus validated by, this approach rather than being seen as a diminished experience in a deficient environment wherein the authenticity claimed by more privileged childhoods could never be realised.

Rethinking 'the child' and rethinking 'the city': Educational possibilities for global futures?

There are some notions that capture our imagination because they seem to extend beyond the specific terms they address and articulate deeper concerns about the world and our place within it. The child in the city can claim to be such a notion, offering more than a straightforward statement about either children, cities or their respective locations in space. Concerns about children's lives and the quality of contemporary childhoods are heightened amongst the imagined anomie, barely graspable scale, and anxiety-inducing uncertainties of the city as emblem for all that denies childhood innocence. In turn, childlike innocence affords opportunities to interrogate and confront the urban society's shortcomings – in ways that Dickens, Jacobs, Mumford and the adventure play activists clearly recognised. Thus, *the child in the city* embodies a rhetorical force that derives from being what cultural theorists term a 'trope'; that is, it serves as an emblem or badge through which deeply embedded concerns about human society are represented and lent force as meaningful propositions. This echoes a particular responsibility placed upon children by the seventeenth and eighteenth century philosophers of the European Enlightenment, namely, that in the new-minted freshness of their imagined child it was possible to glimpse human beings in their original condition, unalloyed by the corrupting influence of society. The arguments of Jean Jacques Rousseau in particular accorded children a special status as natural humans and thus a relationship with nature that continues to inspire many educationists and to shape arguments about what children need. Colin Ward recognised this and drew on the work of cultural theorist Raymond Williams first to underline the deep-seated opposition between the city as a *cultural* world and the countryside as the *natural* world; and then, how this places the child in the city as 'out of place' in an alien environment:

> Moralists and educators all through history, as Raymond Williams has entertainingly illustrated, have polarized the country and the city as environments for children and have concluded that, however much the city may be a necessary provider of civilized life for sophisticated adults, nature is the only true teacher and that there is something 'authentic' or 'organic' about rural childhood.
>
> (Ward, 1978: 19)

However, this also throws up an uncomfortable paradox. On the one hand, the child in the city is deemed to be vulnerable and in need of protection (Mills, 2000); but, where this protection is denied, from Dickens' two children Ignorance and Want, in discourses surrounding delinquency, through Mumford's counter-argument to Jacobs, and underlying the work of the adventure-play theorists, we see that the child is also a thing to be feared. Thus, as much as the city appears to place the child *in danger*, it also reveals the child as *dangerous* (Hendrick, 2015) and frequently as a suitable case for redemptive treatment. Risking a simplistic reduction, the options seem to be to see children as either passive victims or actively villainous, neither of which offer a satisfactory understanding of the world in the twenty-first century nor an acceptable way to characterise children and young people. If this suggests that it is time to re-consider ways of seeing children and childhood, then brute facts about the urbanisation of human life may also demand a rethink about the city that has implications for the currency of the child in the city as a meaningful trope.

According to United Nations and World Bank (2018) sources, a crucial threshold was crossed in 2007 as more than 50 per cent of the world's human population were recorded as living in cities (UNESCO, 2007). In January, 2019 the world's population stands at 7.7 billion and is predicted to grow by 60m per annum, so that according to the United Nations Department of Economic and Social Affairs, by 2050 two-thirds of humans are expected to be urban dwellers (UNDESA, 2018). The significance of this is further underlined by the fact that children in the 'majority world' make up 90 per cent of young people on the planet (Aitken *et al.*, 2007), meaning that the majority of the world's children now grow up in non-western urban environments. Sheer numbers demand that a shift from a dominant focus on liberal individualist constructions of childhood – found in wealthy, economically developed western societies – towards to the diverse experience of young humans across a global scale is made.

Earlier it was suggested that theoretical accounts of the city and the spatiality of its economic and social life has been dominated by the work of the Chicago School in the first half of the twentieth century when Park *et al.* first published *The City*. However, the post-colonial theorists have also turned their attention to urban studies and the privileged position it has accorded the western industrial city, and particularly those that are held to have achieved the status of being a 'Global City'. A leading contributor to this critical work is Jennifer Robinson, a geographer with South African roots, who became increasingly uncomfortable as a young researcher with the assumptions she found in the standard academic literature about cities and its divergence from her experience of growing up in sub-Saharan Africa. In particular, Robinson argues that the dominant influence of the Chicago School elevates a few western cities – such as Chicago and New York in North America or London and Paris in Western Europe – as self-generating pace-setters in the process of urbanisation and the particular forms of economic development that facilitate it. For post-colonial critics, the proposition that 'Global Cities' serve as the standard by which the developed status (or not) of a society is measured is neither appropriate nor in line with emerging realities (see Allen *et al.*, 1998 and Aitken *et al.*, 2007 for a broader argument about stage theories in economic development). For Robinson this privileging of particular cities over the rest is a legacy of colonialist mentalities that seek to justify and maintain the dominance of wealthy, minority world interests, first, by normalising a stage-by-stage pathway to western-style development and then insisting that others must follow that way. As an alternative, Robinson stresses the importance of a fresh curiosity to cities and urbanisation processes that is open to learning from difference. Paddison and McCann describe her position:

> Robinson ... is at best indifferent about Chicago as a point of reference in urban studies. It certainly should not be a privileged referent, she argues. Instead, she suggests that by being open to forms of analysis undertaken in very different places and being willing to learn from their findings and apply their approaches, it is possible to develop more cosmopolitan urban studies in which the innovativeness and mutually constitutive interconnectedness of all places are acknowledged, valorised, researched and used to inform a more worldly urban studies.
>
> (Paddison and McCann, 2014: 224)

This suggests a very different starting point for thinking about urbanisation and the character of cities as social worlds, both, because it renders any and all cities as worthy of enquiry in their own right and, by extension, there is much that we can learn from them. Consequently, Robinson speaks of the whole class as comprising *Ordinary Cities*; thereby rendering any particular city's ordinariness as *extra*-ordinary and a legitimate focus for our curiosity. This invites a more ethnographic encounter at eye-level that challenges the dominance afforded grand-plan theory, such as Burgess' concentric rings and the claim to detached authority built into its view from above. As example, Robinson challenges Louis Wirth's concept of anomie as hallmark disposition of the disinterested urbanite through empirical evidence from anthropological studies of highly industrialised city life in Zambia. She demonstrates that despite the industrial modernity of Zambia's Copperbelt, social relations are far from coldly indifferent to others, rather their social relations demonstrate a cosmopolitan openness that readily embraces diversity: … we learn that urbanites have generated fictive kin, eagerly sought to make connections where none really existed, carefully nurtured neighbours and family, built communities and defended difference' (Robinson, 2006: 9).

Reflection on the post-colonial scholarship of Robinson suggests commonalities with the social constructionism of a broad multidisciplinary coalition of social scientists and humanists contributing to the (New) Social Studies of Childhood (e.g. Blundell, 2012, 2014, 2016; Jenks, 2005; Kehily, 2009; Moran-Ellis, 2010; James and Prout, 2015) and post-colonial childhood theorists (De Boeck and Honwara, 2005; Shallwani, 2010; Taylor, 2013; Taylor and Pacini-Ketchabaw, 2016). Although apparently disparate fields, there is a shared commitment to rejecting essentialist approaches to the city on the one hand, and the child on the other. Further, each challenges the dominance of developmental theories that account for the process of both urbanisation and growing up as a series of stages or steps along a singular pathway by which normative outcomes are calibrated and unwelcome deviations can be disciplined and re-directed. For post-colonial critics these commonalities are not merely coincidental or *ad hoc*, but are rooted in the ways that western interests attempt to rationalise diverse phenomena so that they meet their goals and achieve colonial dominance; for them, both urban studies and the institutions of modern childhood reproduce the interests of the minority world, and naturalise its wealth and material privilege. This overlooks the multiplicity of other possibilities for human social and economic organisation and not only fails to grasp the complexity of children's relationships to schooling, work and family/community, but also tends to promote unhelpful normative judgements about their suitability (Kjørholt, 2007). Globalisation appears to promote convergence through which economic conditions and the production of employable humans through education are brought into alignment; however, this coming together also reveals differences and conflicts demanding dialogic openness in diverse places and multiple scales.

Before concluding the chapter, its analysis has relied on recognising congruencies, or what mathematicians might call homologies, between what appear to be disparate phenomena. This does not mean that they are identical, but that fresh insight might be gained by looking beyond the confines of a single discipline. Sociological approaches run through the chapter, but it has also drawn on literary sources, human geography, economic and social history, philosophy and cultural studies. As such, it proposes that a readiness to take a wider look around is beneficial, and may be essential, to the study of education as a critical agent of change. With this in mind, consideration of the ordinary city directs our attention towards what might be learned from *ordinary childhoods* and understanding how children see the mutually constitutive connections within which they live – not least within education and schooling. Thus, with a nod towards Colin Ward, the *ordinary* child in the *ordinary* city becomes an invitation to be respectfully curious as researchers, and open to difference as educators, educationists and policy-makers, rather than always a problem to be solved.

Questions to consider

- Can educational provision and systems in majority world settings realistically challenge dominant western norms?
- Following on Jennifer Robinson's arguments about ordinary cities, could the concept of the *ordinary child* contribute to making changes to educational institutions and practices that respond constructively to the challenges presented by the global rise of social and political populism over recent years?

Summary

- The chapter explores the impact of urbanisation on children living, playing and learning in city environments as well as educational responses to the challenges it brings.
- The historical provenance of the trope of 'the child in the city' is discussed, along with some educational responses to the dualistic construction of urban children as either *in danger* or *dangerous* that it invites.
- Recognising that nine out of ten children now live in non-western majority-world settings, the chapter discusses challenges to the universal currency of western constructions of childhood and 'the child' found in the work of critical sociologists, children's geographers and post-colonial theorists.
- Post-colonial challenges to the dominance afforded western 'global cities' and assumptions surrounding economic developmentalism are presented, along with their concern to reveal the diverse social realities found in *ordinary cities*. Theoretical commonalities with western constructions of childhood are identified.
- Finally, the reader is encouraged to reflect on ways that a redirection of interest towards the *ordinary child* in the *ordinary city* might open up possibilities for more inclusive and diverse forms of education as humankind faces up to unprecedented challenges in the twenty-first century.

Recommended reading

Hendrick, H. (1997) *Children, Childhood and English Society, 1880-1990.* Cambridge: Cambridge University Press.
Kehily, M. J. (2013) *Understanding Childhood: A Cross-Disciplinary Approach.* Bristol: Policy Press.
Taylor, A. (2013) *Reconfiguring the Natures of Childhood.* London: Routledge.
Wells, K. (2009) *Childhood in a Global Perspective.* Cambridge: Polity Press

References

Aitken, S., Lund, R. and Kjørholt, A. T. (2007) Why children? Why now? *Children's Geographies,* **5**(1–2), pp. 3–14.
Allen, J., Massey, D. and Pile, S. (1998) *City Worlds: Understanding Cities.* London: Routledge.
Allen, M. and Nicholson, M. (1975) *Memoirs of an Uneducated Lady: Lady Allen of Hurtwood.* London: Thames and Hudson.
Benjamin, J. (1974) *Grounds for Play.* London: Imprint unknown.
Blundell, D. (2012) *Education and Constructions of Childhood.* London: Continuum.
Blundell, D. (2014) Childhood and education. In Isaacs, S., Blundell, D., Foley, A., Ginsberg, N., McDonough, B., Silverstone, D. and Young, T. (Eds.). *Social Problems in the UK: An Introduction.* Abingdon: Routledge.
Blundell, D. (2016) *Rethinking Children's Spaces and Places.* London: Bloomsbury bank.

Burns, T., Abegglen, S. and Blundell, D. (2019) Adventure play in 70s East London parts 1 and 2. Online. Available at: https://www.childinthecity.org/2019/02/19/adventure-play-in-70s-east-london-p3/ (Accessed 3 March 2019).

Châtelet, A-M. (2008) A breath of fresh air: Open air schools in Europe. In Gutman, M. and de Coninck-Smith, N. *Designing Modern Childhoods: History, Space, and the Material Culture of Children*. Piscataway: Rutgers University Press.

Collins, P. (1963) *Dickens and Education*. London: MacMillan.

De Boeck, F. and Honwara, A. (2005) Introduction: Children and youth in Africa. In Honwara, A. and De Boeck, F. (Eds.). *Makers and Breakers: Children and Youth in Post-Colonial Africa*. Oxford: James Currey.

Dickens, C. (1837) *Oliver Twist*. London: Bentley's Miscellany.

Dickens, C. (1843) *A Christmas Carol*. London: Chapman and Hall.

Engels, F. (1887) *The Condition of the Working Class in England*. New York: Sonnenschein & Co.

Foley, P. (2001) The development of child health and welfare services in England (1900-1948). In Foley, P., Roche, J., and Tucker, S. (Eds.). *Children in Society: Contemporary Theory, Policy and Practice*. Basingstoke: Palgrave.

Hendrick, H. (2015) Constructions and reconstructions of British childhood: An interpretive survey, 1800 to the present. In James, A., and Prout, A. (Eds.). *Constructing and Reconstructing Childhood: Contemporary Issues in the Sociological Study of Childhood*. Abingdon: Routledge.

Jacobs, J. (1961) *The Death and Life of Great American Cities*. New York: Random House.

James, A. and Prout, A. (Eds.) (2015) *Constructing and Reconstructing Childhood: Contemporary Issues in the Sociological Study of Childhood*. Abingdon: Routledge.

Jenks, C. (2005) *Childhood*. Abingdon: Routledge.

Kehily, M. J. (2009) *An Introduction to Childhood Studies*. Maidenhead: Open University Press.

Kjørholt, A. T. (2007) Childhood as a symbolic space: Searching for authentic voices in the era of globalisation. *Children's Geographies*, **5**(1–2), pp. 29–42.

Kozlovsky, R. (2008) Adventure playgrounds and post-war reconstruction. In Gutman, M. and de Coninck-Smith, N. (Eds.). *Designing Modern Childhoods: History, Space, and the Material Culture of Children*. Piscataway: Rutgers University Press.

Lewis, S. L. and Maslin, M. A. (2018) *The Human Planet: How we Created the Anthropocene*. London: Pelican.

Locke, J, (1693) *Some Thoughts Concerning Education*. London: A. and J. Churchill.

Marx, K. (1867) *Das Kapital: Kritik de politischen oekonomie*. Hamburg: Verlag von Otto Meisner.

Marx, K. and Engels, F. (1848) *The Communist Manifesto*. London: The Workers Educational Association.

Miles, D. (2006) *The Tribes of Britain*. London: Phoenix.

Mills, R. (2000) Perspectives of childhood. In Mills, J. and Mills, R. (Eds.). *Childhood Studies: A Reader in Perspectives on Childhood*. London: Routledge.

Moran-Ellis, J. (2010) Reflections on the sociology of childhood in the UK. *Current Sociology*, **58**(2), pp. 86–205.

Mumford, L. and Miller, D. L. (Eds.). (1995) *The Lewis Mumford Reader*. Athens: The University of Georgia Press.

Paddison, R. and McCann, E. (Eds.) (2014) *Cities and Social Change: Encounters with Contemporary Urbanism*. London: Sage.

Park, R. E., Burgess, E. and McKenzie, R. (1925) *The City*. Chicago: University of Chicago Press.

Robinson, J. (2006) *Ordinary Cities: Between Modernity and Development*. London: Routledge.

Shallwani, S. (2010) Racism and imperialism in the child development discourse: Deconstructing 'developmentally appropriate practice'. In Cannella, G. S. and Soto, L. S. (Eds.). *Childhoods: A Handbook*. New York: Peter Lang.

Taylor, A. (2013) *Reconfiguring the Natures of Childhood*. Abingdon: Routledge.

Taylor, A. and Pacini-Ketchabaw, K. (2016) *Unsettling the Colonial Places and Spaces of Early Childhood Education (Changing Images of Early Childhood)*. Abingdon: Routledge.

Tomes, N. (1985) From useful to useless: The changing social value of children. In Zelitzer, V. (Ed.) *Pricing the Priceless Child: The Changing Social Value of Children*. New York: Basic Books.

UNDESA (2018) 2018 Revision of world urbanization prospects. Online. Available at: https://www.un.org/development/desa/publications/2018-revision-of-world-urbanization-prospects.html (Accessed 7 January 2019).

UNESCO (2007) Global trend towards urbanisation. Online. Available at: http://www.unesco.org/education/tlsf/mods/theme_c/popups/mod13t01s009.html (Accessed 3 March 2019).

Ward, C. (1978) *The Child in the City*. London: Bedford Square Press.

World Bank (2018) Urban Population (% of total). Online. Available at: https://data.worldbank.org/indicator/SP.URB.TOTL.IN.ZS (Accessed 3 March 2019).

12 Enacting the international vision of inclusive education: A UK case study of profound and multiple learning difficulties

Ben Simmons

Introduction

This chapter explores the inclusive education debate as it relates to children with profound and multiple learning difficulties (PMLD). It illuminates a fundamental tension between international policy which promotes inclusive education as a human right (United Nations, 2006), and the challenge of including learners with profound intellectual impairments in the current neoliberal education system (Tomlinson, 2017). This tension is examined through two interpretations of disability found in the field of Disability Studies: the medical model and the social model (Goodley, 2011). A medical model interpretation holds that children with PMLD are excluded from the mainstream because they lack the intellectual ability to learn at the same pace as other children. A social model interpretation holds that children with PMLD are excluded because mainstream education has not been designed with the needs of children with PMLD in mind, resulting in a range of barriers that prevent children with PMLD from meaningful participation. Proponents of the social model of disability call for a radical reform of the education system to reflect the diverse needs of all learners, including children with PMLD (Baglieri and Shapiro, 2017; Greenstein 2016).

According to international policy, one of the key outcomes of inclusive education is social cohesion (UNESCO, 2002) defined in this chapter in terms of a sense of belonging, shared identity and social cooperation (Fonseca *et al.*, 2019; Simmons, 2020). If inclusive education is to be realised for children with PMLD, then any radical reform of the education system must begin with an understanding of how schools can foster social cohesion amongst pupils. This chapter presents research evidence that illuminates the possible conditions of social cohesion, which include specialist staff who perform a dual role of supporting the emerging communication skills of children with PMLD, whilst also providing mainstream school peers with expert knowledge about how each child with PMLD uniquely communicates. The findings also suggest that children benefit from protected time and space to experiment with communication strategies, play together, develop friendships and share roles and responsibilities. The chapter concludes by suggesting that if inclusion is to be actualised for children with PMLD we need to move beyond narrow concepts of inclusion as assimilation into a neoliberal education system, and begin to reimagine inclusive education as a process of enacting the conditions that can lead to social belonging.

Inclusive education

The meaning of 'inclusive education' is highly contested and there are (many) competing interpretations, definitions and models (Armstrong *et al.*, 2010). Inclusive education is often associated with diverse groups of students learning together in a mainstream school. This 'simple' understanding of inclusion focuses on good classroom practice whereby teachers make adaptations and adjustments so that all learners experience educational success (Hodkinson, 2016). Simple models of inclusion describe technical solutions that allow children to be assimilated into an unchanged education system (e.g. through the provision of additional resources and differentiated pedagogy). By contrast, a more radical interpretation of inclusion takes aim at the education system itself, and calls into question the meaning and purpose of education. Radical interpretations of inclusion have their roots in emancipatory movements of the 1980s and 1990s whereby parents, teachers and children expressed dissatisfaction about the two-tier education system (i.e. segregated special schools or integrative mainstream schools not designed for children with complex disabilities). A radical interpretation of inclusion is a reform programme that ultimately aims to restructure the education system (Armstrong *et al.*, 2010).

Inclusive education has received international support, particularly from intergovernmental organisations such as the United Nations and its agencies who have produced numerous documents enshrining the right of all children to a mainstream education. For example, the *Salamanca Statement* (UNESCO, 1994), adopted by 92 governments and 25 international organisations, set the policy agenda for inclusion on an international scale (Goodley, 2011) and declared that inclusion was 'essential to human dignity and to the exercise and enjoyment of human rights' (11). The *Salamanca Statement* also linked inclusion to economic benefits, claiming that inclusive education 'improve[s] the efficiency and ultimately the cost effectiveness of the entire education system' (ix). The *Convention of the Rights of Person with Disabilities* claimed that inclusion can 'maximize academic and social development' (United Nations, 2006: 17) whilst the *Declaration on Cultural Diversity* claimed that 'policies for the inclusion and participation of all citizens [act] as guarantees of social cohesion, the vitality of civil society and peace (UNESCO, 2002: 13). More recently, the *Incheon Declaration and Framework for Action* declared that inclusive education was 'essential for peace, tolerance, [and] human fulfilment' (UNESCO 2015: 7).

Despite international support for inclusive education, there is ongoing resistance to the view that mainstream education is appropriate for *all* children. For example, Mary Warnock – a champion of 'integration' in the 1970s (DES, 1978) – suggested that some children find it 'impossible' (2010: 33) to participate in mainstream schools, and that inclusion is better understood in terms of children 'being involved in a common enterprise of learning, rather than being necessarily under the same roof' (ibid: 32). This view has been extended to children with PMLD who are the focus of this chapter (Imray and Colley, 2017).

Profound and multiple learning difficulties

'PMLD' is a label used in the UK to refer to children who are said to experience the severest of impairments to cognition resulting in significant developmental delay. A review of the literature in this field has demonstrated that the cognitive abilities of children with PMLD are often compared to those of the neonate or infant insofar as children with PMLD are described as oper-ating at the preverbal stages of development (Simmons and Watson, 2014). For example, children with PMLD are understood as being 'pre-volitional': they lack free will or agency and cannot move with intent (Farrell, 2004); 'pre-contingency aware': they do not show awareness of cause–effect relationships (Ware, 2003); 'pre-intersubjective': they do not represent other people as subjects 'like me', and cannot differentiate between subject and object; 'pre-symbolic' or 'pre-intentional': they do not intentionally communicate meaning to others (Coupe O'Kane and Goldbart, 1998); and 'stereotypic in behaviour': they display reflexive, non-volitional behaviour (Tang *et al.*, 2003). In addition to profoundly delayed cognitive development, children with PMLD are also said to experi-ence a range of additional impairments, including physical impairments (Neilson *et al.*, 2000) and sensory impairments (Vlaskamp and Cuppen-Fonteine, 2007), mental health and complex med-ical conditions (Pawlyn and Carnaby, 2009). Hence, children with PMLD are described as being dependent on others for the most rudimentary care needs and are deemed to require a lifetime of support (Tadema and Vlaskamp, 2010). With optimal intervention, it is hoped that children with PMLD will make some progress through the pre-verbal stages of development.

Relatively few children with PMLD attend mainstream schools, and it appears that the older children with PMLD get, the less likely they are to access a mainstream education. In England it is estimated that out of approximately 9,000 children with PMLD, 82 per cent attend special school, five per cent attend mainstream primary school and three per cent attend mainstream secondary school (Salt, 2010). Lyons and Arthur-Kelly (2014: 446) suggest that segregated provision for chil-dren with PMLD is an international trend and that 'if they [children with PMLD] have access to any school education, are educated in "special" schools or classes by "special" educators'. Advocates of special-school provision argue that children with PMLD are too cognitively impaired to engage with the mainstream and require developmentally-appropriate curricula, pedagogy, and resources found in special schools (Imray and Colley, 2017).

Conceptualising (profound) disability: The medical model and the social model

Definitions of PMLD are typically rooted in developmental psychology which present a medicalised and deficit-based account of children with the PMLD label. However, by drawing conceptual resources from Disability Studies we can redefine the meaning and location of disability, and in doing so shed new light on why children with PMLD are excluded from the mainstream. Disability Studies is a broad field of theory, research and practice that challenges the common view of disability as personal tragedy (Goodley, 2011). Its roots can be found in the disability rights movements which emerged during the 1960s when disabled people, 'like feminists, African Americans, and gay and lesbian activists … insisted that their bodies did not render them defective, [and] could even be sources of political, sexual, and artistic strength' (Neilsen, 2012: 160, in Baglieri and Shapiro, 2017: 5). UK activists in the 1970s have been particularly influential in the development of Disability Studies, with groups such as the *Union of the Physically Impaired Against Segregation and the Disability Alliance* making key distinctions between medical and sociological accounts of disability.

The medical model of disability is the dominant perspective about disability in our society and equates disability with an 'abnormal' or 'disordered' body or mind (Baglieri and Shapiro, 2017).

A disability is a professionally diagnosed condition which is characterised in terms of functional limitations, meaning that the disabled person is unable to independently perform basic tasks required to fulfil daily routines that may be taken for granted by non-disabled people (Barnes and Mercer, 2010). Societies predisposed to understanding disability through the prism of the medical model view disability as a personal tragedy which requires medical intervention (treatment, rehabilitation and/or cure) to make the body function as 'normal' as possible (Baglieri and Shapiro, 2017; Goodley, 2011). From a medical model perspective, a person's disability is the main reason for their social exclusion.

The social model of disability presents a counter-perspective to the medical model by redefining the meaning of disability and the problem to be addressed. The social model rests heavily on a distinction between impairment and disability. Impairment is described as a form of bodily, sensory or mental difference that is often defined within a medical context (Goodley, 2011). By contrast, the social model defined disability as:

> The disadvantage or restriction of activity caused by a contemporary social organisation which takes little or no account of people who have physical impairments and thus excludes them from participation in the mainstream of social activities.
>
> (UPIAS, 1975, in Shakespeare, 2017: 197)

The social model defines disability not in terms of bodily difference, but in terms of how society responds to those differences. Disability is a culturally, socially and politically produced form of social exclusion which stems from the way in which society creates barriers that prevent disabled people from social participation. From a social model perspective, it is society that disables people with impairments (Shakespeare, 2017). Hence, whereas the medical model locates the problem in the individual and the solution in the treatment of the individual, the social model aims to remove society's disabling barriers (Swain *et al.*, 1993).

Medical model and social model concepts of disability have been applied to the context of special and inclusive education. Special schools are conceptualised as embodying the medical model of disability insofar as children are excluded or extracted from the mainstream and treated through educational interventions until they are capable of independently participating with their non-disabled counterparts:

> Students perceived as having problems, like something broken, are sent to resource rooms, special classes, even special schools or institutions, to be repaired and later returned. Unlike a repair shop, however, many students in special education – indeed the preponderance of them never escape the special label and placement […] They stay in the repair shop.
>
> (Biklen *et al.*, 1989: 8, in Baglieri and Shapiro, 2017: 6).

By contrast, the social model of disability has been aligned with inclusive education which shifts the focus away from how best to remediate disabled children to an examination of how the school environment can support or disable young people. The social model of inclusive education prioritises the removal of obstacles that prevent access to mainstream education: 'it is about removing all forms of barriers to access and learning for all children who are experiencing disadvantage' (Barton and Armstrong, 2001: 708). Of particular importance for those who embrace the social model is the development of diverse communities. By focusing primarily on the diagnosis and remediation of impairments the medical model limits the experiences and social opportunities of children. However, by 'framing disability in its social dimensions, attention is instead focused on how schools and curriculum may be constructed and reformed to enable students with disabilities to gain access to learning and participation with their peers' (Baglieri and Shapiro, 2017: 7).

From a social model perspective, children with PMLD experience social exclusion, not because of their learning impairments but because of discriminatory practices which prevent children with PMLD accessing a common curriculum. Segregated education (special schools) contribute to the oppression of disabled people by removing them from wider society. Instead of trying to change children with PMLD (curing them of their profound developmental delay), advocates of the social model of disability argue that there should be a focus on removing the barriers which prevent disabled people from participating in mainstream social life. These barriers include physical barriers to social spaces, discriminatory practices and, and private prejudice. However, a more radical reading of the social model of disability holds that inclusive education should not be understood as a simple technical solution to managing or assimilating children who struggle to 'fit' into an existing school system, but as an ongoing education reform programme that challenges the meaning of education (Armstrong *et al.*, 2010). From this perspective, inclusive education is a doomed project unless we call into question the neoliberal ideology that shapes our current school system.

Inclusion into what? A social model critique of neoliberal education

Neoliberalism is a free market ideology that is heavily implicated in the educational policy and practice of late-capitalist, industrialised society. In such a society the production of profit is the basic organising principle of economic life, and this requires the disciplining of labour power to increase capital accumulation (Armstrong *et al.*, 2010). Businesses and employers are freed from state intervention in order to allow increased productivity and economic growth. The state is 'rolled back', welfare spending is reduced, and public services are deregulated, privatised, contracted out or shaped by business principles (Goodley, 2011). From a neoliberal perspective, the function of the education system is to provide a steady supply of young people who have developed work-related competencies, knowledge and dispositions that allow individuals to compete in the labour market (Tomlinson, 2017).

Central to the development of education policy is the concept of a 'knowledge economy' which treats knowledge as a high-value commodity (Ball, 2008). In our current economic context, knowledge is overtaking capital and energy as the primary wealth-creating asset (Greenstein, 2016). The National Curriculum (for England)(DfE, 2014) plays a central role in the knowledge economy insofar as it prescribes the body of knowledge deemed necessary for economic competitiveness. Drawing on Freire (1972), Greenstein (2016) argues that the National Curriculum presents as an objective body of facts that lends itself to the banking model of education, whereby teachers posit facts in the minds of learners who are required to patiently receive, memorise and repeat what is prescribed. Literacy and numeracy are privileged and rewarded whilst other subject such as art and dance are minimised, and the 'vital human capacities' (Greenstein, 2016: 50) such as love, care and solidarity fail to be recognised or appreciated. The increasingly narrow curriculum is linked to the standards agenda, defined in terms of a continual driving up of attainment standards, workforce skills and ultimately the nation's competitiveness in a globalised economy (Ainscow *et al.*, 2006; Hodkinson, 2016). Schools are assessed according to the collective attainment of students (the results of which are published as league tables) and schools that fail to achieve government standards are penalised through funding retention and closure (Greenstein, 2016). What emerges in this context is a fundamental contradiction for children with PMLD. On the one hand education policy advocates an inclusive education whereby diverse students are educated in the same room, with adaptation or differentiation of pedagogy, curriculum and assessment in order to make the learning objectives accessible to all. On the other hand, educational policy promotes the rapid learning of facts and the development of business entrepreneurship deemed necessary to support the economy. This leads to a narrow curriculum and a fast-paced, information processing or banking model of education which is inappropriate for children with PMLD (Greenstein, 2016; Imray and Colley, 2017). Hence, there is a mismatch between the neoliberal ideologies of schooling that aim to produce obedient citizens for the global market economy (Greenstein, 2016) and the needs of children with PMLD who are defined as not being able to engage cognitively in the National Curriculum. What emerges from this tension is a view that inclusion for children with PMLD is impossible because of the pathology of 'PMLD'.

From a social model perspective, the failure to include children with PMLD stems not simply from a lack of appropriate 'environmental' adaptations, but from an education system that prioritises the acquisition of subject knowledge, competition between individuals, schools and nations, and the segregation of children who cannot keep up with similarly aged peers. Such a system works against the goal of creating social cohesion through inclusive education (UNESCO, 2002) by creating the conditions of exclusion for certain groups of children (such as children with PMLD).

If a key goal of inclusion is to maximise social development and tolerance (United Nations, 2006; UNESCO, 2015) then an examination of how the education system can support the social inclusion of children with PMLD is needed. The following section describes a research project that examined the social opportunities that children with PMLD can experience across both mainstream schools and special schools, which in turn sheds light on the complexity of social inclusion.

Refocusing the inclusion debate: Researching the social

The research presented in this chapter comes from a three-year research project funded through a British Academy Postdoctoral Fellowship (2014–2017) which investigated the social inclusion of children with PMLD who experienced both special and mainstream educational opportunities. The research aimed to (i) investigate how different educational settings (mainstream and special) afforded different opportunities for social interaction, (ii) examine how children with PMLD respond to different opportunities, and (iii) explore how different opportunities impact on the growth of social awareness and communication skills of children with PMLD. The data presented is based on an analysis of three children with the pseudonyms of Emma, Harry and Charlie. Emma was five years old, Harry was eight years old and Charlie was ten years old during data collection. Emma and Harry attended the same special school in England and were educated in the school's PMLD class. The PMLD class doubled up as a reception class for younger children with special educational needs. For the purposes of this project, Emma and Harry attended an age-equivalent class in a local mainstream school for one day a week (these placements were set up for the project, but continued after the project had ended, which indicates their successful nature). Each child was observed once a week in the mainstream school and once a week in a special school for ten weeks (20 observations per child). Emma and Harry participated in the project at different times (Emma in the autumn term, and Harry in the winter). A special school teaching assistant (SSTA) accompanied Emma and Harry on each visit. Charlie's entire class attended mainstream school one afternoon a week. All the staff from Charlie's class supported the mainstream placement. Charlie's school had been running mainstream placements for all children for many years.

The methodology resembled a participatory or ethnographic approach which has been described extensively elsewhere (e.g. Simmons and Watson, 2014, 2017; Simmons, 2018). Prior to under-taking fieldwork, the researcher engaged in pre-observation focus groups with school staff and semi-structured interviews with the children's parents. The aim was to explore the children's interests, abilities and methods of communication by consulting those who knew the children intimately. This led to the development of an initial lens through which to interpret and understand the children's action. Participatory observation was undertaken to develop understandings of the children's behaviours by working with them in context. Participatory observation helped the researcher to develop trust and rapport with members of staff and provided the researcher with opportunities for informal discussion with staff in real time. These informal conversations allowed the researcher to share and discuss his interpretations of Charlie's, Harry's and Emma's actions, ask questions and seek out staff members' expertise and wisdom (e.g. to resolve the researcher's confusion about the meaning of newly-observed or unexpected behaviours).

Research data primarily consisted of written fieldnotes or 'vignettes' composed during periods of non-participatory observation. Vignettes are rich and prosaic renderings of fieldnotes about social interactions. They have a story-like structure and adhere to chronological flow. Vignettes are restricted to a particular place, time and actor (or group of actors), and can vary from a few lines of descriptions to several paragraphs. When opportunities for social interaction were observed, the researcher would write detailed, descriptive accounts as the interaction unfolded, paying attention to who initiated the interaction and how, the actions of the interactive participants over time and contextual variables such as location, context of the interaction and the objects involved. The data were thematically analysed, the findings of which are presented below.

Findings

Special school interactions: Teaching to communicate and care-based routines

Each child participating in the research was described by teaching staff as functioning at the pre-verbal stages of communication. Given this, teachers and teaching assistants regularly focused on developing children's emerging social cognition and communication skills. Daily routines involved staff working one-to-one 'dyadically' with children and encouraging them to express a preference for an object or event (e.g. Emma was asked to smile at food to express 'want', or to turn away from food to express 'not want'). Children were sometimes asked to make a choice between two objects (e.g. Charlie was encouraged to choose between a flashing ball or a tambourine by prolonged looking at an object). Some children were encouraged to request prolonged access to an object or event by vocalising (or rather, shouting) upon request. (e.g. staff would lay Harry down on a trampoline and bounce him up and down until he laughed. They would then stop bouncing until he shouted loudly, at which point the bouncing would resume). In each of these examples the teaching staff aimed to develop children's awareness that they can have control over the physical environ- ment by communicating their preferences and choices to others. If the children failed to express a preference, choice, or request for more, teaching staff would employ a range of prompts, including verbal prompts (e.g. repeating a question using dramatic intonation: 'Do you want *more* bouncing, Harry?'), gestural and visual prompts (e.g. staff would wiggle two objects in front of Charlie's face to get his attention), and physical prompts (e.g. staff dabbed yogurt on Emma's lips to see if she would lick her lips with delight or express disgust at the flavour). The vignette below embodies this style of interaction:

> It's lunchtime and Charlie is wheeled to the end of the table. The other children around him open up their lunchboxes and begin to eat. Charlie stares at the ceiling and appears to be daydreaming. The TA [teaching assistant] sits down beside him, suggests that Charlie must be hungry, then holds up two pictures – a yogurt and a drink bottle. She tries to get his attention by clearing her throat ('ahem!'), repeating and singing his name (|Charlie, Charlie, Chaaaaarlie....') and tapping her feet on the ground. He continues to stare at the ceiling until the TA tickles his tummy, which makes him jump and gasp. He looks forward and has a grumpy expression on his face. The TA chuckles at his response. She asks him if he would like a drink or a yogurt. Charlie doesn't appear to choose anything so she wiggles the water bottle in front of his face, then a spoon. Charlie shouts, and his gaze moves between the children eating and the objects in front of his face. He stares at the drink bottle and licks his lips. The TA celebrates ('Good choice, Charlie!') and puts the bottle to his lips. He drinks.

In addition to a formal dyadic approach to teaching communication skills during lesson time, spe- cial school staff regularly engaged in a range of care-based routines such as providing comfort to children by massaging aching arms and legs, helping children eat and drink, get changed, go to the toilet and administer medication. The above vignette demonstrates how care-based routines provided a context for teaching communication skills. However, not all interactions aimed to teach communication skills, care-based routines often revolved around reassurance (e.g. staff would offer verbal reassurance, speak in a soothing tone and narrate what was happening (e.g. 'We're just clipping you in the hoist, Harry. Are you ready? One, two, three… up we go…'). Staff described an on-going 'battle' with managing the side-effects of medication. Whilst medication was deemed imperative to sustain bodily functioning and reduce discomfort, it also made the children heavily drowsy. Staff would attempt to negate the effects of the medication by singing to children, talking to them using dramatic intonation, 'shake-to-wake' (e.g. rubbing and shaking limbs) as well as other forms of physical stimulation, including massage. This frustrated children who verbally protested (they exhibited startle responses before shouting out loud in a grumpy manner and turning away from staff trying to wake them).

Outside of the special school: The fluidity of staff interaction styles

Whilst the weight of the data suggests that staff interactions in the special school were largely functional (i.e. oriented towards the development of children's emerging communication skills) and/or care-based, the interactive style changed during school trips or when supporting children with PMLD in the mainstream. When on school trips (e.g. to the beach or woods), staff interactions were more pluralistic or group-based (e.g. involving children and several members of staff interacting at the same time). These interactions were playful in nature and incorporated games (e.g. playing 'Piggy in the middle' by throwing a beach ball over Harry) or teasing (e.g. during a trip to the beach staff sang 'dip him in the sea!'). There was clear evidence of group effect, meaning that the group as a whole was excited, smiling and/or laughing. These playful interactions lacked pedagogic purpose, were often spontaneous (not timetabled or planned) and joyful in nature:

> Harry is lying on the beach and having fun. The teacher pretends to jump on Harry before hovering above him on all fours. He smiles lots and verbalises loudly whilst looking up at the teacher above him. The sun comes out from behind a cloud and Harry jumps. He vocalises and smiles, whilst changing the modulation of his voice ('lalalala-ug-aaaaaah'). Harry is engaged in group affection – he is the focus of interaction and affection and looks around at the staff. Staff around him joke and ask if he's having fun. Harry responds by smiling and vocalises loudly and the staff laugh. A teaching assistant pours warm sand over Harry's feet and she giggles. He continues smile and vocalises ('aaaaah').

In the above vignette Harry is excited and focused on the adults around him. Harry is not simply surrounded by a group, but the group form around him because of his interactions with the teacher. He acts as a beacon or focus of attention (the subject of affection) and the adults near appear mutually engaged and happy.

Whilst the interactions between Harry and special school staff during school trips can be described as informal and playful, interactions between school staff and children with PMLD in the mainstream school were functional and pedagogical in nature. Whilst some interactions resembled those described in the special school (i.e. development of communication skills and care-based routines), a central theme that emerged during analysis of the mainstream data was 'narrated bodily appropriation'. Narrated bodily appropriation refers to a particular style of dyadic physical interaction whereby SSTA would move or control Charlie's, Harry's or Emma's bodies (or, more specifically, body parts such as limbs) in accordance with the contextual demands of the situation. If a teacher asked a question, the specialist staff would raise the hands of children with PMLD to indicate a response (e.g. the SSTA raised Harry's hand when the teacher asked the class 'Who would like to play outside?'). During literacy the SSTA would play an audiobook for Emma whilst holding Emma's finger to point to the words and pictures on the physical page. The SSTA raised Charlie's hand and hit them on a drum during music. The physical control of children's limbs was also observed during care-based interactions. If Emma's 'ticks' appeared to be resulting in harm (e.g. her skin began to redden after rubbing her face too much) the SSTA would put splints on Emma's arms to prevent her from reaching her nose. Charlie would slump in his chair and put his chin on his chest when he was tired and/or uninterested, and his SSTA would sit him up and sometimes hold his head up so he would face whoever or whatever he was meant to be paying attention to (a teacher, an interactive whiteboard, etc.) These forms of interaction were typically narrated, meaning that the interactions were accompanied by a description of what was about to happen and why. The SSTA would also issue verbal instructions (e.g. 'Sit up please'), ask questions ('Did you like the story?') and offer lots of praise (e.g. 'Good looking, Harry!').

Peer interaction in the mainstream: Embodying specialist styles and naturalistic engagement

During the research project there was very little observed interaction between the children with PMLD and other children in the special schools, outside of greetings or farewells at the beginning or end of the day. By contrast, the research data described a range of interactions between children with PMLD and the mainstream children. SSTAs played a central role in supporting these interactions, particularly at the beginning of the project. SSTAs would support interaction by sitting children with PMLD next to mainstream peers and giving the PMLD children the same material to use (pens, paper, musical instruments, rulers, paintbrushes, jigsaw pieces). The SSTAs would celebrate the mainstream school peers' achievements with the children with PMLD (e.g. when a group finished completing a jigsaw puzzle in a reception class, an SSTA raised Emma's hands and cheered, or told peers that Emma liked her paintings). Peers would be invited to sit beside children with PMLD and given explicit communication strategies to help peers interact with PMLD children (e.g. 'Tell her your name.' 'Tell her what you've done today'. 'Can you choose a story for Emma?'). The SSTAs suggested how to play with the PMLD children (e.g. 'Can you roll the ball to Emma?' 'Emma likes to have her hands held'). Sometimes the SSTAs would provide manual support for the children with PMLD so that they could participate in other children's games (e.g. Charlie was sitting on the carpet, leaning back on the SSTA so she supported his weight, whilst she helped Charlie roll a ball to other children hand-on-hand). Peers received praise and encouragement for interacting with children with PMLD, and the SSTA would answer children's questions (e.g. 'Why is she in a wheelchair?' 'Can Harry speak?' 'Does Charlie understand what he's supposed to do?'). Sometimes the SSTA would play games that attracted the attention of groups of children (such as Emma's SSTA blowing bubbles in the playground). What emerged from this explicit support was a style of peer interaction that was specialist in nature. Without seeking permission, peers began to assume the role of the SSTA during lessons and to employ similar interaction strategies as the SSTAs. For example, peers began to help children with PMLD through hand-on-hand support during writing or painting, engaged in 'shake-to-wake' (e.g. rubbing the shoulders, or wiggling the arms and legs of sleepy PMLD children to wake them up), and began to use verbal and physical prompts if the children with PMLD did not respond in a desired way (e.g. Harry was asked whether he would like to taste pineapple or banana, and when he did not respond the children repeated the question in more dramatic tone, provided time for Harry to reply, etc.).

Whilst peers developed specialist communication strategies to engage with PMLD children, they also engaged in their own rich and diverse forms of communication, particularly as they became more confident over time. The theme of 'interaction-for-interaction's-sake' describes this data. During this style of interaction mainstream peers would recontextualise classroom resources in order to interact with PMLD children. For example, they would tickle Harry's nose with a paintbrush to gain his attention or make animals out of playdough for Harry to squeeze. Charlie was given a tambourine during a music lesson and played 'tug of war' with peers who attempted to prise it from his hands (resulting in much laughter from both Charlie and peers). Peers would play 'hide and seek' or 'tag' with and through PMLD children, sometimes running away in the playground pushing the children with PMLD so they would not get caught, or hiding behind their wheelchairs. Harry and Emma became the audience for peers who sang, danced and pulled silly faces to make Harry and Emma laugh. During these interactions Harry (and eventually Emma) were excited, alert, smiling and observant. Peers in the mainstream would give children with PMLD objects of affection (friendship bracelets, daisy chains, home-made cards, party invites) and interact in physical and affectionate ways (e.g. hugging children with PMLD, stroking their arms whilst saying 'hello', putting their ears on Harry's chest to determine if he was hiccupping or pay attention to how tense his body was during hugging). Children would rub Harry's arms to help warm him up, tuck in Emma's poncho if it started to rain, and report if Charlie was being sick.

Physical exchanges sometimes appeared subversive. During carpet time, peers were expected to sit still and quietly whilst watching and listening to the teacher. Whilst peers typically did this, they still engaged with Harry and Emma in non-verbal ways, such as holding their hands, rubbing their legs, resting against their wheelchairs and legs, using Harry's out-stretched legs as a 'table' to rest their whiteboards on. Harry would watch children raise their hands, locate the source of children speaking, and become increasingly happy and eventually shouting out in excitement. During these moments Harry began to develop new forms of symbolic communication – he would straighten his arm out and open his palm which was taken as an attempt to initiate interaction. Children would hold his hand and stroke his palm, much to Harry's delight.

Discussion

This chapter has described the tension between the international vision of inclusive education (e.g. United Nations, 2006; UNESCO, 2015) and the idea of a neoliberal education which creates the conditions for *exclusion* (Greenstein, 2016; Tomlinson, 2017). The extent to which inclusion is achievable for children with PMLD is called into question when debate about inclusive education revolves around a 'simple' definition of inclusion which involves making adaptations to classroom environments to support the participation of children with PMLD in the enterprise of subject know-ledge acquisition (Imray and Colley, 2017; Warnock, 2010). This simple definition of inclusion risks invoking a medical model of disability which suggests that no amount of environmental adaptations can facilitate children with PMLD acquiring subject knowledge at the same rate as their non-disabled counterparts. If inclusion means the assimilation of children with PMLD into an unchanging neo-liberal mainstream education then the inclusion project may never succeed.

However, if definitions of inclusive education embody a more radical social model interpretation which calls into question the very meaning of education, then we can begin to imagine alternative arrangements. Radical inclusionists call for a reform of the education system as a whole to reflect the diverse learning needs of all children, including children with PMLD (Baglieri and Shapiro, 2017; Goodley, 2011). If we begin with the idea that inclusive education aims to foster social cohesion, as suggested by international policy (UNESCO, 2002), then for inclusion to succeed we need to develop understanding of the conditions that lead to social cohesion. In this chapter social cohesion was defined in terms of a sense of belonging, shared identity and social cooperation (Fonseca *et al.*, 2019; Simmons, 2020). The research findings presented above suggest that this requires deployment of specialist staff who can support the emerging communication skills of children with PMLD, whilst also providing mainstream school peers with knowledge about the communication strategies of children with PMLD. This led to mainstream peers supporting Harry, Emma and Charlie by assuming the role of a specialist TA (e.g. by providing hand-on-hand support, or engaging in care-based routines such as tucking in Emma's poncho in the cold weather). However, the findings also suggest the importance of providing children with protected time and place to experiment with communication strategies, play together, develop friendships and share roles and responsibilities. Mainstream peers played games with Harry, Emma and Charlie, sang and danced for them, gave them objects of affection and engaged in physical interaction such as hugging, stroking arms and playing tug-of-war. The children with PMLD responded positively, with smiles, laughter, increased openness to mainstream peers and clear evidence of increased alertness. Descriptions of such social inclusion are largely absent from the inclusion debate for children with PMLD, though they appear to offer much promise for thinking about the meaning of social cohesion and how this can be supported.

One of the arguments for the segregation of children with PMLD is that special school staff have training and expertise to work with profoundly disabled children. However, the findings of this research suggest that specialist staff were not consistent in their interaction style with children with PMLD, but instead appeared to be influenced by the context of the interaction. The special school staff interactions were timetabled (planned for), normative (in the sense of developing children's interaction ability according with an early developmental stage) and functional (the interactions aimed to help children develop communication skills). During school trips the interactions were playful, spontaneous and rarely embodied the pedagogical style of interaction found in the special school. By contrast, in the mainstream school the specialist staff attempted to support children with PMLD to access the mainstream curriculum (e.g. through narrated bodily appropriation, such as hand-on-hand support with writing). These different interactive styles appear to emerge under different environmental conditions. Staff interactions in different schools (mainstream/special) were shaped by the routines, objects and curriculums on offer. However, during school trips and away from routines practices, curricular and the material infrastructure of both the mainstream school and the special school, the staff appeared to be 'freer' or more playful, they laughed more and engaged with children with PMLD in a similar manner to that of mainstream children. This suggests that the material environment influences the nature or style of staff interaction. More research is needed to examine this relationship further, and to explore how environments also constrain and support social interaction opportunities between children with PMLD and mainstream peers.

Conclusion

This chapter has introduced social complexity to debates about whether children with PMLD are 'includable'. It has suggested that arguments that focus on physical place (either a mainstream school or a special school) overlook rich variations in social participation that occur when staff engage outside of special school contexts, and the ways that mainstream peers and special school staff can create engaging social environments for children with PMLD. The chapter has supported a radical social model perspective of inclusion which calls into question the neoliberal focus of education which emphasises a competitive approach to subject knowledge acquisition. If UNESCO's vision of inclusion is to be taken seriously then we need to move beyond binary models of education that separate children according to 'type', and begin to develop understandings about the conditions that lead to social belonging. To date there has been no published research that has examined inclusive education for children with PMLD from a radical social model perspective. This chapter calls for more theoretical and empirical work to develop this view further.

Questions for discussion

- What is your definition of 'inclusive education'? To what extent do you agree with the definitions given in this chapter?
- According to international policy makers, inclusive education leads to social cohesion. What does social cohesion mean to you, and how could inclusive education lead to social cohesion?
- Children with PMLD are defined as belonging to the earliest, pre-verbal stages of development. What could be the benefits of including children with PMLD in a mainstream school?
- Can an education system rightfully claim to be 'inclusive' if it provides special schools for children with special educational needs?

Summary

- Inclusive education has been a key focus of international education policy since the 1990s. Policy makers claim that inclusive education plays a central role in enhancing society, particularly with regards to social cohesion, tolerance and peace.
- However, not all children have been successfully included in mainstream schools, and in certain countries (like the UK) special schools continue to exist.
- Children with profound and multiple learning difficulties (PMLD) belong to the group who present the biggest challenge to inclusive education. Some commentators argue that children with PMLD are too intellectually impaired to meaningfully participate in mainstream schools and thus require specialist settings which offer specially trained staff, better material resources and a tailored curriculum and pedagogy.
- A radical social model perspective of inclusive education holds that the problem lies not with children with PMLD, but with the neoliberal education system that narrowly frames education in terms of subject knowledge acquisition. A radical perspective of inclusion calls for the redesign of the entire education system to reflect the diverse needs of all learners.
- This chapter presents research that appeals to a radical vision of inclusion. It examines the conditions that lead to social inclusion, and suggests that successful models of inclusive education must focus on developing a sense of belonging, shared identity and social cooperation across diverse peers.

Recommended reading

Armstrong, A., Armstrong, D. and Spandagou, I. (2010) *Inclusive Education: International Policy and Practice*. London: Sage.

Davis, L. (Ed.) (2017) *The Disability Studies Reader*, (5th ed.). London: Routledge.

Greenstein, A. (2016) *Radical Inclusive Education: Disability, Teaching and Struggles for Liberation*. Hove: Routledge.

Simmons, B. and Watson, D. (2014) *The PMLD Ambiguity: Articulating the Lifeworlds of Children with Profound and Multiple Learning Difficulties*. London: Routledge.

Acknowledgements

The research presented in this chapter was funded through a British Academy Postdoctoral Fellowship (2014–2017). Data collection took place whilst the researcher was based at the Graduate School of Education, University of Bristol (UK).

The project received full ethical approval from the University of Bristol's Research Governance Office and favourable opinion from the National Social Care Research Ethics Committee/NHS Health Research Authority.

References

Ainscow, M., Booth, T., and Dyson, A. (2006) Inclusion and the standards agenda: negotiating policy pressures in England. *International Journal of Inclusive Education*, **10**(4–5) pp. 295–308.

Armstrong, A., Armstrong, D. and Spandagou, I. (2010) *Inclusive Education: International Policy and Practice.* London: Sage.

Baglieri, S. and Shapiro, A. (2017) *Disability Studies and the Inclusive Classroom: Critical Practices for Embracing Diversity in Education*, (2nd ed.). New York: Routledge.

Ball, S. (2008) *The Education Debate.* Bristol: The Policy Press.

Barnes, C. and Mercer, G. (2010) *Exploring Disability*, (2nd ed.). Cambridge: Polity Press.

Barton, L. and Armstrong, F. (2001) Disability, education and inclusion: Cross-cultural issues and dilemmas. In Albercht, G., Seelman, K. and Bury, M. (Eds.). *Handbook of Disability Studies.* California: Sage.

Coupe O'Kane, J. and Goldbart, J. (1998) *Communication Before Speech: Development and Assessment*, (2nd ed.). London: David Fulton.

DES (1978) *Special Educational Needs (The Warnock Report).* London: HMSO.

DfE (2014) *The National Curriculum in England: Framework Document.* London: Crown Copyright.

Farrell, M. (2004) *Inclusion at the Crossroads.* London, David Fulton.

Fonseca, X., Lukosch, S. and Brazier, F. (2019) Social cohesion revisited: A new definition and how to characterize it. *Innovation: The European Journal of Social Science Research*, **32**(2), pp. 231–253.

Freire, P. (1972) *Pedagogy of the Oppressed.* London: Penguin Books.

Goodley, D. (2011) *Disability Studies: An Interdisciplinary Introduction.* London: Sage.

Greenstein, A. (2016) *Radical Inclusive Education: Disability, Teaching and Struggles for Liberation.* Hove: Routledge.

Hodkinson, A. (2016) *Key Issues in Special Educational Needs and Inclusive Education*, (2nd ed.). London: Sage.

Imray, P. and Colley, A. (2017) *Inclusion is Dead: Long Live Inclusion.* London: Routledge.

Lyons, G. and Arthur-Kelly, M. (2014) UNESCO inclusion policy and the education of school students with profound intellectual and multiple disabilities: Where to now? *Creative Education*, **5**, pp. 445–456.

Neilson, A., Hogg, J., Malek, M. and Rowley, D. (2000) Impact of surgical and orthotic intervention on the quality of life of people with profound intellectual and multiple disabilities and their carers. *Journal of Applied Research in Intellectual Disabilities*, **13**, pp. 216–238.

Pawlyn, J. and Carnaby, S. (2009) *Profound Intellectual and Multiple Disabilities: Nursing Complex Needs.* Oxford: Wiley-Blackwell.

Salt, T. (2010) *Salt Review: Independent Review of Teacher Supply for Pupils with Severe, Profound and Multiple Learning Difficulties (SLD and PMLD).* Nottingham: Crown Copyright.

Shakespeare, T. (2017) The social model of disability. In Davis, L. (Ed.). *The Disability Studies Reader*, (5th ed.). London: Routledge.

Simmons, B. (2018) The phenomenology of intersubjectivity and research with profoundly disabled children: Developing an experiential framework for analysing lived social experiences. In Twomey, M. and Carroll, C. (Eds.). *Seen and Heard: Exploring Participation, Engagement and Voice for Children with Disabilities.* Oxford: Peter Lang.

Simmons, B. (2020) Exploring the situated social being of children with PMLD across educational contexts: A study of belonging. In Nind, M. and Strnadova, I. (Eds.) *Belonging for People with Profound Intellectual and Multiple Disabilities: Pushing the Boundaries of Inclusion.* London: Routledge.

Simmons, B. and Watson, D. (2014) *The PMLD Ambiguity: Articulating the Lifeworlds of Children with Profound and Multiple Learning Disabilities.* London: Routledge.

Simmons, B. and Watson, D. (2017) From individualism to co-construction and back again: Rethinking research methodology for children with profound and multiple learning disabilities. In Kelly, B. and Byrne, B. (Eds.). *Valuing Disabled Children and Young People: Research, Policy and Practice.* London: Routledge.

Swain, J., Finkelstein, V., French, S. and Oliver, M. (1993) *Disabling Barriers: Enabling Environments.* London: Sage.

Tadema, A. C. and Vlaskamp, C. (2010) The time and effort in taking care for children with profound intellectual and multiple disabilities: A study on care load and support. *British Journal of Learning Disabilities,* **38**, pp. 1–48.

Tang, J. C., Patterson, T. G. and Kennedy, C. H. (2003) Identifying specific sensory modalities maintaining the Stereotypy of students with profound multiple disabilities. *Research in Developmental Disabilities,* **24**, pp. 433–451.

Tomlinson, S. (2017) *A Sociology of Special and Inclusive Education: Exploring the Manufacture of Inability.* Abingdon: Routledge.

UNESCO (1994) *The Salamanca Statement and Framework for Action on Special Needs Education.* Spain: UNESCO.

UNESCO (2002) *Universal Declaration on Cultural Diversity.* Paris: UNESCO.

UNESCO (2015) *Education 2030 Incheon Declaration and Framework for Action for the Development of Sustainable Development Goal 4.* Incheon: UNESCO.

United Nations (2006) *Convention on the Rights of Persons with Disabilities and Optional Protocol.* New York: United Nations.

Vlaskamp, C. and Cuppen-Fonteine, H. (2007) Reliability of assessing the sensory perception of children with profound intellectual and multiple disabilities: a case study. *Child Care Health Development,* **33**(5), pp. 547–551.

Ware, J. (2003) *Creating a Responsive Environment for People with Profound and Multiple Learning Difficulties,* (2nd ed.). London, David Fulton.

Warnock, M. (2010) *Special Educational Needs: A New Look,* (2nd ed.). London: Continuum.

Index

Dumay, X. 53
Durkheim, E. 1, 5, 12, 86
Dyer, R. 59

ecology 125
economics ix, 1, 13–14
Economist 100
economy 68, 72–6
Education Action Zones 88
Education Acts UK (chronological): Elementary
    Education Act (or Forster Act) (1870) 27–9, 30,
    32, 72, 81, 90, 95, 124; Endowed Schools Acts
    (1874) 82; Elementary Education Act (or Mundella
    Act) (1880) 28, 72, 82; Education Act (or Butler
    Act) (1944) 72; Education Act (1979) 94;
    Education Reform Act (1988) 95; Further and
    Higher Education Act (1992) 95; Education
    (Schools) Act (1997) 98; Education and Skills Act
    (2008) 99; Apprenticeships, Skills, Children and
    Learning Act (2009) 99; Academies Act (2010)
    102; Education Act (2011) 102
Education for All (EFA) 114
Education Studies ix–x
egalitarian education 88
Elias, N. 12
Ellis, A. 83
Ellison, R. 60
Eltis, W. 80
emerging powers 109, 114
empiricism 4–5
Engels, F. 81, 122, 125
Englishness 62
Enlightenment 130
environmental education 129
ethnicity 12, 13, 14, 16, 18–21
ethnocentrism 117
ethnographic research 38–41
ethics, in research 117
Eton College 80
Europe 27–8
European Union 76, 102
Every Child Matters 124
exclusion, school 38, 40, 46
expenditure on education 81

Factory Act (1833) 70
Fairclough, N. 6, 30, 32, 34
Fanon, F. 59, 60
Farrell, M. 137
Feinstein, L. 6, 35
Ferguson, A. 49
field 14–15, 17–20, 22
Flynn, N. 19, 20
Foley, P. 125, 127
Fonseca, X. 135, 145
Forster, W.E. 7, 27, 28, 29, 30 31
fossil fuels 121

Foucault, M. 7–8, 38, 46, 69 72, 73
France 26, 80, 82, 103
Francis, B. 72
Frank, A.G. 79
free schools 102
Freire, P. 139
French Revolution 49
Friedman, M. 86, 105
Froebel, J.F. 124
functionalism 112, 117
Further Education Funding Council 95

Garden City Movement 125
Garner, S. 59
Gazdula, J.H. 79, 93
gender 13, 14, 58, 60, 62, 65, 66
General Teaching Council for England 102
Ghana 100
Giddens, A. 98, 109, 111
Gill, O. 64
Gillard D. 5, 9, 28, 58, 81, 88, 99, 102, 105
Gilpin, R. 116
Glass R. 88
Glennerster, H. 95
global citizens 112–13, 115
global human capital 104
global political economy 79–92, 93–108
globalisation 34, 76, 85, 109–16, 132
Glorious Revolution (1688) 49
Goldblatt, D. 116
Goodley, D. 135, 136, 138, 139, 145
Gove, M. 7, 33, 102, 106
grammar schools 31, 80, 82, 88
Gramsci, A. 25
Grant, R. 53
Green, A. 7, 8, 10, 27, 28, 32, 35, 36
Greenstein, A. 139, 140, 145, 147
Gristy, C. 72
Guba, E. 116
Gypsy Travellers 39–40, 42–3, 46

habitus 1, 2, 12–24, 39; critiques of 21–2;
    definition of 13–14; and ethnicity 18–20
Hackney 65, 98
Hall, S. 6, 69, 78
Halliday, J. 8
Hamilton, P. 46
Hancock, A.M. 5
Harbison, F.H. 87, 105, 110
Hardy, S.A. 51
Härma, J. 101
Harrison, J.F.C. 26
Harrow School 80
Harvey, D.I. 87
Hatcher, R. 73, 76, 77
Hayek, F. 74, 86
hegemony 1, 2, 8, 9, 25–37, 59, 61

Printed in Great Britain
by Amazon

65879680R00097